STOCKWELL-MUDD LIBRARIES

3 5044 00177 3370

The person borrowing this item is responsible for its return to the library on or before the **Latest Date** stamped below.

Overdue charges accrue until the maximum fine is reached. Consult the library fine schedule for details.

A **minimum** $50.00 replacement bill will be issued after maximum fine has accumulated.

STOCKWELL-MUDD LIBRARIES, Albion College

WITHDRAWN
FROM
ALBION COLLEGE LIBRARY

D1214821

The Photographic History
of The Civil War

In Ten Volumes

A VISION OF THE BY-GONE
THE SLOOP-OF-WAR "PORTSMOUTH" OF THE OLD NAVY

Here is a sight the like of which never will be seen again—the U. S. sloop-of-war "Portsmouth" at anchor and drying out her sails. An honorable record did this old corvette leave behind her. Of the type of vessel that had fought in the War of 1812, she had gone through the Mexican War, and had chased and captured many a slaver. But a year or so ago, she was still afloat as the training-ship of the New Jersey state militia. She has every sail up except her head-sails and studding sails. As can be seen at a glance, she was a very lofty craft, and though clewed up, she has her sky-sails, her royals, her topgallant-sails, her topsails, set on every mast. "Excellent, whether sailing, steering, working, scudding, lying to, or riding at anchor in a seaway, she sometimes got her sternboard in stays." With this single exception, reported Commander Armstrong, "she possesses the finest qualities of any ship I ever sailed in; rolls as easy as a cradle, and stands up under her canvas like a church." Lying under her stern is the captain's gig; her other boats seem to have been called away; probably one of the watches has gone ashore.

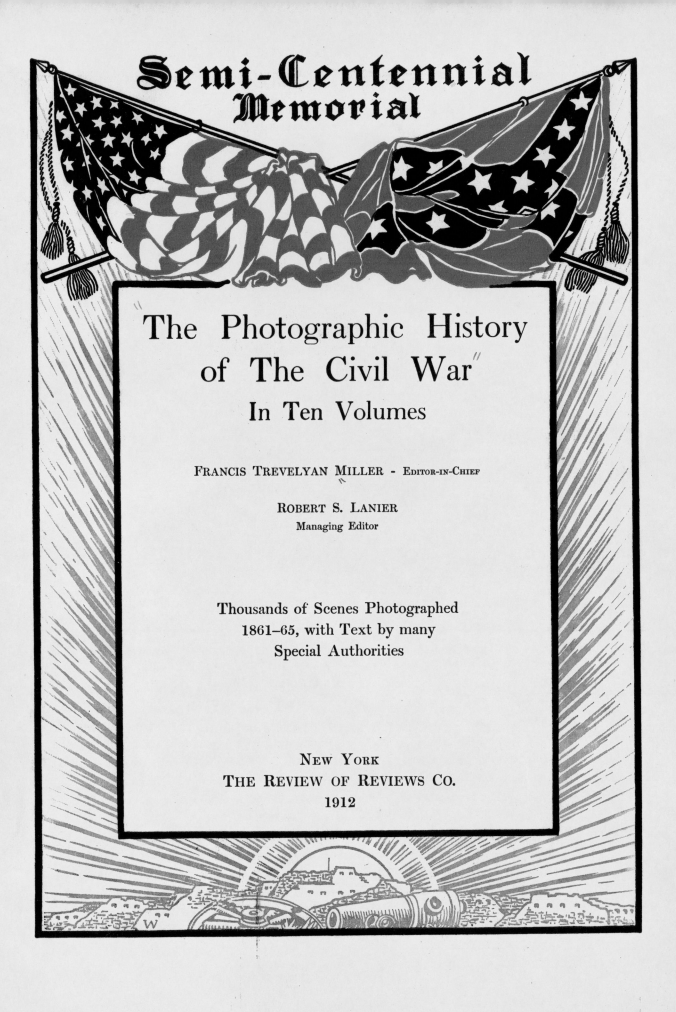

Semi-Centennial Memorial

The Photographic History of The Civil War"

In Ten Volumes

FRANCIS TREVELYAN MILLER - EDITOR-IN-CHIEF

ROBERT S. LANIER
Managing Editor

Thousands of Scenes Photographed
1861–65, with Text by many
Special Authorities

NEW YORK
THE REVIEW OF REVIEWS CO.
1912

The Photographic History
of The Civil War
In Ten Volumes

Volume Six

The Navies

BY

JAMES BARNES

Author of "David G. Farragut," "Naval Actions of 1812," "Yankee Ships and
Yankee Sailors," "Commodore Bainbridge," "The Blockaders,"
and other naval and historical works

With an Introduction

BY

FRENCH E. CHADWICK

Rear-Admiral, United States Navy

New York
The Review of Reviews Co.
1912

Copyright, 1911, by Patriot Publishing Co., Springfield, Mass.

ALL RIGHTS RESERVED, INCLUDING THAT OF TRANSLATION
INTO FOREIGN LANGUAGES, INCLUDING THE SCANDINAVIAN

Printed in New York, U.S.A.

E
468
.7
.M64
1912
v. 6

oversize
with
book

THE TROW PRESS
NEW YORK

65396

CONTENTS

Photograph Descriptions Throughout the Volume
    James Barnes
    Robert Sloss

PREFACE

FEW annals in the history of the United States are of greater and more compelling interest than those connected with the achievement of its sailors. The descendants of Drake and Frobisher, led by John Paul Jones, Perry, Bainbridge, Porter, and other illustrious naval heroes in the days of lofty spars and topsails, made a name for themselves both on the sea and on the lasting scrolls of history. Their records, penned by historians and novelists, form brilliant pages in American literature. Therefore, it was not strange that a conflict in which officers and seamen of the same race and speech, graduates of the same historic Naval Academy and sailing the same seas and along the same shores, met in heroic struggle, should form a story second to none in its fascination and interest.

The Civil War ships and the men who fought them are distinctive in naval history, not for immensity of single battles or extent of total destruction, but for diversity of action, the complete realization of the ironclad as a fighting vessel, and the development of the torpedo as a weapon of destruction. Readers are fortunate in finding, at the outset of this volume, the scholarly appreciation by Admiral Chadwick of the essential part played by the navies in the war, while the battles at sea and on inland waters are described by Mr. Barnes with a vividness possible only to a naval historian to whom the sea and its sailors long have been objects of sympathetic study.

The photographic record of the great American conflict

Preface

is particularly striking in this volume. Never before has there been assembled such a pictorial and actual record of fleets and sailors, Union and Confederate. The stately frigate with walls of live-oak, the newly born ironclad, the swift blockade-runner, the commerce-destroying cruiser, which left its indelible mark on the American merchant marine no less than on international law, and last, but not least, the actors in scenes of the great naval drama appear on the pages that follow, in an illustrated "catalogue of the ships" that even Homer in his stately Iliad could have envied.

INTRODUCTION

BY

FRENCH E. CHADWICK

THE VALUE OF DISCIPLINE—PRACTICE ON THE "MENDOTA"

THOUGH LAMENTABLY UNPREPARED FOR WAR IN '61, THE FEDERAL NAVY BY 1864 SET AN
EXAMPLE OF CONSTANT ARDUOUS TRAINING AND DRILL, EVEN DURING LULLS IN THE ACTUAL
FIGHTING SUCH AS WHEN THIS PHOTOGRAPH WAS TAKEN, ON THE JAMES RIVER IN 1864

CUSTODIANS OF THE COAST

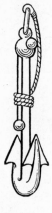

Looking out from the mouth of every important harbor along the Southern seacoast, the Confederates were confronted by just such a grim menace as this. Riding at anchor or moving swiftly from point to point, the Federal fighting-ships, with sleepless vigilance, night and day sought every opportunity to destroy the vessels which attempted to keep up the commercial intercourse of the Confederacy with the outside world. At first it was chiefly a "paper blockade," and the fact that its mere announcement accorded to the Confederacy the status of belligerents was hailed at the South as a fortunate diplomatic mistake. Swift merchantmen abroad were easily induced to enter the bold enterprise which meant such profitable trade; laughing at the inadequate Federal patrol, they began to dump huge cargoes of the munitions of war at every Southern port, taking in return cotton, so necessary to keep the looms of Europe going. With the rapid growth of the Federal navy the blockade, whose early impotence had been winked at by European powers, became more and more a fact. The cordon was drawn tighter and tighter from the Potomac to the Rio Grande. One venturesome vessel after another was overhauled or driven ashore and both they and their cargoes became the rich prizes of the Federal navy. While this served vastly to increase the difficulty and danger of dealing

COPYRIGHT, 1911, PATRIOT PUB. CO

A FLEET OF FEDERAL BLOCKADERS IN 1864

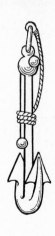

with the South, it did not deter greatly the bold spirits to whom this war-time commerce was so profitable and necessary, and down to the fall of the last Southern seaport swift blockade-runners were found that could continue to show
the beleaguering fleet a clean pair of heels. From the war's very beginning the Confederates were hopeful of being
able to oppose the Federal navy with fighting-vessels that would raise the blockade, but they could not build boats
fast enough, and almost as soon as they were finished they were captured or destroyed in one bold attempt after another
to contend with the superior numbers that opposed them. Once at Mobile and again at Charleston, after a naval victory the Confederates proclaimed the blockade raised, only to find that in a few days the investing fleet had been
doubled in strength. Meanwhile the blockade-runners continued to ply between Nassau, Bermuda, and other con-
venient depots and the ports of the Confederacy. Charleston, S. C., and Wilmington, N. C., the two most closely
guarded ports, continued to be made by these greyhounds of the sea until the Federal land forces at last compassed
the evacuation of the towns. Enormous as was the quantity of the merchandise and munitions of war that got by
the blockade, it was the work of the Federal navy that first began to curtail the traffic, and finally ended it.

CONFEDERATES IN THE NEWLY–CAPTURED PENSACOLA FORT—1861

Full of enthusiasm and military spirit, but suspecting little what trials lay before them, the Confederate volunteers pictured here are drilling at one of the forts that had been abandoned by the Federal Government, even before the momentous shot was fired at Sumter. Fort Pickens, through the forethought of Commander Henry Walke, who disobeyed his orders most brilliantly and successfully, had been saved to the Federal Government. The other batteries and forts at Pensacola, however, had been handed over to the Confederacy, and here we see the men in gray, early in '61, taking advantage of the gift. Note the new uniforms, the soldierly and well-fed appearance of the men, the stores of ammunition for the great guns.

COPYRIGHT, 1911, REVIEW OF REVIEWS CO.

WHERE THE BLOCKADERS CAME TOO LATE

Many of these soldiers pictured here were soon fighting miles away from where we see them now; a great many were drafted from New Orleans, from Mobile, Savannah, and Charleston; Florida and Georgia furnished their full quota to the Confederate army. This photograph was taken by Edwards, of New Orleans, who, like his confrère Lytle, succeeded in picturing many of the stirring scenes and opening tableaux of the war; they afterward took advantage of their art and used their cameras as batteries at the command of the Confederate secret service, photographing ships and troops and guns of the Federal forces, and sending them to the commanding generals of their departments. Over the chase of the gun is Pensacola harbor.

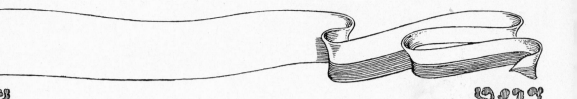

INTRODUCTION—THE FEDERAL NAVY AND THE BLOCKADE

By F. E. Chadwick
Rear-Admiral, United States Navy

THE American Civil War marks one of the great social reconstructions which are ever taking place as we advance from plane to plane of mentality. The American and the French revolutions; the overthrow of European feudalism by Napoleon, who was but the special instrument of a great movement, are among the special reconstructions more immediately preceding that of 1861, but all had, in a way, a common impulse—the impulse which comes from having arrived at a new mental outlook.

Such revolutions may be bloodless if mental development is equal to meeting the emergency, as it was in the formation of the American Constitution, in 1787. They are, however, far more apt to be in blood, as was that of 1861, which was brought about by the immense and rapid development, in the last century, of mechanism, the press, and the mobility of populations. We had to step to a new mental, moral, and psychic plane, and war was made certain by the want of a wisdom and foresight which, in the circumstances, it was, perhaps, too much to expect.

The present volume deals with the part taken by the navy in the great contest—a part of vastly greater importance than has generally been recognized. Historians are, however, beginning to see that the rôle of the navy was a vital one, absolutely necessary to success; that the blockade was a constrictive force which devitalized Southern effort. Whatever doubt may have existed at the outset as to the strategy of the

COPYRIGHT, 1911, REVIEW OF REVIEWS CO.

THE "SABINE," THE FIRST BLOCKADER IN THE SOUTH ATLANTIC

The towering masts of this fine sailing frigate arrived in Pensacola Harbor on April 12, 1861, the day Fort Sumter was fired upon. With the "Brooklyn," she landed reënforcements at Fort Pickens. On May 13th, Captain H. A. Adams of the "Sabine" issued notice of the blockade at Pensacola, the first Atlantic port to be thus closed. The "Sabine," like her prototypes, the "United States" and the "Constitution," mounted 44 guns. She sailed on the expedition to Paraguay in 1858–9, and became one of the first ships of the old navy to see active service in the Civil War. She served in Admiral Du Pont's squadron on the expedition to Port Royal in November, 1861. Her commander on that expedition was Captain Cadwalader Ringgold. It was largely due to the heroic efforts of his officers and crew that 650 marines were saved from drowning when the transport "Governor" foundered on the 3d. In February, 1862, when the "new-fangled" "Monitor," the latest "Yankee notion" in war vessels, was going begging for officers and men, a crew was at last formed largely of volunteers from the "Sabine." Of such stuff were made the tars of the old American sailing-ships of war

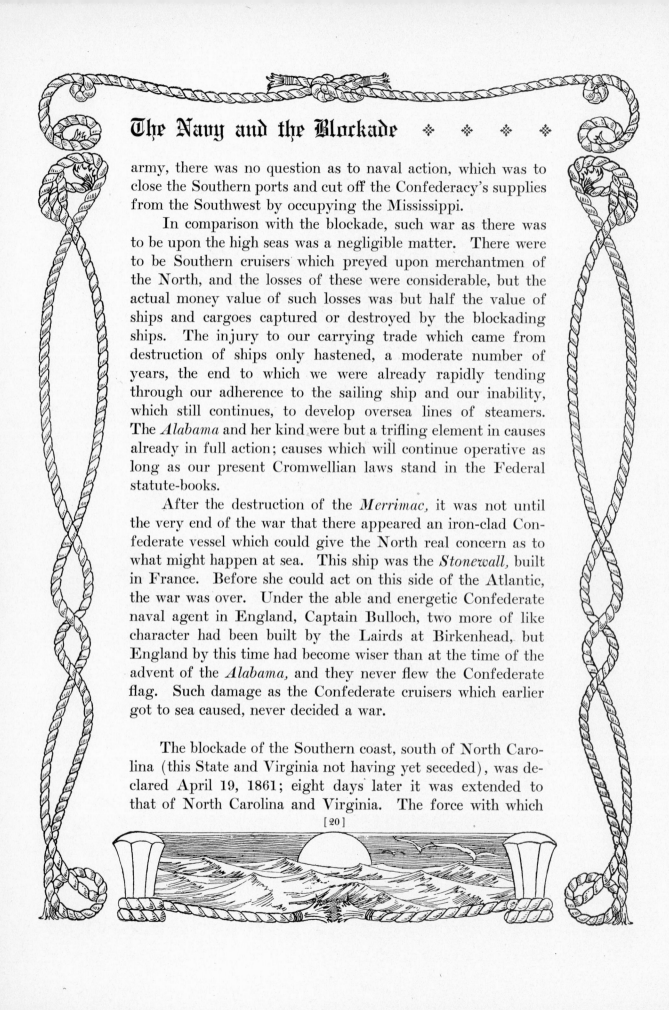

army, there was no question as to naval action, which was to close the Southern ports and cut off the Confederacy's supplies from the Southwest by occupying the Mississippi.

In comparison with the blockade, such war as there was to be upon the high seas was a negligible matter. There were to be Southern cruisers which preyed upon merchantmen of the North, and the losses of these were considerable, but the actual money value of such losses was but half the value of ships and cargoes captured or destroyed by the blockading ships. The injury to our carrying trade which came from destruction of ships only hastened, a moderate number of years, the end to which we were already rapidly tending through our adherence to the sailing ship and our inability, which still continues, to develop oversea lines of steamers. The *Alabama* and her kind were but a trifling element in causes already in full action; causes which will continue operative as long as our present Cromwellian laws stand in the Federal statute-books.

After the destruction of the *Merrimac,* it was not until the very end of the war that there appeared an iron-clad Confederate vessel which could give the North real concern as to what might happen at sea. This ship was the *Stonewall,* built in France. Before she could act on this side of the Atlantic, the war was over. Under the able and energetic Confederate naval agent in England, Captain Bulloch, two more of like character had been built by the Lairds at Birkenhead, but England by this time had become wiser than at the time of the advent of the *Alabama,* and they never flew the Confederate flag. Such damage as the Confederate cruisers which earlier got to sea caused, never decided a war.

The blockade of the Southern coast, south of North Carolina (this State and Virginia not having yet seceded), was declared April 19, 1861; eight days later it was extended to that of North Carolina and Virginia. The force with which

COPYRIGHT, 1911 REVIEW OF REVIEWS CO.

CAUGHT BY HER OWN KIND

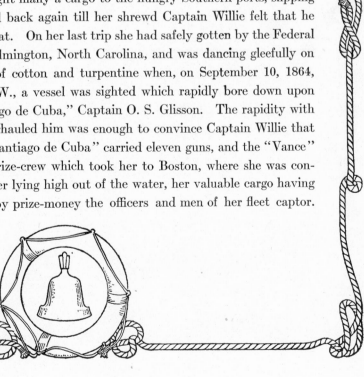

The blockade-runner "A. D. Vance." It frequently took a blockade-runner to catch a blockade-runner, and as the Federal navy captured ship after ship of this character they began to acquire a numerous fleet of swift steamers from which it was difficult for any vessel to get away. The "Vance" brought many a cargo to the hungry Southern ports, slipping safely by the blockading fleet and back again till her shrewd Captain Willie felt that he could give the slip to anything afloat. On her last trip she had safely gotten by the Federal vessels lying off the harbor of Wilmington, North Carolina, and was dancing gleefully on her way with a bountiful cargo of cotton and turpentine when, on September 10, 1864, in latitude 34° N., longitude 76° W., a vessel was sighted which rapidly bore down upon her. It proved to be the "Santiago de Cuba," Captain O. S. Glisson. The rapidity with which the approaching vessel overhauled him was enough to convince Captain Willie that she was in his own class. The "Santiago de Cuba" carried eleven guns, and the "Vance" humbly hove to, to receive the prize-crew which took her to Boston, where she was condemned. In the picture we see her lying high out of the water, her valuable cargo having been removed and sold to enrich by prize-money the officers and men of her fleet captor.

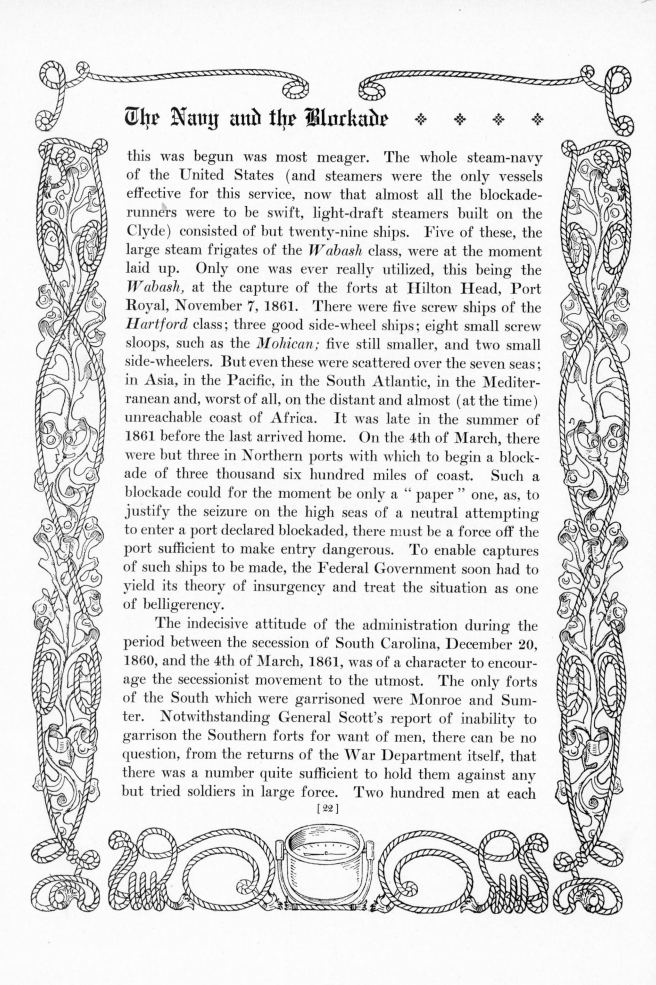

this was begun was most meager. The whole steam-navy of the United States (and steamers were the only vessels effective for this service, now that almost all the blockade-runners were to be swift, light-draft steamers built on the Clyde) consisted of but twenty-nine ships. Five of these, the large steam frigates of the *Wabash* class, were at the moment laid up. Only one was ever really utilized, this being the *Wabash,* at the capture of the forts at Hilton Head, Port Royal, November 7, 1861. There were five screw ships of the *Hartford* class; three good side-wheel ships; eight small screw sloops, such as the *Mohican;* five still smaller, and two small side-wheelers. But even these were scattered over the seven seas; in Asia, in the Pacific, in the South Atlantic, in the Mediterranean and, worst of all, on the distant and almost (at the time) unreachable coast of Africa. It was late in the summer of 1861 before the last arrived home. On the 4th of March, there were but three in Northern ports with which to begin a blockade of three thousand six hundred miles of coast. Such a blockade could for the moment be only a " paper " one, as, to justify the seizure on the high seas of a neutral attempting to enter a port declared blockaded, there must be a force off the port sufficient to make entry dangerous. To enable captures of such ships to be made, the Federal Government soon had to yield its theory of insurgency and treat the situation as one of belligerency.

The indecisive attitude of the administration during the period between the secession of South Carolina, December 20, 1860, and the 4th of March, 1861, was of a character to encourage the secessionist movement to the utmost. The only forts of the South which were garrisoned were Monroe and Sumter. Notwithstanding General Scott's report of inability to garrison the Southern forts for want of men, there can be no question, from the returns of the War Department itself, that there was a number quite sufficient to hold them against any but tried soldiers in large force. Two hundred men at each

COPYRIGHT, 1911, PATRIOT PUB. CO.

A FIGHTING INVENTOR
REAR–ADMIRAL JOHN A. DAHLGREN ON BOARD THE U. S. S. "PAWNEE" IN
CHARLESTON HARBOR

Over the admiral's right shoulder can be seen the ruins of the still unsurrendered Fort Sumter. It was for his services on land that Dahlgren was made rear-admiral, Feb. 7, 1863. He had been employed on ordnance duty between 1847–57. With the exception of a short cruise, he had spent the ten years in perfecting the Dahlgren gun, his own invention. In 1862 he was chief of the Bureau of Ordnance. From this he stepped into command of the South Atlantic blockading squadron, July 6, 1863. From that time on he showed the qualities of a great commander in active service. Not only did he bravely and wisely direct the naval activities in Charleston Harbor, but in February, 1864, he led the naval expedition up the St. John's River that was to coöperate with the troops in gaining a hold in Florida. In December, 1864, he coöperated with General Sherman in the capture of Savannah, and on Feb. 18, 1865, he had the satisfaction of moving his vessels up to Charleston, the evacuated city that he had striven so long to capture.

would have been ample to hold the important forts below New Orleans, at Mobile, Pensacola, Savannah, and Wilmington. There were at the Northern posts, which might, of course, have been completely denuded of men with safety, over one thousand men. Fort Monroe was sufficiently garrisoned for protection; the total garrison of Sumter was but eighty-four. As it was, the other forts had simply to be entered and occupied by the raw secessionist volunteers. Such occupancy, which gradually took place, naturally gave an immense impetus to the Southern movement. Had these forts been occupied by Federal troops and had Sumter been properly reenforced, there can be little question that secession would have ended with the act of South Carolina. For with her ports in Federal hands, the South was powerless. Communication with the exterior world was to her a necessity in the strongest meaning of the word, because she was lacking in many things of vital importance. She could not have gone to war; she would not have gone to war, in so helpless a situation.

Even the one effort to hold any of these forts, the retention of which was so vital, was made abortive by the action of Scott in causing to be embarked in New York, in the merchant steamer *Star of the West,* a raw company of artillery under a lieutenant for the reenforcement of Fort Sumter, instead of a force of the older soldiers from Fort Monroe, in the *Brooklyn.* The *Star of the West* made a feeble effort to enter Charleston Harbor. She was fired upon, and seeing no colors hoisted at Sumter or sign of assistance from the fort, turned and went to sea. Had the *Brooklyn* been sent, as President Buchanan, to his credit be it said, intended, and as had been first arranged, the secessionist battery would not have dared to fire upon the powerful man-of-war, or, had it dared, the few guns of the battery or of all of the improvised defenses, none of which had before fired a shot, would have been quickly silenced by the *Brooklyn's* guns; the ship would have occupied the harbor; Sumter would have been manned and provisioned, and

[24]

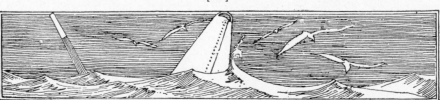

COPYRIGHT, 1911, REVIEWS OF REVIEWS CO.

LEADERS OF DIPLOMACY IN 1863

SECRETARY SEWARD AND NINE FOREIGN DIPLOMATS AT THE TIME WHEN CONFEDERATE CRUISERS ABROAD WERE AN INTERNATIONAL PROBLEM

No military picture of moving troops, no group of distinguished generals, could possibly hold the interest for students of the history of the Civil War that this photograph possesses. It is the summer of 1863. Gathered at the foot of this beautiful waterfall, as if at the end of a day's outing for pleasure, are ten men of mark and great importance. Here are William H. Seward, American Secretary of State, standing bareheaded, to the right. With him, numbered so that the reader can easily identify them, are (2) Baron De Stoeckel, Russian Minister; (3) M. Molena, Nicaraguan Minister; (4) Lord Lyons, British Minister; (5) M. Mercier, French Minister; (6) M. Schleiden, Hanseatic Minister; (7) M. Bertenatti, Italian Minister; (8) Count Piper, Swedish Minister; (9) M. Bodisco, Secretary Russian Legation; (10) Mr. Sheffield, Attaché British Legation; (11) Mr. Donaldson, a messenger in the State Department. These were ticklish times in diplomatic circles. Outwardly polite to one another, and on an occasion such as this probably lowering the bars of prescribed convention, many of these men would have liked to know what was going on in the brains of their associates, for diplomacy is but a game of mental hide-and-seek. More than any one else would Mr. Seward have desired at this moment to be gifted in the art of mind-reading. He would have liked to hear from Lord Lyons exactly what stand the British Government was going to take in relation to the Confederate cruisers that had been outfitted in Great Britain. He would have liked to hear also from Minister Mercier more on the subject of the vessels building in France that he had been in correspondence with John Bigelow about, and he would have liked to know exactly what Napoleon III was trying to do in Mexico, in the ambitious game of which Maximilian was a pawn. The Nicaraguan Minister would have appreciated a word himself on the latter subject; and Lord Lyons, in view of the presence of the Russian fleet, would have liked to pick the brain of Baron De Stoeckel, whose royal master, the Czar, had made such firm offers of friendship to the United States at just this hour. Mr. Schleiden, in view of what was to happen in the next few years, would have welcomed an outburst of confidence from M. Mercier, and for that matter, so would M. Bertenatti. But here they are, sinking all questions of statecraft and posing for the photographer as if the game of diplomacy was far from their minds and they were ordinary "trippers" seeing the sights

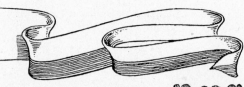

Charleston Harbor would have been permanently in the hands of the Federal authorities.

Equal folly, inefficiency, and, in cases, disloyalty were shown in the failure to take steps to protect the great navy-yard at Norfolk and in the surrender of that at Pensacola. The former could have been saved had the incoming administration acted more promptly; the latter could, at any moment in the two months succeeding its surrender in January, have been reoccupied, had there been a show of wisdom in government affairs. With the loss of these two great establishments went the loss of some thousands of cannon, which went to arm the Southern batteries. Had these untoward events not happened, affairs would have assumed a very different phase; for a time, at least, war would have been deferred, and soberer thought might have had its weight.

Whether it were better that the war should be fought, and the pick of the manhood of the South and much of that of the North perish, need not be discussed; but the patent fact remains that the failure to employ the *Brooklyn* instead of the *Star of the West,* the failure to garrison the other forts of the South, the failure to save Norfolk and Pensacola were governmental failures of surpassing ineptitude and folly, only to be made good by four years of a war which brought three millions of men into the field, six hundred ships to close the Southern ports, engulfed the treasure of the North, and laid waste the South. The change to our new mental and psychical plane, a change which had to be made, was dearly bought for want of wisdom and foresight beyond our powers at the moment.

Leaving aside the what-might-have-beens and coming to things as they happened, the blockade, by the end of 1861, had become so effective that in the governmental year of 1861–62, the total cotton exported from the South was but thirteen thousand bales as against the two million of the previous season. During the quarter beginning September 1, 1861, less

COPYRIGHT, 1911, REVIEW OF REVIEWS CO.

FOREIGN ALLIES

Here in the harbor of Alexandria, Va., the crew of the Russian frigate "Osliaba" have climbed into the rigging to view with the officers on the bridge the strange land to which they had been sent on a friendly mission. England was almost openly hostile to the North at the beginning of the war, while France better concealed its sympathies. Its diplomats were highly in favor of joining with Germany and Italy to aid Maximilian in setting up his monarchy in Mexico. The Federal navy was confronted from the start, not only with the problem of the blockade, but with that of providing sufficient fighting-ships to enable it to contend successfully with the navies of foreign powers in case complications arose. When Emperor Alexander ordered his warships to proceed to American waters, there was an end to rumors of foreign hostilities; and when one division of the Russian fleet entered New York Harbor and the other the Golden Gate, feasts of welcome awaited both officers and men who had come to augment the Federal navy at its most critical period.

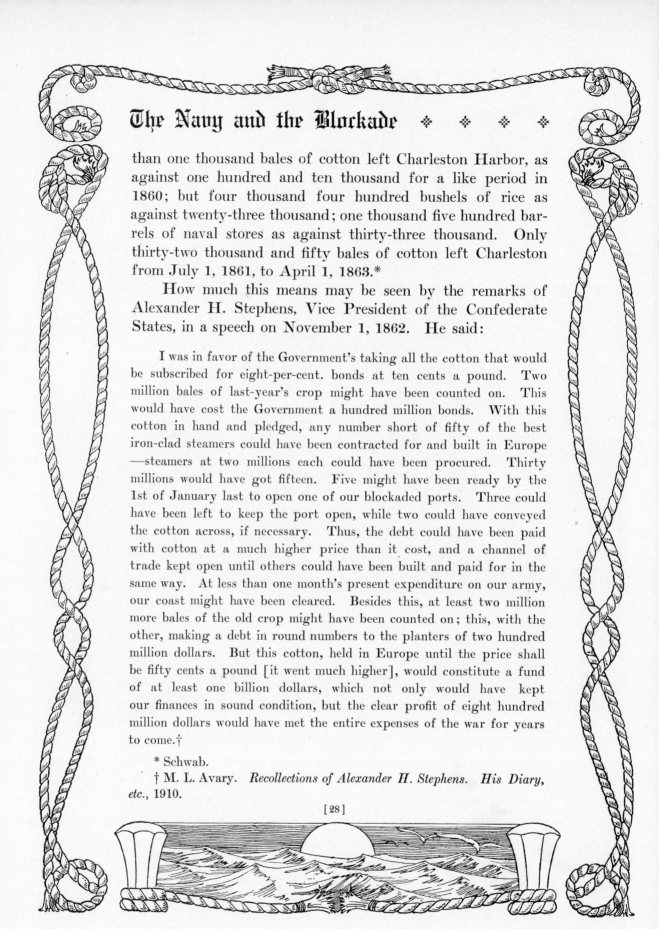

than one thousand bales of cotton left Charleston Harbor, as against one hundred and ten thousand for a like period in 1860; but four thousand four hundred bushels of rice as against twenty-three thousand; one thousand five hundred barrels of naval stores as against thirty-three thousand. Only thirty-two thousand and fifty bales of cotton left Charleston from July 1, 1861, to April 1, 1863.*

How much this means may be seen by the remarks of Alexander H. Stephens, Vice President of the Confederate States, in a speech on November 1, 1862. He said:

> I was in favor of the Government's taking all the cotton that would be subscribed for eight-per-cent. bonds at ten cents a pound. Two million bales of last-year's crop might have been counted on. This would have cost the Government a hundred million bonds. With this cotton in hand and pledged, any number short of fifty of the best iron-clad steamers could have been contracted for and built in Europe —steamers at two millions each could have been procured. Thirty millions would have got fifteen. Five might have been ready by the 1st of January last to open one of our blockaded ports. Three could have been left to keep the port open, while two could have conveyed the cotton across, if necessary. Thus, the debt could have been paid with cotton at a much higher price than it cost, and a channel of trade kept open until others could have been built and paid for in the same way. At less than one month's present expenditure on our army, our coast might have been cleared. Besides this, at least two million more bales of the old crop might have been counted on; this, with the other, making a debt in round numbers to the planters of two hundred million dollars. But this cotton, held in Europe until the price shall be fifty cents a pound [it went much higher], would constitute a fund of at least one billion dollars, which not only would have kept our finances in sound condition, but the clear profit of eight hundred million dollars would have met the entire expenses of the war for years to come.†

* Schwab.

† M. L. Avary. *Recollections of Alexander H. Stephens. His Diary, etc.*, 1910.

COPYRIGHT. 1911, REVIEW OF REVIEWS CO.

A FRIENDLY VISITOR

The Russians, although in some degree a maritime nation, did not devote much attention to their navy, as can be seen from a glance at this picture of one of the visiting Russian vessels during the Civil War, the "Osliaba." In another photograph has been shown a group of their sailors. They are as different in appearance from the trim American and English men-of-warsmen as their vessel is different from an American or English man-of-war. The Russian sailors were all conscripts, mostly taken from inland villages and forced to take up a sea-faring life in the service of the Czar. There had to be a sprinkling of real seamen among the crew, but they, like the poor serfs from the country, were conscripts also. The Russian harbors are practically cut off from the world by ice for at least five months of the year. This fact has prevented Russia from taking a place among maritime nations. It has been Russia's purpose to reach warm-water harbors that has brought on two of its greatest wars.

Albion
College
Library

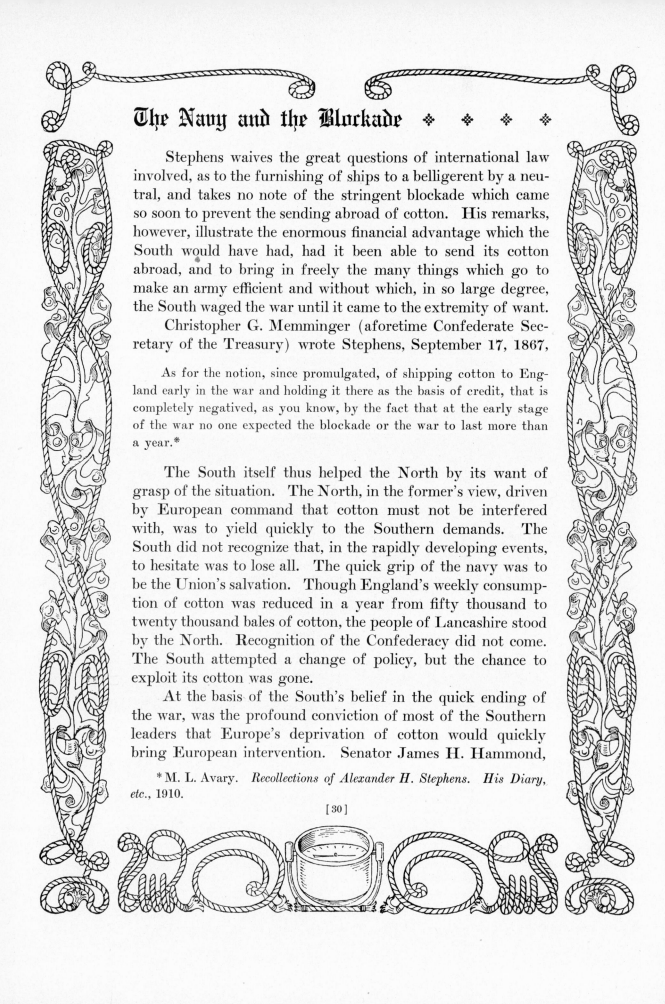

The Navy and the Blockade ❖ ❖ ❖ ❖

Stephens waives the great questions of international law involved, as to the furnishing of ships to a belligerent by a neutral, and takes no note of the stringent blockade which came so soon to prevent the sending abroad of cotton. His remarks, however, illustrate the enormous financial advantage which the South would have had, had it been able to send its cotton abroad, and to bring in freely the many things which go to make an army efficient and without which, in so large degree, the South waged the war until it came to the extremity of want.

Christopher G. Memminger (aforetime Confederate Secretary of the Treasury) wrote Stephens, September 17, 1867,

> As for the notion, since promulgated, of shipping cotton to England early in the war and holding it there as the basis of credit, that is completely negatived, as you know, by the fact that at the early stage of the war no one expected the blockade or the war to last more than a year.*

The South itself thus helped the North by its want of grasp of the situation. The North, in the former's view, driven by European command that cotton must not be interfered with, was to yield quickly to the Southern demands. The South did not recognize that, in the rapidly developing events, to hesitate was to lose all. The quick grip of the navy was to be the Union's salvation. Though England's weekly consumption of cotton was reduced in a year from fifty thousand to twenty thousand bales of cotton, the people of Lancashire stood by the North. Recognition of the Confederacy did not come. The South attempted a change of policy, but the chance to exploit its cotton was gone.

At the basis of the South's belief in the quick ending of the war, was the profound conviction of most of the Southern leaders that Europe's deprivation of cotton would quickly bring European intervention. Senator James H. Hammond,

*M. L. Avary. *Recollections of Alexander H. Stephens. His Diary, etc.,* 1910.

COPYRIGHT, 1911, REVIEW OF REVIEWS CO.

MESSENGERS FROM THE CZAR OF RUSSIA

Here again the reader is introduced to some guests of the North—the officers of one of the little fleet that put into the Hudson and paid visits along the coast. It was not the Russian people at large who showed any friendliness to the United States during the Civil War; they knew little, cared less, and were not affected by the results of the conflict more than if it had been waged between two savage tribes in the heart of Africa. It was the Czar, for reasons of state or for his own purposes—which are much the same thing—who made the friendly overtures. Still smarting from the crushing disaster of the Crimea, where England, France, and Sardinia had combined to aid the hated Turk in keeping the Russians from the Bosphorus and the Mediterranean, the Czar would have given a great deal to have seen the "Trent" affair open hostilities between America and the mother country. Great Britain then would have its hands full in guarding its own shores and saving its Canadian possessions. The eyes of Napoleon III. were directed westward also at this time. King Victor Emmanuel, of Sardinia, who in '61 had had placed on his head the crown of United Italy, was trying to juggle the disjointed states of his new kingdom into harmony. Besides this, the Czar had unproductive land to sell—Alaska. It was Russia's chance. This friendship was in the game of diplomacy. But different from what Russia expected was the attitude of England.

of South Carolina, in a speech in the Senate on March 4, 1858, had said:

> But if there were no other reason why we should never have war, would any sane nation make war on cotton? Without firing a gun, without drawing a sword, should they make war on us we could bring the whole world to our feet. . . . What would happen if no cotton was furnished for three years? I will not stop to depict what everyone can imagine, but this is certain: England would topple headlong and carry the whole civilized world with her, save the South. No, you dare not make war on cotton. No power on earth dares to make war upon it.

And again:

> I firmly believe that the slaveholding South is now the controlling *power* of the world—that no other power would face us in hostility. This will be demonstrated if we come to the ultimate . . . cotton, rice, tobacco, and naval stores command the world, and we have sense enough to know it.

With such views, and they were practically the views of the whole South, it is not surprising that, with the belief that to withhold cotton would bring the world to terms, the South was slow to adopt such ideas as those put forth by Stephens. It was soon to be reduced largely to its own resources. " Buttons were made of persimmon seeds; tea of berry leaves; coffee of a variety of parched seeds; envelopes and writing-paper of scraps of wall-paper; shoes of wood and canvas." *

The South, however, aided by adventurous British merchants and her own able secret service abroad, of which Captain Bulloch, formerly of the United States navy, was the head, displayed a wondrous energy. Notwithstanding the blockade, the advent of very fast shallow-draft steamers, built principally on the Clyde and specially for the purpose of running the blockade, did much to alleviate the situation for the Confederacy until the Federal navy's hold on the coast gradually tightened. The

* Schwab.

MANNING THE YARDS—A VISITOR FROM BRAZIL

The lack of skill at manning yards that is pictured here shows that in Civil War times the Brazilians, never a maritime nation, had much to learn. Occasionally during the war, along the South Atlantic coast, while the blockade was still in existence and rigidly enforced, strange vessels would be seen by the cordon of outlying scouts, and more than once mistakes were narrowly averted. It was hard to tell under what guise a blockade-runner might approach the starting-line for the final dash for shore. In July, 1864, late one evening, a vessel was seen approaching and her actions were so peculiar that a little gunboat started at once for the guard-ships and made report. Two vessels were despatched to intercept the stranger. There was a slight fog and the moon was bright, a combination that made it impossible to see more than a few yards ahead. All at once the mist lifted, and there—lying within half pistol-shot between the two Federal cruisers—lay the suspected one. Immediately she was hailed and told to surrender. A voice replied through the speaking trumpet in broken English, stating that she was the French sloop-of-war "Alerte," and wished to make the nearest port, as she was suffering from "occasional discomposure of her engines." This having been ascertained to be the truth, the Frenchman was allowed to drop anchor for repairs. Now and then visitors from South American ports would also drop in, and in this picture of the barkentine-rigged side-wheeler is shown a Brazilian warship.

The Navy and the Blockade

United States was backward then, as in fact it always has been, if the truth be spoken, in marine engineering. Changes came in machinery and material of construction abroad which we were slow to follow, so that the high-powered and lean model of the Clyde iron-built blockade-runner had a distinct advantage in speed over her chasers. Thus, even during the last two months of 1864, the imports of Charleston and Wilmington comprised over eight million five hundred thousand pounds of meat, one million five hundred thousand pounds of lead, nearly two million pounds of saltpeter, five hundred thousand pairs of shoes, three hundred and sixteen thousand pairs of blankets, over five hundred thousand pounds of coffee, sixty-nine thousand rifles, forty-three cannon, ninety-seven packages of revolvers, and two thousand six hundred and thirty-nine packages of medicine. The traffic across the Mexican border was of the same character, but there was still the gantlet to be run of the Mississippi River, now in Federal possession through the dauntless spirit of Farragut, greatest of naval commanders, not excepting Nelson himself.

But the grip of the navy was closing upon the Confederate ports. Charleston was, with the aid of the army, at last closed. Savannah was sealed; Mobile and New Orleans had, of course, long before been lost, as also Pensacola. Wilmington, so long closely watched, finally fell after the capture of Fort Fisher, and then happened that which, as already explained, might have occurred in the beginning had the Buchanan administration but acted with vigor, that is, the complete segregation of the South from the rest of the world. She still had men in plenty, but men to be effective must be fed and clothed. With open ports the war could have been indefinitely continued. With ports closed, the Southern armies were reduced to a pitiful misery, the long endurance of which makes a noble chapter in heroism.

The whole naval warfare of the secession period was thus one of closure. It was a strife to control the waters of the

COPYRIGHT, 1911, PATRIOT PUB. CO.

THE FLEET THAT CLEARED THE RIVER

"A spear-thrust in the back" was delivered to the Confederacy by the inland-river fleet that cut it in two. The squadron of Flag-Officer Davis is here lying near Memphis. Thus appeared the Federal gunboats on June 5, 1862, two miles above the city. Fort Pillow had been abandoned the previous day, but the Confederate river-defense flotilla still remained below and the Federals, still smarting from the disaster inflicted on the "Cincinnati," were determined to bring on a decisive engagement and, if possible, clear the river of their antagonists. Meanwhile four new vessels had joined the Federal squadron. These were river steamers which Charles Ellet, Jr., had converted into rams in the short space of six weeks. Their principle was as old as history, but it was now to be tried for the first time in aid of the

MEMPHIS, TENNESSEE ON THE HEIGHTS

Federal cause. On these heights above the river the inhabitants of Memphis were crowded on the morning of June 6, 1862, as the Federal squadron moved down-stream against the Confederate gunboats that were drawn up in double line of battle opposite the city. Everyone wanted to see the outcome of the great fight that was impending, for if its result proved adverse to the Confederates, Memphis would fall into Federal hands and another stretch of the Mississippi would be lost to the South. In the engagement at Memphis two of the Ellet rams accompanied the squadron—the "Queen of the West" commanded by Charles Ellet, and the "Monarch" commanded by his younger brother, Major Alfred Ellet. The Confederate flotilla was destroyed, but with the loss of Charles Ellet, from a mortal wound.

LIEUTENANT–COLONEL
ALFRED W. ELLET

ONE OF THE THREE
ELLETS AT MEMPHIS

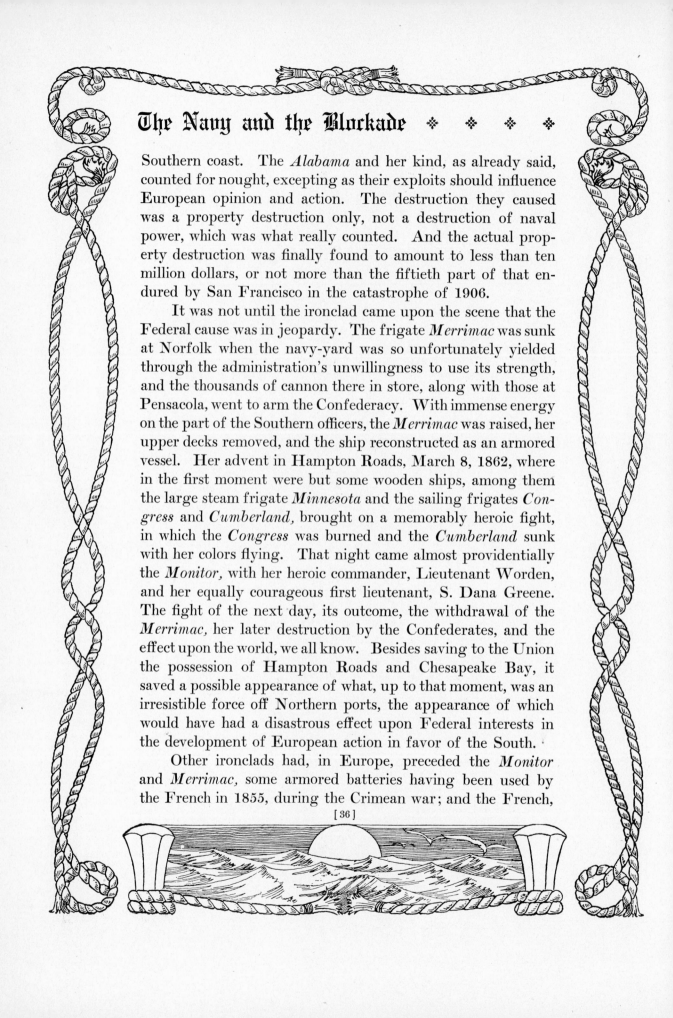

Southern coast. The *Alabama* and her kind, as already said, counted for nought, excepting as their exploits should influence European opinion and action. The destruction they caused was a property destruction only, not a destruction of naval power, which was what really counted. And the actual property destruction was finally found to amount to less than ten million dollars, or not more than the fiftieth part of that endured by San Francisco in the catastrophe of 1906.

It was not until the ironclad came upon the scene that the Federal cause was in jeopardy. The frigate *Merrimac* was sunk at Norfolk when the navy-yard was so unfortunately yielded through the administration's unwillingness to use its strength, and the thousands of cannon there in store, along with those at Pensacola, went to arm the Confederacy. With immense energy on the part of the Southern officers, the *Merrimac* was raised, her upper decks removed, and the ship reconstructed as an armored vessel. Her advent in Hampton Roads, March 8, 1862, where in the first moment were but some wooden ships, among them the large steam frigate *Minnesota* and the sailing frigates *Congress* and *Cumberland*, brought on a memorably heroic fight, in which the *Congress* was burned and the *Cumberland* sunk with her colors flying. That night came almost providentially the *Monitor*, with her heroic commander, Lieutenant Worden, and her equally courageous first lieutenant, S. Dana Greene. The fight of the next day, its outcome, the withdrawal of the *Merrimac*, her later destruction by the Confederates, and the effect upon the world, we all know. Besides saving to the Union the possession of Hampton Roads and Chesapeake Bay, it saved a possible appearance of what, up to that moment, was an irresistible force off Northern ports, the appearance of which would have had a disastrous effect upon Federal interests in the development of European action in favor of the South.

Other ironclads had, in Europe, preceded the *Monitor* and *Merrimac*, some armored batteries having been used by the French in 1855, during the Crimean war; and the French,

COPYRIGHT, 1911, REVIEW OF REVIEWS CO.

THE "BLACKHAWK," PORTER'S FAMOUS MISSISSIPPI FLAGSHIP
PHOTOGRAPHED OFF MEMPHIS, JUNE, '64

This wooden vessel, formerly a powerful river steamer, was armed and added to the Mississippi squadron soon after Porter took command. She was the admiral's flagship on the first expedition up the Yazoo. As the Stars and Stripes were run up on the court-house at Vicksburg, July 4, 1863, the "Blackhawk," bearing Admiral Porter and his staff, swept proudly up to the levee and received on board General Grant, with many of his officers. They "were received with that warmth of feeling and hospitality that delights the heart of a sailor." Outwardly unmoved, Grant received the congratulations of the officers of the navy upon the greatest victory of the war so far—a victory which the river squadron had helped so materially to win. Again the "Blackhawk" steamed away on active service as Porter's flagship to lead the futile Red River expedition.

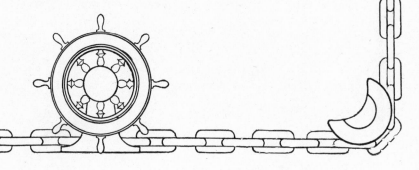

following their success, had built the *Gloire*. The British were
building four large broadside ships of the *Warrior* type; others
were to follow in the Confederate navy, the *Tennessee* at Mobile, the *Atlanta* in Wassaw Sound, the *Albemarle* in the
North Carolina sounds, and the formidable French-built *Stonewall;* but it was the *Monitor* which was to give the standard
for future types. Said the London *Times* after the Hampton
Roads fight, "Whereas we had one hundred and forty-nine
first-class war-ships, we have now two, [the large broadside
ships *Warrior* and *Black Prince*] . . . There is not a ship in
the English navy apart from those two that it would not be
madness to trust to an engagement with that little *Monitor*."
The type of hull of the latter has now been wholly discarded,
but the revolving turret remains the basic principle in the
mounting and protection of heavy guns. Notwithstanding
the defects of the system, the *Monitor* was the forerunner and
type of fifty-eight turreted vessels built or laid down during
the Civil War.

The Federal navy during the war rose to a force of five
hundred and sixty-nine steam vessels and over fifty thousand
seamen. Three hundred and thirteen steamers had been purchased and two hundred and three had been built or were well
advanced to completion. Over seven thousand five hundred
volunteer officers from the merchant service, many of great ability and value, were employed, some of whom, at the end of the
war, were taken into the regular service, rising to the highest
ranks and filling with credit most important posts.

The fight of the *Monitor* and *Merrimac,* the passage of
the Mississippi forts (April 24, 1862), Port Hudson (March
14, 1863), Mobile (August 5, 1864), the fight between the
Weehawken and *Atlanta,* the destruction of the *Albemarle,* and
the duel of the *Kearsarge* and *Alabama* were notable battles,
three of which rank in the forefront of naval actions in daring
and in effect. It is not too much to say that Farragut's deeds
in the Mississippi and at Mobile have not their parallel in

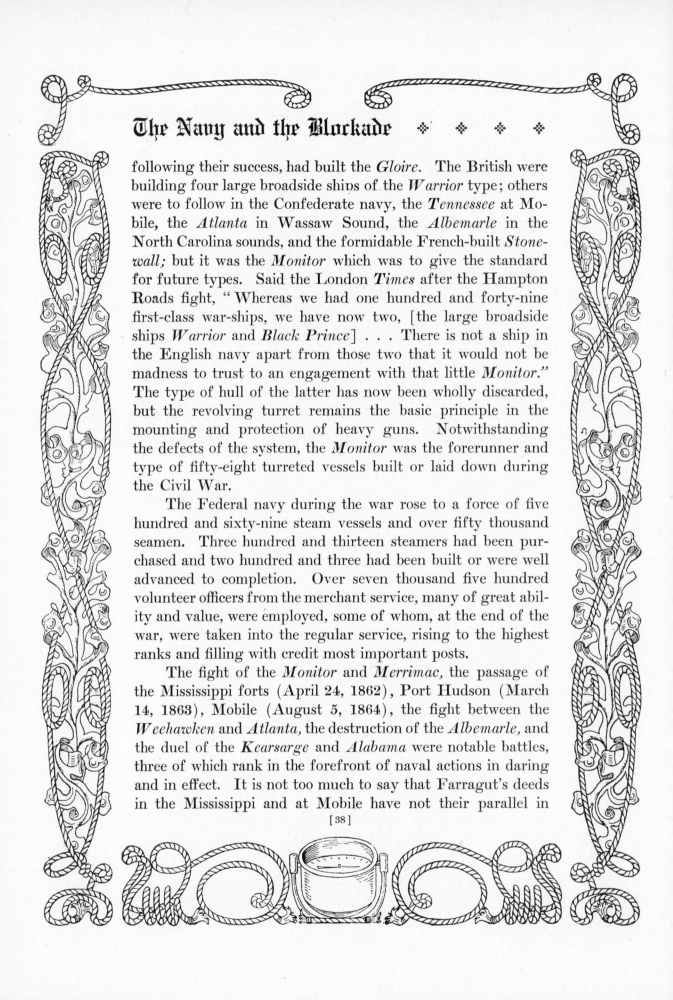

COPYRIGHT, 1911, PATRIOT PUB. CO.

THE SILENCED GUNS AT FORT FISHER—THE FINAL LINK IN THE BLOCKADING CHAIN, 1865

The wreckage in this picture of the dilapidated defenses of Fort Fisher marks the approaching doom of the Confederate cause. The gun dismounted by the accurate fire of Porter's fleet and the palisade broken through by the attackers from the sea-front are mute witnesses to the fact that the last port of the South has been effectually closed and that all possibility of securing further supplies and munitions of war from the outside world is at an end. Since the beginning of hostilities Fort Fisher had kept open the approach to Wilmington,

North Carolina, and even at the beginning of 1865 the blockade-runners were able in many cases to set at naught the efforts of the Federal squadron to keep them out of Wilmington. The fall of Fort Fisher, making the blockade at last a complete accomplished fact from the Potomac to the Rio Grande, marked the last act in the long drama of achievements by the navy in a war that could never have been won so soon without its help. Nor could the navy alone have closed the port. In the second attack the army had to help.

naval history. Says Charles Francis Adams, "It may safely be claimed that the running of the forts at the mouth of the Mississippi and the consequent fall of New Orleans was as brilliant an operation, and one as triumphantly conducted, as Sherman's march through Georgia," which, as he mentions later, was itself made possible by the undisputed maritime supremacy of the North. "Throttling the Confederacy by the blockade throughout," he says, "the navy was also a spear-thrust in its back."

Great, however, as was the effect of cutting in twain the Confederacy by the occupancy of the Mississippi, much greater was the effect of the monotonous and unheroic work of the blockade in Atlantic waters. By the end of the war there were captured and destroyed, in all, one thousand five hundred and four vessels, of a value of over thirty million dollars, much of which was British property. Large as was the money value, it was as nothing in comparison with the effect in deciding the great question at issue, through the loss of that without which the South could not live.

The failure of historians, with few exceptions, through nearly fifty years to recognize this great service done by the navy, shows a want of philosophic perception without which history is but a diary of events. Blockade is from a dramatic standpoint but a poor offset to great battles with thousands killed and wounded, the losses in which come keenly to tens of thousands of men and women. The fortunes of a million men in an army thus overshadow in the mind of the great public those of a comparatively meager fifty thousand in ships, and a blockade may go unnoticed by the public in war, much as the constant diplomacy of the navy goes unnoticed in peace.

To place New Orleans, Mobile, and Hampton Roads in the category of commonplace events is not to know war. As acts, they are among the lime-lights of history; in results, two, at least, were among the most momentous; for whatever went far to save this Union must be in such a category.

[40]

THE ORGANIZATION
OF THE
FEDERAL NAVY

___

GEORGE BANCROFT—FOUNDER
OF THE NAVAL ACADEMY

ALREADY NOTABLE AS A HISTORIAN IN 1845, BANCROFT
SIGNALIZED HIS ENTRANCE INTO PRESIDENT POLK'S CAB-
INET, AS SECRETARY OF THE NAVY, BY FOUNDING THE
NAVAL SCHOOL, LATER THE ACADEMY AT ANNAPOLIS

JACK–TARS OF THE OLD NAVY

A glance at these seasoned men ranged alongside the 9-inch pivot-gun of the sloop-of-war "Wissahickon" gives us an idea of the appearance of the men of the old navy.   The face of the gun-captain standing near the breach of his gun shows that he is a sailor through and through.   There are very few landsmen pictured here.   The old Jack-tar, standing fourth in the right row, who has turned his cap into a ditty bag, harks back to the fighting days when steam had hardly been thought of.   He is a survivor of the War of 1812, and remembers the days of Bainbridge, of Decatur, Stewart, and Biddle.   Even the younger men have no look of the volunteer about them; they are deep-sea sailors, every one.   The "Wissahickon" was one of the Federal cruisers that had put out in search of the

COPYRIGHT, 1911, REVIEW OF REVIEWS CO.

THE PIVOT-GUN OF THE "WISSAHICKON" AND ITS CREW

Confederate commerce-destroyers. She was in the fleet of Admiral Farragut at New Orleans and ran the batteries at Vicksburg. Late in 1862 she was in Carolina waters and in January, 1863, participated in the first attacks on Fort McAllister. She was in Admiral Dahlgren's fleet during the stirring operations in Charleston harbor and returned to South Carolina waters toward the close of 1864, where she captured numerous prizes, enriching her officers and crew. The sailors on few of the Federal vessels had a more varied and adventurous experience of the war than did those of the "Wissahickon," and the faces in the picture, both old and young, are those of men ready at any and all times for a fight or a frolic on their beloved ship.

THE OLD NAVY—THREE VETERANS OF THE LINE

In the center of this war-time photograph rides the famous frigate "Constitution." She was one of the four fighting-ships the construction of which, under Act of Congress of March 27, 1794, marked the birth of an adequate navy to protect the commerce of the young republic. She was the third to be launched, October 21, 1797, at Boston. Her exploits in the harbor of Tripoli in 1804 and her great fight with the "Guerrière" soon made her name a household word to all Americans. Full of years and honors in 1861, she was lying at Annapolis as a training-ship at the outbreak of the War of the Rebellion, and was in great danger of falling into the hands of the Confederates. General Benjamin F. Butler, who was in the vicinity with the Eighth Massachusetts Regiment, sent a detachment that guarded the old ship till she was towed to New-port, where she arrived May 9th under Lieutenant-Commander G. W. Rodgers, with officers and midship-men from the Military Academy aboard. At the extreme right of the picture is the "Macedonian," originally a British sloop-of-war captured by the U. S. frigate "United States" in 1812. She was a spick-and-span new

COPYRIGHT, 1911, REVIEW OF REVIEWS CO.

"SANTEE," "CONSTITUTION," AND "MACEDONIAN"

vessel then. In 1852–4 she sailed in Commodore Perry's fleet that opened Japan to American commerce. The outbreak of the war found her lying at Vera Cruz. The frigate on the left, the "Santee," was a later addition to the navy, also mounting fifty guns. She served on blockade duty, chiefly in the Gulf, during the war. There, while lying off Galveston, November 7, 1861, in command of Captain Henry Eagle, some of her crew performed one of the most brilliant naval exploits that marked the beginning of hostilities. Lieutenant James E. Jouett volunteered to run into the harbor and destroy the Confederate steamer "General Rusk" and the schooner "Royal Yacht." Near midnight the little party in two launches pulled boldly into the harbor. When almost upon the "General Rusk," Lieutenant Jouett's launch grounded and was run into by the second launch. With the Confederates thus aroused and several steamers speeding to find him in the darkness, Lieutenant Jouett nevertheless determined to board. After a thrilling encounter, he made prisoners of the crew and destroyed the schooner, returning with a loss of one killed and six wounded.

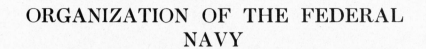

ORGANIZATION OF THE FEDERAL NAVY

WHEN President Lincoln and his administration found themselves confronted with the most stupendous problem that any nation had had as yet to face, there was one element in their favor that counted more heavily than any other, an element whose value has been overlooked by the early historians of the war. It was the possession not only of a navy but of shipyards and a vast merchant marine from which to draw both vessels and men, and thus to increase the Northern fighting efficiency at sea.

Though both North and South were wholly unprepared for the gigantic struggle, at the command of the Federal Government were inexhaustible resources. Manufactories and establishments of all kinds were at hand, together with ship-building yards that had turned out a merchant marine which, previous to the outbreak of hostilities, had gained the commerce-carrying supremacy of the world. These factors and advantages were of tremendous importance in contributing to the final success of the Federal cause. Not only was the part of the trained sailor significant, but the mechanic and inventor found a peculiar scope and wide field for development in the application of their genius and talents to the navy's needs. In five years, the whole science of naval warfare was to be changed; the wooden fleets of Europe were to become antiquated and practically useless, and the ironclad whose appearance had been adumbrated was now to become a reality for all sea fighting.

Ninety ships of war made up the United States navy at the opening of the year 1861, but of these only forty-two were in any measure ready for active service; the remainder were

COPYRIGHT, 1911, REVIEW OF REVIEWS CO.

THE FLAGSHIP "WABASH"—THE PRIDE OF THE NAVY IN '61

Sights such as this photograph conveys have passed forever. The type of vessel pictured here is now as obsolete as the great "Harry" of King Henry VIII or a Spanish galleon of King Philip. But what a beautiful sight she presents; the long clean sweep of her spar-deck, her standing rigging as taut as fiddle-strings, and all her running gear coiled and flemished down—no wonder that the "Wabash" was the pride of the navy, and that her crew pointed to the name on their caps with pride when they were ashore. The "Wabash" was a steam frigate of the first rating. No finer vessel could have been found in any foreign navy. She displaced 3,274 tons, carried two 10-inch pivot guns on her spar-deck and a broadside of fourteen 8-inch guns; on her gun-deck she carried twenty-eight 9-inch guns and two 12-pounders. On the deck stands a little group of three—Admiral Du Pont, who was in command of the South Atlantic blockading squadron, her Captain, C. R. P. Rodgers, and Commander Corbin. Until the ironclad appeared, such ships as the "Wabash", though small in number, gave to the United States navy a prestige wherever the flag was flown.

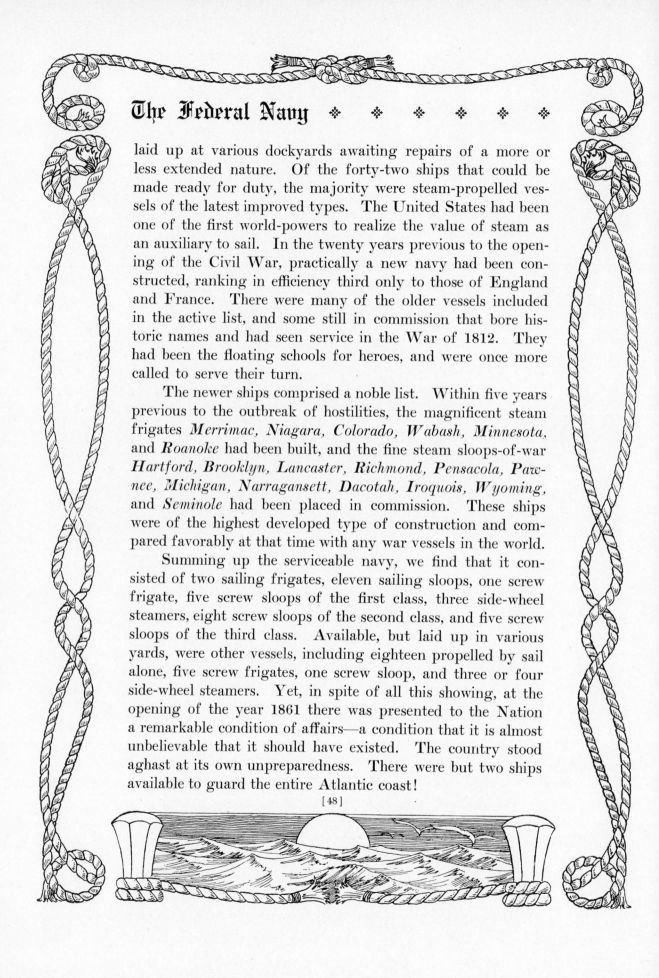

laid up at various dockyards awaiting repairs of a more or less extended nature. Of the forty-two ships that could be made ready for duty, the majority were steam-propelled vessels of the latest improved types. The United States had been one of the first world-powers to realize the value of steam as an auxiliary to sail. In the twenty years previous to the opening of the Civil War, practically a new navy had been constructed, ranking in efficiency third only to those of England and France. There were many of the older vessels included in the active list, and some still in commission that bore historic names and had seen service in the War of 1812. They had been the floating schools for heroes, and were once more called to serve their turn.

The newer ships comprised a noble list. Within five years previous to the outbreak of hostilities, the magnificent steam frigates *Merrimac, Niagara, Colorado, Wabash, Minnesota,* and *Roanoke* had been built, and the fine steam sloops-of-war *Hartford, Brooklyn, Lancaster, Richmond, Pensacola, Pawnee, Michigan, Narragansett, Dacotah, Iroquois, Wyoming,* and *Seminole* had been placed in commission. These ships were of the highest developed type of construction and compared favorably at that time with any war vessels in the world.

Summing up the serviceable navy, we find that it consisted of two sailing frigates, eleven sailing sloops, one screw frigate, five screw sloops of the first class, three side-wheel steamers, eight screw sloops of the second class, and five screw sloops of the third class. Available, but laid up in various yards, were other vessels, including eighteen propelled by sail alone, five screw frigates, one screw sloop, and three or four side-wheel steamers. Yet, in spite of all this showing, at the opening of the year 1861 there was presented to the Nation a remarkable condition of affairs—a condition that it is almost unbelievable that it should have existed. The country stood aghast at its own unpreparedness. There were but two ships available to guard the entire Atlantic coast!

COPYRIGHT, 1911, REVIEW OF REVIEWS CO.

WITH ALL SAILS SET

Despite the presence of magnificent force and might in the great modern vessel of war that rates from twelve to twenty thousand tons, there is little that suggests the romance of the sea about the huge mass of steel, magnificent and formidable though it may appear. The modern ship is sexless, or rather masculine. But no one would apply to such a fine old war-vessel as is pictured here, the training-ship "Saratoga," anything less than the sailor's half-endearing term of femininity. Ships, just as we see this one, fought in the War of the Revolution, and, with hardly a change, the "Saratoga" appears here as in the Mediterranean she forged ahead in chase of one of the Barbary pirates, or maneuvered to escape from a British seventy-four in the War of 1812. In the older days, she would not have had the handy double topsails which give her one more yard to each mast. Perhaps with single topsails she looked still handsomer. It required seamanship in those days to make a landfall. Dead reckoning was "dead reckoning" with a vengeance. Nowadays, after the departure has been taken and the ship laid on her course, the revolutions of the engines, the knowledge of ocean currents, and the spinning taffrail log give a navigating officer a technical knowledge of his whereabouts. It was different when they depended on the wind alone. It was in the school of the sailing-ship that most of the officers who fought in the Civil War had been trained. The "Saratoga" was one of Commodore Perry's fleet when he sailed to Japan, in 1852. Just previous to the outbreak of the war she had been engaged in putting down piracy in the West Indies, and long after the war was started she was hovering off the western coast of Africa, capturing the "Nightingale," a slaver with over 960 slaves herded between decks. During the war she was used mainly as a school-ship.

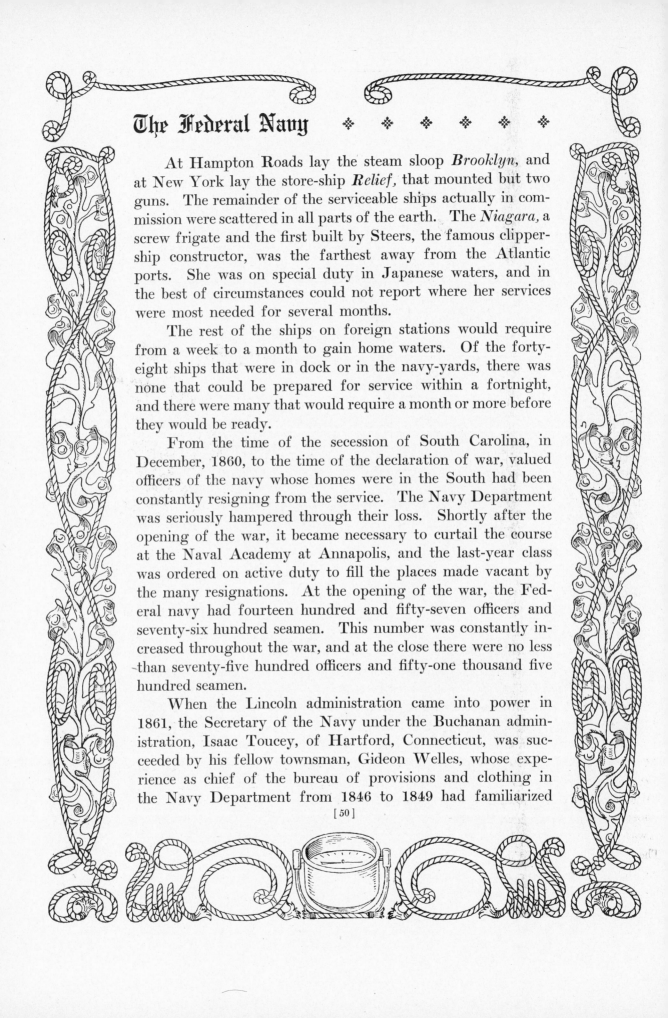

The Federal Navy ✦ ✦ ✦ ✦ ✦ ✦

At Hampton Roads lay the steam sloop *Brooklyn*, and at New York lay the store-ship *Relief,* that mounted but two guns. The remainder of the serviceable ships actually in commission were scattered in all parts of the earth. The *Niagara,* a screw frigate and the first built by Steers, the famous clipper-ship constructor, was the farthest away from the Atlantic ports. She was on special duty in Japanese waters, and in the best of circumstances could not report where her services were most needed for several months.

The rest of the ships on foreign stations would require from a week to a month to gain home waters. Of the forty-eight ships that were in dock or in the navy-yards, there was none that could be prepared for service within a fortnight, and there were many that would require a month or more before they would be ready.

From the time of the secession of South Carolina, in December, 1860, to the time of the declaration of war, valued officers of the navy whose homes were in the South had been constantly resigning from the service. The Navy Department was seriously hampered through their loss. Shortly after the opening of the war, it became necessary to curtail the course at the Naval Academy at Annapolis, and the last-year class was ordered on active duty to fill the places made vacant by the many resignations. At the opening of the war, the Federal navy had fourteen hundred and fifty-seven officers and seventy-six hundred seamen. This number was constantly increased throughout the war, and at the close there were no less than seventy-five hundred officers and fifty-one thousand five hundred seamen.

When the Lincoln administration came into power in 1861, the Secretary of the Navy under the Buchanan administration, Isaac Toucey, of Hartford, Connecticut, was succeeded by his fellow townsman, Gideon Welles, whose experience as chief of the bureau of provisions and clothing in the Navy Department from 1846 to 1849 had familiarized

COPYRIGHT, 1911, REVIEW OF REVIEWS CO.

THE "COLORADO"—A FRIGATE OF THE OLD NAVY

The "Colorado" was one of six 40-gun screw frigates, the pride and strength of the Federal navy in '61. Like most of her sister-ships of the old navy, the "Colorado" (built for sea fighting) was prevented by her size from getting up the narrow channels, and her gallant commander, Theodorus Bailey, had to lead the fleet at New Orleans past the forts in another vessel. On September 14, 1861, at Pensacola, volunteers from the "Colorado's" crew in four boats, led by Lieutenant J. H. Russell, carried off a "cutting out" expedition. They drove the stubbornly resisting crew from the Confederate privateer "Judah" and destroyed the vessel.

[E—4]

him with the details of department work. Under Welles, as assistant secretary, was appointed Gustavus V. Fox, a brilliant naval officer, whose eighteen years in the service had well fitted him for the work he was to take up, and whose talents and foresight later provided valuable aid to the secretary. At the head of the bureau of yards and docks was Joseph Smith, whose continuous service in the navy for nearly a half-century and whose occupancy of the position at the head of the bureau from 1845 had qualified him also to meet the unlooked-for emergency of war.

Under the direction of the secretary, there were at this time a bureau of ordnance and hydrography, a bureau of construction, equipment, and repair, a bureau of provisions and clothing, and a bureau of medicine and surgery. It was soon found that these bureaus could not adequately dispose of all the business and details to come before the department, and by act of Congress of July 5, 1862, there was added a bureau of navigation and a bureau of steam engineering. The bureau of construction, equipment, and repair was subdivided into a bureau of equipment and recruiting and a bureau of construction and repair.

In William Faxon, the chief clerk of the Navy Department, Secretary Welles found the ablest of assistants, whose business ability and mastery of detail were rewarded in the last months of the war by his being appointed assistant secretary while Mr. Fox was abroad.

With the organization of the new Navy Department, steps were taken at once to gather the greater number of the ships of the Federal fleets where they could be used to the utmost advantage. Work on the repairing and refitting of the ships then laid up in the various navy-yards was begun, and orders were given for the construction of a number of new vessels. But in the very first months of the actual opening of the war, the Navy Department dealt itself the severest blow that it received during the whole course of hostilities.

GIDEON WELLES, WAR SECRETARY OF THE FEDERAL NAVY

Rarely has so stupendous a task confronted a man as that which fell to the lot of Lincoln's Secretary of the Navy. In ordinary times the man fit for that office must be a statesman, a constitutional lawyer, a judge of international law and national obligations, as well as a man of sound judgment and executive ability of the highest order. These qualities Gideon Welles possessed in a marked degree. At the time he took his seat in the Cabinet the Navy Department was entirely unprepared for the work that was immediately required of it, work perhaps more arduous than had ever before been demanded of the maritime power of any government. The whole management of the navy during the war indicated the most remarkable administrative ability on the part of the Secretary. The herculean tasks required were performed without ostentation, with a firm and sagacious hand that never wavered before ungenerous and ignorant criticism. Not only was the physical side attended to with marvelous promptness and efficiency, but the policies of the Administration were frequently shaped by his wise influence.

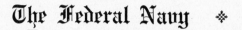

The Federal Navy ❖

Lying at the Gosport Navy-Yard at Norfolk, Virginia, were some of the navy's strongest, most formidable, and most historic ships—the steam frigate *Merrimac*, of forty guns, that was soon to make the world ring with her name; the sloop-of-war *Germantown*, of twenty-two guns; the *Plymouth*, of the same number, and the brig *Dolphin*.

There were, besides, the old sailing vessels whose names were dear to the country: to wit, the *Pennsylvania*, a line-of-battle ship; the *United States, Columbus, Delaware, Raritan,* and *Columbia.* There was also on the stocks, and unfinished, a ship of the line, the *New York*.

There is not time or space in this short preamble to enter into the reasons for what happened, but through blunders and a feeling of panic, the fiat went forth that the navy-yard and all it contained should be destroyed. On the night of April 20th, this order was carried into effect, and over two million of dollars' worth of Federal property was destroyed, besides vast stores and ammunition. Thousands of cannon fell into the hands of the new-born Secessia. It was a bitter chapter for the cooler heads to read. All along the coast of the Southern States, other vessels which could not be removed from docks or naval stations were seized by the Confederate Government or destroyed by orders from Washington.

As if suddenly recovered from the fever of apprehension that had caused so much destruction, the Federal Government soon recognized its necessities, and the Navy Department awoke to the knowledge of what would be required of it. Immediately, the floating force was increased by the purchase of great numbers of vessels of all kinds. Of these, thirty-six were side-wheel steamers, forty-two were screw steamers, one an auxiliary steam bark, and fifty-eight were sailing craft of various classes. These vessels mounted a total of five hundred and nineteen guns, of which the steam craft carried three hundred and thirty-five. In addition to these, the navy-yards were put to work at the building of new vessels, twenty-three being

FROM THE OLD NAVY TO THE NEW

THE SLOOP–OF–WAR "PENSACOLA," FIRST IN LINE WITH FARRAGUT

The "Pensacola" was the type of United States fighting-ship that marks the transition from the old navy to the new, consummated by the Civil War. Steam had superseded sail, armor plate was still to come. Farragut could never get used to it, contending that in old wooden ships like the "Hartford" a shot would pass clean through both sides, doing less damage than when penetrating an ironclad. The "Pensacola" formed a splendid type of the steam sloop-of-war, of which the "Hartford," Farragut's famous flagship, was the latest addition to the navy at the outbreak of the war. When Farragut fought his way past the forts below New Orleans, the "Pensacola" (after the grounding of the "Cayuga") was first in line. Her captain, Henry W. Morris, deliberately slowed up and stopped frequently opposite the forts, as did the "Mississippi," so that their powerful batteries might take effect while the smaller vessels got by.

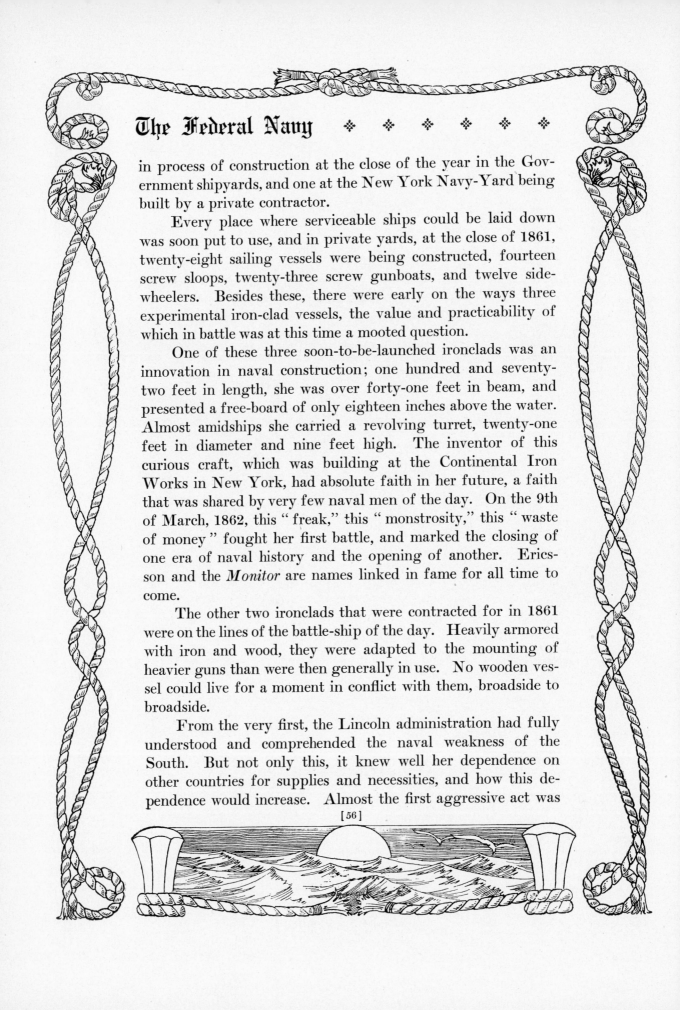

in process of construction at the close of the year in the Government shipyards, and one at the New York Navy-Yard being built by a private contractor.

Every place where serviceable ships could be laid down was soon put to use, and in private yards, at the close of 1861, twenty-eight sailing vessels were being constructed, fourteen screw sloops, twenty-three screw gunboats, and twelve side-wheelers. Besides these, there were early on the ways three experimental iron-clad vessels, the value and practicability of which in battle was at this time a mooted question.

One of these three soon-to-be-launched ironclads was an innovation in naval construction; one hundred and seventy-two feet in length, she was over forty-one feet in beam, and presented a free-board of only eighteen inches above the water. Almost amidships she carried a revolving turret, twenty-one feet in diameter and nine feet high. The inventor of this curious craft, which was building at the Continental Iron Works in New York, had absolute faith in her future, a faith that was shared by very few naval men of the day. On the 9th of March, 1862, this " freak," this " monstrosity," this " waste of money " fought her first battle, and marked the closing of one era of naval history and the opening of another. Ericsson and the *Monitor* are names linked in fame for all time to come.

The other two ironclads that were contracted for in 1861 were on the lines of the battle-ship of the day. Heavily armored with iron and wood, they were adapted to the mounting of heavier guns than were then generally in use. No wooden vessel could live for a moment in conflict with them, broadside to broadside.

From the very first, the Lincoln administration had fully understood and comprehended the naval weakness of the South. But not only this, it knew well her dependence on other countries for supplies and necessities, and how this dependence would increase. Almost the first aggressive act was

FORERUNNERS OF THE LIGHT–DRAUGHT GUNBOAT—FERRYBOATS CONVERTED INTO WAR–VESSELS

In these pictures are seen two of the navy's converted ferryboat fleet. The "McDonough" (above) was taken while on duty near Hilton Head by a lieutenant of volunteers who possessed one of those rare new instruments, a camera. She was quite thoroughly armored. Under command of Lieutenant-Commander Bacon she was lying in Stono River, February 1, 1863, when the "Isaac Smith," going up the river to make a reconnaissance, was entrapped by three concealed Confederate batteries. The "McDonough" got under way to the assistance of the "Isaac Smith," but was unable to stand the fire of the heavy rifled guns that finally caused the surrender of the "Isaac Smith." Thus these improvised gunboats went bravely to their tasks, sometimes winning single-handed against superior force, sometimes paying the penalty of their boldness in cruising up rivers and about sounds and bayous where hostile batteries and gunboats lay concealed or where troops were ambushed ready to pick off the pilot and anyone else who showed himself. The necessities of this sort of inland warfare taught the navy the value of the light-draught.

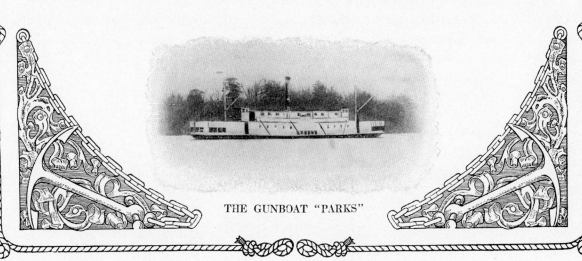

THE GUNBOAT "PARKS"

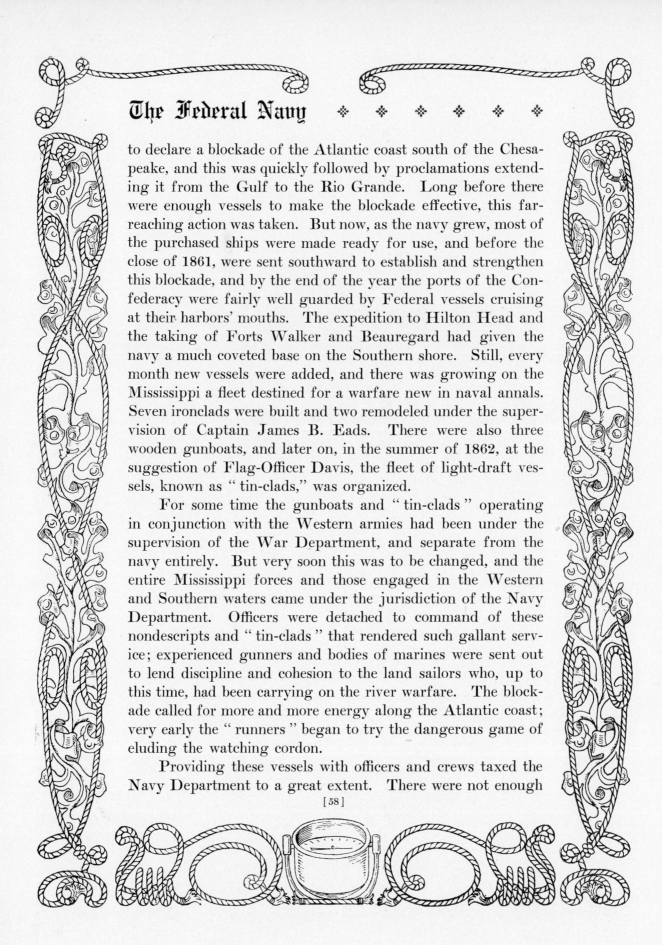

to declare a blockade of the Atlantic coast south of the Chesapeake, and this was quickly followed by proclamations extending it from the Gulf to the Rio Grande. Long before there were enough vessels to make the blockade effective, this far-reaching action was taken. But now, as the navy grew, most of the purchased ships were made ready for use, and before the close of 1861, were sent southward to establish and strengthen this blockade, and by the end of the year the ports of the Confederacy were fairly well guarded by Federal vessels cruising at their harbors' mouths. The expedition to Hilton Head and the taking of Forts Walker and Beauregard had given the navy a much coveted base on the Southern shore. Still, every month new vessels were added, and there was growing on the Mississippi a fleet destined for a warfare new in naval annals. Seven ironclads were built and two remodeled under the supervision of Captain James B. Eads. There were also three wooden gunboats, and later on, in the summer of 1862, at the suggestion of Flag-Officer Davis, the fleet of light-draft vessels, known as " tin-clads," was organized.

For some time the gunboats and " tin-clads " operating in conjunction with the Western armies had been under the supervision of the War Department, and separate from the navy entirely. But very soon this was to be changed, and the entire Mississippi forces and those engaged in the Western and Southern waters came under the jurisdiction of the Navy Department. Officers were detached to command of these nondescripts and " tin-clads " that rendered such gallant service; experienced gunners and bodies of marines were sent out to lend discipline and cohesion to the land sailors who, up to this time, had been carrying on the river warfare. The blockade called for more and more energy along the Atlantic coast; very early the " runners " began to try the dangerous game of eluding the watching cordon.

Providing these vessels with officers and crews taxed the Navy Department to a great extent. There were not enough

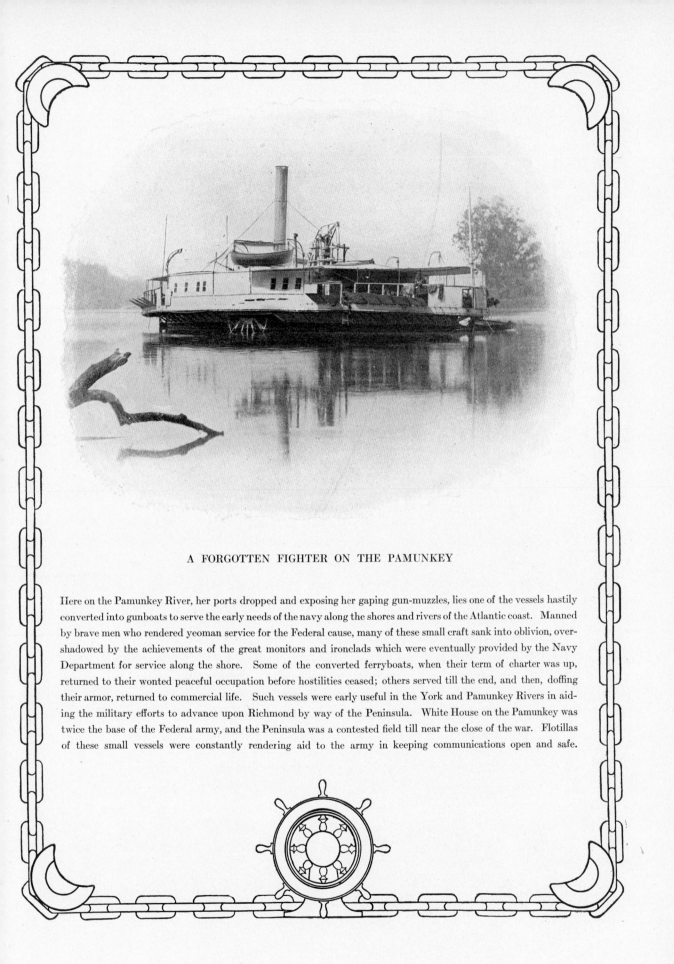

A FORGOTTEN FIGHTER ON THE PAMUNKEY

Here on the Pamunkey River, her ports dropped and exposing her gaping gun-muzzles, lies one of the vessels hastily converted into gunboats to serve the early needs of the navy along the shores and rivers of the Atlantic coast. Manned by brave men who rendered yeoman service for the Federal cause, many of these small craft sank into oblivion, overshadowed by the achievements of the great monitors and ironclads which were eventually provided by the Navy Department for service along the shore. Some of the converted ferryboats, when their term of charter was up, returned to their wonted peaceful occupation before hostilities ceased; others served till the end, and then, doffing their armor, returned to commercial life. Such vessels were early useful in the York and Pamunkey Rivers in aiding the military efforts to advance upon Richmond by way of the Peninsula. White House on the Pamunkey was twice the base of the Federal army, and the Peninsula was a contested field till near the close of the war. Flotillas of these small vessels were constantly rendering aid to the army in keeping communications open and safe.

experienced men then in the navy to officer more than a small portion of the ships brought into service, and it was necessary to call for recruits. The merchant marine was drawn on for many valuable men, who filled the stations to which they were assigned with credit to themselves and the navy. It may be said to the credit of both the merchant marine and the "service," however, that the consequent jealousy of rank that at times was shown resulted in nothing more serious than temporary dissatisfaction, and was seldom openly expressed. The men of both callings had been too well trained to the discipline of the sea to question the orders of their superiors, and after the distribution of commissions usually settled down to a faithful and efficient discharge of the duties to which they had been assigned.

From the outset of the war, it appeared more difficult to secure enlistments for the navy than for the army, and with the constant addition of ships it finally became necessary to offer large bounties to all the naval recruits in order to keep the quota up to the required numbers. During the war the United States navy built two hundred and eight vessels and purchased four hundred and eighteen. Of these, nearly sixty were ironclads, mostly monitors.

With the introduction of the ironclad and the continual increase of the thickness and efficiency of the armor as the war progressed, the guns of the navy also changed in weight and pattern. The advent of the ironclad made necessary the introduction of heavier ordnance. The manufacturers of these guns throughout the North were called upon to provide for the emergency. At the beginning of the war, the 32-pounder and the 8-inch were almost the highest-power guns in use, though some of the steam vessels were provided with 11-inch Dahlgren guns. Before the war had closed, the 11-inch Dahlgren, which had been regarded as a "monster" at the start, had been far overshadowed, and the caliber had increased to 15-inch, then 18-inch, and finally by a 20-inch that came so

COPYRIGHT, 1911, PATRIOT PUB. CO.

FROM THE MERCHANT MARINE—THE "FORT JACKSON"

Here the U. S. S. "Fort Jackson" lies in Hampton Roads, December, 1864. This powerful side-wheel steamer of 1,770 tons burden was a regular river passenger-steamer before she was purchased by the Federal Government and converted into a gunboat of the second class. Her armament consisted of one 100-pounder rifle, two 30-pound rifles, and eight 9-inch smooth-bores. The navy had come to know the need of her type during the latter half of the war. By the end of 1862, 180 purchased vessels had been added to its force. But many of these, unlike the "Fort Jackson," were frail barks in which officers and men "had to fight the heaviest kind of earthworks, often perched at a great height above the water, where their plunging fire could perforate the vessels' decks and boilers or even pass down through their bottoms." But so splendid was the organization and discipline of the navy from the first that inadequacies of equipment were compensated for in a most remarkable degree. The personnel of the navy, both regular and volunteer, was of such a quality that men never questioned the peril which the mere embarking in some of the earlier gunboats entailed. The "Fort Jackson," under Captain B. F. Sands, was in the third line of the fleet that on December 24 and 25, 1864, hurled more than a million and a quarter pounds of shot and shell at Fort Fisher on the Cape Fear River, North Carolina. After the fall of that fort the "Fort Jackson" continued on blockade duty off the North Carolina coast, and during 1865 captured three blockade-runners with valuable cargoes.

late in the war as never to be used. Rifled cannon were also substituted for the smooth-bore guns.

The navy with which the Federals ended the war belonged to a different era from that with which it started, the men to a different class. Very early in 1862, the number of artisans and laborers employed in the Government navy-yards was increased from less than four thousand to nearly seventeen thousand, and these were constantly employed in the construction and equipment of new ships, embracing all the improvements that could be effectively used, as soon as they were shown to be practical. In addition to these seventeen thousand men, there were fully as many more engaged by private contractors, building and equipping other vessels for the service.

One of the features of the navy in the Civil War, and before referred to, was the "tin-clad" fleet, especially constructed to guard the rivers and shallow waters of the West and South. The principal requirement of these "tin-clads" was that they be of very light draft, to enable them to navigate across the shoals in the Mississippi and other rivers on which they did duty. The lighter class of these vessels drew less than two feet of water, and it was a common saying that they could "go anywhere where the ground was a little damp." They were small side- or stern-wheel boats, and were armored with iron plating less than an inch in thickness, from which they derived the name of "tin-clads." Though insufficient protection to resist a heavy shell, this light plating was a good bullet-proof, and would withstand the fire of a light field-piece, unless the shell chanced to find a vulnerable spot, such as an open port-hole.

These boats were armed with howitzers, and their work against field-batteries or sharpshooters on shore was particularly effective. The heavier class of boats that were used in the river offensive and defensive work was armed with more guns of larger caliber, and their armor-plating was somewhat heavier than that of the little vessels designed to get close to

COPYRIGHT, 1911, REVIEW OF REVIEWS CO.

FIGHTERS AFLOAT—GUNBOAT MEN ON THE "MENDOTA"

Here on the deck of the "Mendota" on the James River, late in '64, has gathered a typical group of gunboat men. While there are some foreign faces among them, many (particularly the younger ones) betoken the native American that responded to the call to arms by enlisting in the navy. At the outbreak of the war there were but seven thousand six hundred sailors in the Federal navy. It was a matter of no small difficulty to procure crews promptly for the new vessels that were being converted and constructed so rapidly, especially when the military service was making such frequent and sweeping requisitions upon the able-bodied men of the country. Nevertheless, at the close of the war the number of sailors in the navy had been increased to fifty-one thousand five hundred. It was an even more difficult problem to secure competent officers. Volunteers were called for by the Navy Department at the very outset of the struggle. As many of these enrolled as there had been sailors in the navy at the war's outbreak. Many vessels were officered entirely by volunteers, and these men acquitted themselves in a manner no less distinguished than the officers of the regular service. The gun in the picture is one of the "Mendota's" 200-pounder rifles, of which she carried two. In the war the American navy broke away from the old tradition that the effectiveness of a fighting-vessel is in proportion to the number of guns she carries. The distinct tendency became not to divide the weight she could safely bear among numerous guns of small caliber, but rather to have fewer guns of higher efficiency. Many of the small Federal gunboats carried 100-pounder rifles.

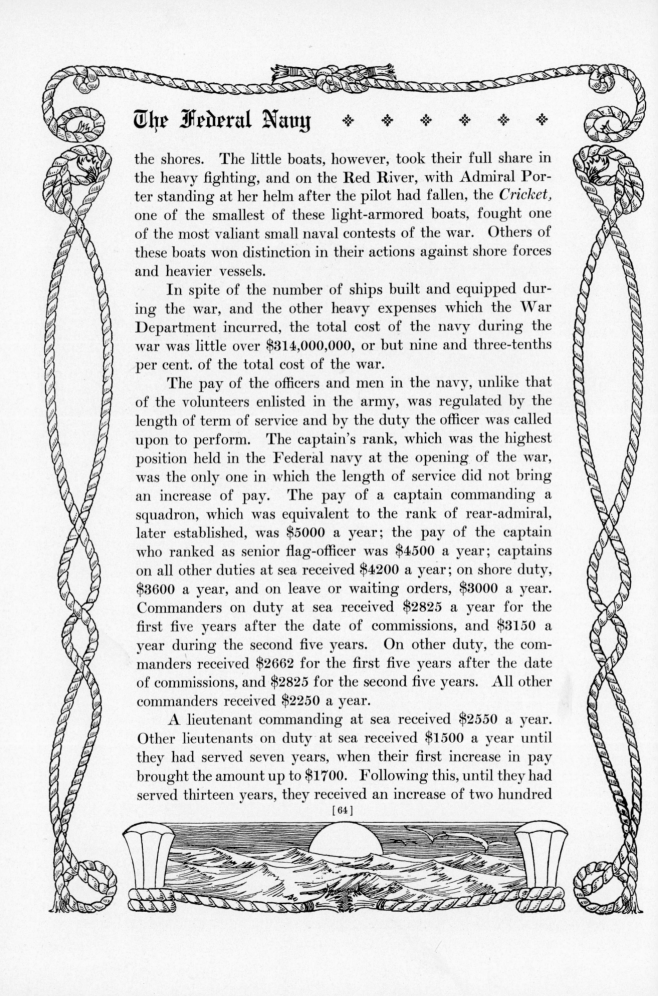

the shores. The little boats, however, took their full share in the heavy fighting, and on the Red River, with Admiral Porter standing at her helm after the pilot had fallen, the *Cricket*, one of the smallest of these light-armored boats, fought one of the most valiant small naval contests of the war. Others of these boats won distinction in their actions against shore forces and heavier vessels.

In spite of the number of ships built and equipped during the war, and the other heavy expenses which the War Department incurred, the total cost of the navy during the war was little over $314,000,000, or but nine and three-tenths per cent. of the total cost of the war.

The pay of the officers and men in the navy, unlike that of the volunteers enlisted in the army, was regulated by the length of term of service and by the duty the officer was called upon to perform. The captain's rank, which was the highest position held in the Federal navy at the opening of the war, was the only one in which the length of service did not bring an increase of pay. The pay of a captain commanding a squadron, which was equivalent to the rank of rear-admiral, later established, was $5000 a year; the pay of the captain who ranked as senior flag-officer was $4500 a year; captains on all other duties at sea received $4200 a year; on shore duty, $3600 a year, and on leave or waiting orders, $3000 a year. Commanders on duty at sea received $2825 a year for the first five years after the date of commissions, and $3150 a year during the second five years. On other duty, the commanders received $2662 for the first five years after the date of commissions, and $2825 for the second five years. All other commanders received $2250 a year.

A lieutenant commanding at sea received $2550 a year. Other lieutenants on duty at sea received $1500 a year until they had served seven years, when their first increase in pay brought the amount up to $1700. Following this, until they had served thirteen years, they received an increase of two hundred

LEARNING NEW LESSONS—THE NAVAL ACADEMY CLASS OF '66

The faces of the graduates of '66, and the view below of part of the Naval Academy grounds at Annapolis, taken in 1866, are the evidence of the peace-footing to which the institution has been restored within a year. The cadets and instructors have returned from Newport in 1865 and resumed their old quarters, from which they had been precipitately driven by the first Confederate move on Washington. The grand veteran "Constitution," the "Old Ironsides" of the navy, had given her pet name to her more powerful descendant, and lying near the center of the picture is now relegated to the position of receiving-ship. At the end of the wharf is tied up the "Santee," on whose deck many a midshipman has paced out the sentry duty with which he was punished for the infringement of regulations. Between the two lies the "Saratoga," now a supply-ship. New students had come to take the places of those who learned the theories and practice of naval warfare with the current exploits of the navy ringing in their ears day by day. Some of the officers who had fought through the great struggle were adding their practical experience, so lately gained, to the curriculum. However, the traditions of the old navy were still predominant; the training of the seaman was still considered essential for the cadets and was enforced as in the old sailing days as the foundation of their education. It was nevertheless the Naval Academy which kept alive for a future generation the valuable experience that had been gained at such a cost in the four years of Civil War.

COPYRIGHT, 1911, REVIEW OF REVIEWS CO.

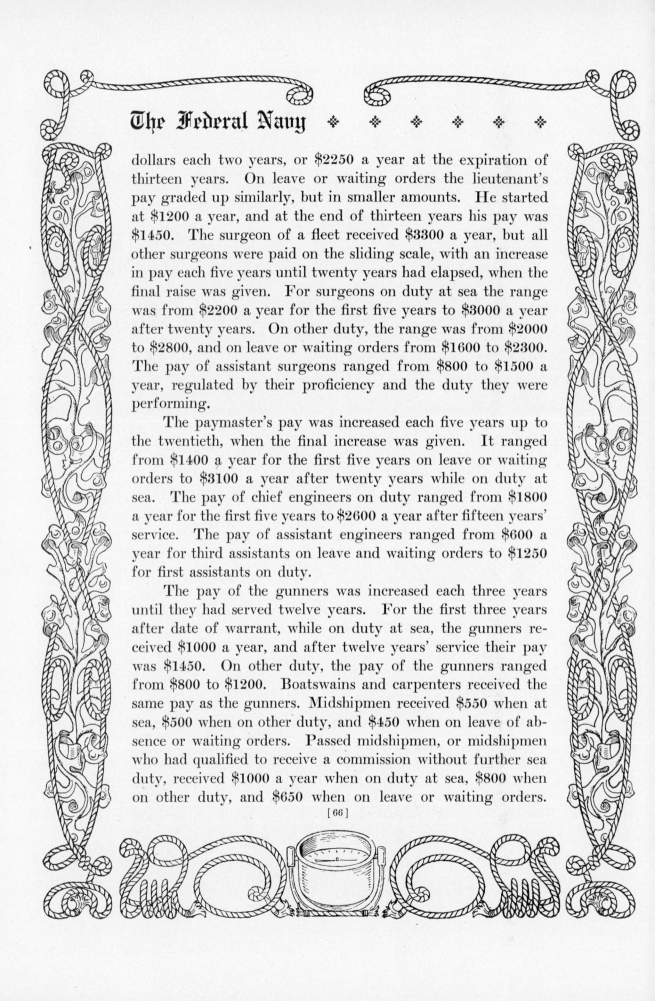

dollars each two years, or $2250 a year at the expiration of thirteen years. On leave or waiting orders the lieutenant's pay graded up similarly, but in smaller amounts. He started at $1200 a year, and at the end of thirteen years his pay was $1450. The surgeon of a fleet received $3300 a year, but all other surgeons were paid on the sliding scale, with an increase in pay each five years until twenty years had elapsed, when the final raise was given. For surgeons on duty at sea the range was from $2200 a year for the first five years to $3000 a year after twenty years. On other duty, the range was from $2000 to $2800, and on leave or waiting orders from $1600 to $2300. The pay of assistant surgeons ranged from $800 to $1500 a year, regulated by their proficiency and the duty they were performing.

The paymaster's pay was increased each five years up to the twentieth, when the final increase was given. It ranged from $1400 a year for the first five years on leave or waiting orders to $3100 a year after twenty years while on duty at sea. The pay of chief engineers on duty ranged from $1800 a year for the first five years to $2600 a year after fifteen years' service. The pay of assistant engineers ranged from $600 a year for third assistants on leave and waiting orders to $1250 for first assistants on duty.

The pay of the gunners was increased each three years until they had served twelve years. For the first three years after date of warrant, while on duty at sea, the gunners received $1000 a year, and after twelve years' service their pay was $1450. On other duty, the pay of the gunners ranged from $800 to $1200. Boatswains and carpenters received the same pay as the gunners. Midshipmen received $550 when at sea, $500 when on other duty, and $450 when on leave of absence or waiting orders. Passed midshipmen, or midshipmen who had qualified to receive a commission without further sea duty, received $1000 a year when on duty at sea, $800 when on other duty, and $650 when on leave or waiting orders.

THE NAVY'S SEAT OF LEARNING

COPYRIGHT, 1911, REVIEW OF REVIEWS CO.

Among the multifarious distinguished services of the scholarly and versatile Bancroft was his founding of the Naval School while Secretary of the Navy in 1845. It was reorganized and renamed the Naval Academy in 1850. In the picture above we see part of the water-front and the landing as it appeared after the war when the peaceful study of naval science had again been resumed here, the Academy having been moved to Newport, Rhode Island, during the war. While George Bancroft, approaching three-score years and ten, was writing history in New York during the great civil struggle, the graduates of the school he founded were making history as officers on the fighting-ships of both North and South. As West Point furnished the military brains for both armies, so Annapolis produced the men whose famous deeds afloat were the glory of both navies. No less than 322 officers resigned from the United States navy and entered the Confederate navy, and 243 of these were officers of the line. Thus nearly a fourth of the officers of the navy at the beginning of 1861 espoused the cause of the South. It was classmate against classmate afloat as well as ashore.

COPYRIGHT, 1911, PATRIOT PUB. CO.

MARINES AT THE WASHINGTON NAVY YARD

AMPHIBIOUS SOLDIERS—1865

This striking picture of an officer and five privates in the United States Marine Corps shows the quality of the men who made up that highly important branch of the service. The United States Marine Corps was established by Act of Congress on July 11, 1798, "as an addition to the present military establishment." On June 30, 1834, another Act for its better organization was passed. The marines were early in the war, not only in minor engagements along the coast incidental to the blockade, but in the first battle of Bull Run, July 21, 1861, where they coöperated with the regular military forces. The marines proved especially useful in the fighting along the Western rivers. When Admiral D. D. Porter took command of the Mississippi squadron, he applied for a force of marines to be carried in suitable vessels accompanying the fleet of gunboats so that the forces could be landed at various points. It was necessary to have trained soldiers at hand to pursue and annihilate these irresponsible raiders, who pillaged on the property of non-combatants

COPYRIGHT, 1911, PATRIOT PUB. CO.

OFFICER AND MEN OF THE U. S. MARINE CORPS

on both sides.   The Navy Department at the time could not furnish the marines that Porter wanted, but the War Department undertook to organize a marine brigade and also to furnish the necessary transports to carry them about.   The command of this was given to Brigadier-General Alfred Ellet.   Ellet's marine brigade, numbering about 2,000 strong, first sailed up the Tennessee River in April, 1863, to join the flotilla of Lieutenant-Commander Fitch, which was trying to suppress marauding bands in that territory.   On April 25th, the marine brigade was attacked at Duck River by 700 Confederates under Colonel Woodward, who had mistaken the Federal vessels for transports.   They were disagreeably surprised when the marines, landing promptly, discomfited them in a sharp engagement and pursued them for twelve miles inland.   On May 7th, since the waters of the Tennessee had become too low, the marine brigade joined Admiral Porter's squadron and rendered important service along the Mississippi and the Yazoo.

The Federal Navy ❖ ❖ ❖ ❖ ❖ ❖

Naval chaplains received the same pay as lieutenants. The pay-scale tapered down through the various grades of seamen, until the " boys," which included all the youngsters engaged in the positions of " powder-monkeys," " water-boys," and various other duties, received ten dollars a month and their rations.

Early in the war, the Navy Department was confronted by a serious problem that manifested itself in the numbers of "contrabands," or runaway slaves that made their way into the navy-yards and aboard the Federal ships, seeking protection. These contrabands could not be driven away, and there was no provision existing by which they could be put to work and made useful either on board the ships or in the navy-yards. The situation was finally brought to the attention of the Secretary of the Navy, and he was asked to find some remedy. Under date of the 25th of September, 1861, he issued an order that from that date the contrabands might be given employment on the Federal vessels or in the navy-yards at any necessary work that they were competent to do. They were advanced to the ratings of seamen, firemen, and coal-heavers, and received corresponding pay.

The principal yards where the construction work of the Federal navy was carried on were those at New York, Philadelphia, Portsmouth, and Boston.

Early in the war, the Naval Academy was removed to Newport, Rhode Island, "for safe-keeping," but in 1865, when invasion was an impossibility and the dwindling forces of the South were mostly confined to the armies of Johnston and Lee, south of the James, the academy once more returned to its old home. There were many young men of the classes of 1861 and 1862 who found themselves shoulders high above the rank generally accredited to officers of their years. For deeds of prowess and valor they had been advanced many numbers in the line of promotion. The classes of 1865 and 1866 were very large, and for a long time after the reduction of the naval establishment, promotion in the service became exceedingly slow.

II

ORGANIZATION
OF THE
CONFEDERATE NAVY

1863—BUILDING THE "INDIANOLA," SOON TO BE CAPTURED BY CONFEDERATES

THE "INDIANOLA," ONE OF THE MOST FORMIDABLE IRONCLADS ON THE MISSISSIPPI RIVER, WAS CAP-
TURED BY CONFEDERATE TROOPS ON FEBRUARY 24, 1863. SUCH WAS THE PAUCITY OF SHIPYARDS
AT THE SOUTH, AND THE SCARCITY OF MATERIALS AND SKILLED MECHANICS, THAT THE CAPTURE OF
A FEDERAL VESSEL OF ANY KIND WAS AN EVENT FOR GREAT REJOICING IN THE CONFEDERATE NAVY

THE ORGANIZATION OF THE CONFEDERATE NAVY

O N looking over the history of the rise of the Confederacy, viewed even from the writings of the earlier and more or less partisan historians, a reader will not fail to be impressed with the wonderful resourcefulness that was displayed in meeting the unexpected exigencies of war. Viewed from an absolutely impartial standpoint, the South apparently accomplished the impossible. The young Confederacy succeeded against heavy odds in making something out of almost nothing. There was no naval warfare in the proper sense of the word during the four years' conflict; there were no fleets that met in battle at sea, and only two or three actions that could be touched upon in strictly naval annals. But at the outset, in the making up of the Government of the new republic, there was formed a Navy Department whose accomplishments, struggling against the difficulties that confronted it, were little short of marvelous, considering the limited time, available for preparation, in a country almost barren of ship-yards and other means of providing and equipping sea-going vessels, not to mention warships.

In the closing days of 1860, the secession of South Carolina made the fact apparent to the people of the North and South that the breach was constantly widening between the two sections of the country. Very soon it was perceived that the ever-growing chasm could not be bridged by diplomatic means, and that to sustain the stand they had taken the seceding States would be forced by the urging voices of their leaders to make an appeal to arms.

The South was immeasurably handicapped in more ways than one, but principally by its utter lack of any war-ships,

The Confederacy was able to enter upon the seas early, with a naval force that had to be reckoned with, as a result of its enterprise in seizing the undefended Norfolk Navy-yard only nine days after Sumter was fired upon. As early as February 21, 1861, Jefferson Davis appointed Stephen Mallory as Secretary of the Confederate Navy. He resigned from the United States Senate, where he had represented his State, Florida, and before he joined the Confederate Cabinet the navy-yard in his home town, Pensacola, had been seized, January 10, 1861, by Florida and Alabama State troops. The Federal navy-yards in the South were neither so active nor so well equipped as those at the North. But Norfolk Navy-yard, one of the oldest and most extensive, was provided with everything for the building and finishing of vessels of the largest size. At the time

STEPHEN RUSSELL MALLORY
SECRETARY OF THE CONFEDERATE STATES NAVY

of the secession of Virginia it contained at least 2,000 pieces of heavy cannon, including 300 new Dahlgren guns. The aggregate value of the property there was close to $10,000,000. Most of this fell into the hands of the Confederates. Owing to the possession of the yard equipment, it was here that the Southern naval constructors were first able to exemplify their ideas in ironclad construction by raising the hull of the sunken "Merrimac" and converting her into the armored "Virginia," to strike terror at the heart of the North by her performances in Hampton Roads in 1862. Although the Federals regained possession of Norfolk soon afterward and compelled the destruction of the "Virginia," her record stirred the Confederates to almost superhuman efforts. Secretary Mallory was most active in founding enterprises both at home and abroad for the construction of vessels.

COPYRIGHT, 1911, REVIEW OF REVIEWS CO.

THE BEGINNING OF THE CONFEDERATE NAVY—RUINS OF THE NORFOLK NAVY-YARD, 1862

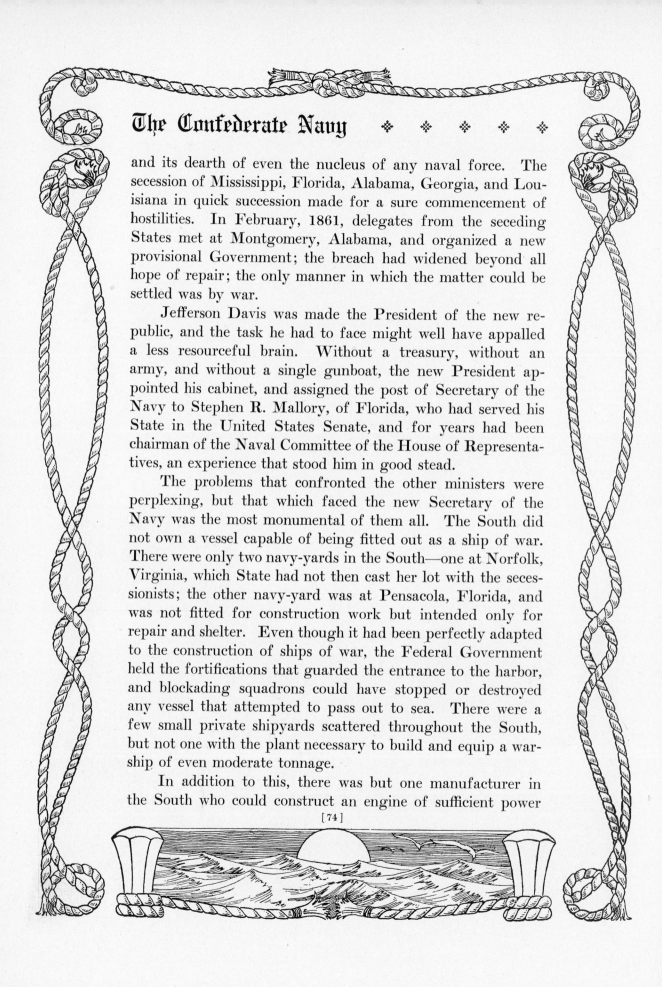

and its dearth of even the nucleus of any naval force. The secession of Mississippi, Florida, Alabama, Georgia, and Louisiana in quick succession made for a sure commencement of hostilities. In February, 1861, delegates from the seceding States met at Montgomery, Alabama, and organized a new provisional Government; the breach had widened beyond all hope of repair; the only manner in which the matter could be settled was by war.

Jefferson Davis was made the President of the new republic, and the task he had to face might well have appalled a less resourceful brain. Without a treasury, without an army, and without a single gunboat, the new President appointed his cabinet, and assigned the post of Secretary of the Navy to Stephen R. Mallory, of Florida, who had served his State in the United States Senate, and for years had been chairman of the Naval Committee of the House of Representatives, an experience that stood him in good stead.

The problems that confronted the other ministers were perplexing, but that which faced the new Secretary of the Navy was the most monumental of them all. The South did not own a vessel capable of being fitted out as a ship of war. There were only two navy-yards in the South—one at Norfolk, Virginia, which State had not then cast her lot with the secessionists; the other navy-yard was at Pensacola, Florida, and was not fitted for construction work but intended only for repair and shelter. Even though it had been perfectly adapted to the construction of ships of war, the Federal Government held the fortifications that guarded the entrance to the harbor, and blockading squadrons could have stopped or destroyed any vessel that attempted to pass out to sea. There were a few small private shipyards scattered throughout the South, but not one with the plant necessary to build and equip a warship of even moderate tonnage.

In addition to this, there was but one manufacturer in the South who could construct an engine of sufficient power

THE "ATLANTA"—FIRST TO RUN THE BLOCKADE FOR THE CONFEDERACY

The "Atlanta" was bought in September, 1861, by Captain James D. Bulloch, secret-service agent of the Confederate States in Europe. She was a new Clyde-built ship, and had made but one or two trips to the north of Scotland, attaining a speed of thirteen knots. She was the first to run the blockade inward for the account of the Confederate Government. She reached Savannah safely on November 12th with a cargo of Enfield rifles, ball cartridges, percussion caps, and various sorts of arms and ammunition. "No single ship," says Captain Bulloch, "ever took into the Confederacy a cargo so entirely composed of military and naval supplies." The "Fingal," as she was originally named, was bottled up by the blockade in Savannah. In January 1862, the Confederates began converting her into an ironclad of the "Merrimac" type. She was cut down to the main deck and widened amidships. A casemate was built upon her deck. Then she was heavily armored and fitted with a formidable ram and a spar torpedo. On July 3d she steamed down the Savannah River on her trial trip, causing great apprehension among the Federals for the safety of the fleet about Port Royal. After her capture by the Federals on June 17, 1863, the Confederates attempted to build other ironclads at Savannah. The "Savannah" was completed, fully armed, and manned, and the "Milledgeville," the same armored type, was nearly so when the city was evacuated in 1865.

COPYRIGHT, 1911, REVIEW OF REVIEWS CO.

RUINS OF THE MACHINE-SHOP AT THE NORFOLK NAVY-YARD

properly to propel a serviceable gunboat; there was a scarcity of iron, and there were no factories equipped to roll the two-and-one-half-inch plate that served to armor the ironclads soon to replace the wooden ships. There was but one plant in the South that could supply large-caliber guns, and that was the Tredegar Iron Works in Richmond, Virginia, which was out of the jurisdiction of the Confederate States until after the firing on Fort Sumter. There was wood enough in the South to have built a mighty fleet of ships, but it was standing in the forests, uncut and unseasoned, and in everything necessary for the equipment and construction of serviceable war-ships, the South was lacking or very poorly supplied. There was no money in the Confederate coffers to buy all these necessities, and while the existence of the Confederacy as a revolutionary body was recognized by the world-powers, its stability as a Government was not acknowledged, and its credit was not established.

An additional obstacle in the path of the formation of a Confederate navy was the fact that the great powers of Europe issued proclamations of neutrality almost immediately after the first gun had been fired at Fort Sumter, and the lesser powers soon followed the lead of the greater ones. In substance, these proclamations allowed ships of either navy harbor for the purpose of making repairs or of securing supplies. No ship might reenforce her crew in any of these foreign ports or make any alterations other than repairs necessary to make their crafts seaworthy; they were to receive on board no ordnance supplies or any other " contraband " articles; they might not take on board more than enough coal to carry them to the nearest port in their own country, and they could not coal in the harbor of any one power more than once in three months, except by special permission.

This was the situation that faced the Secretary of the Navy of the Confederacy after the opening of hostilities. But even before the war-cloud had broken over the Nation,

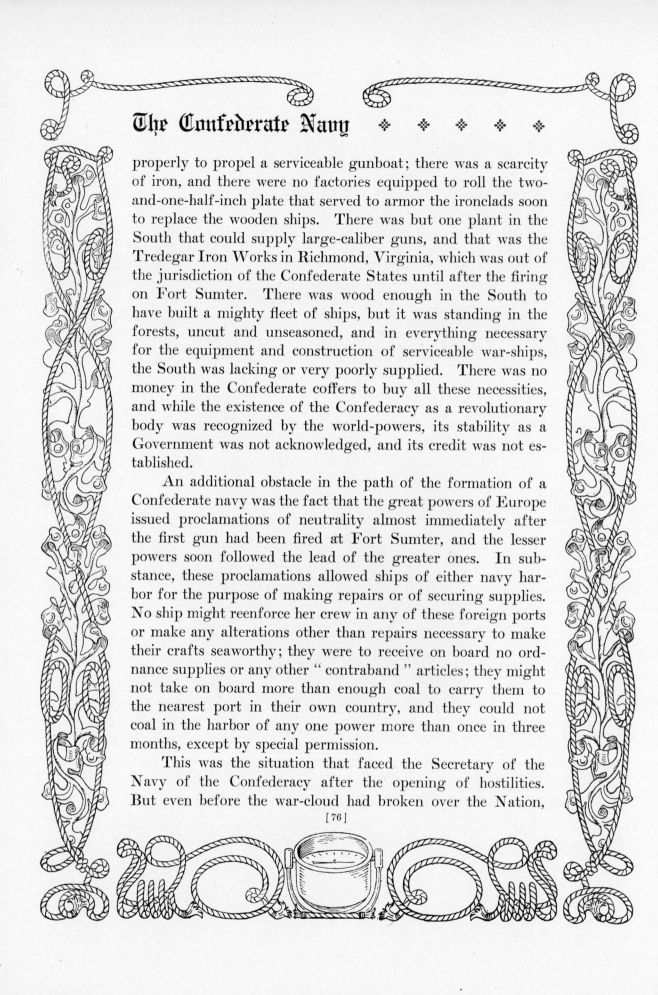

COPYRIGHT 1911, PATRIOT PUB. CO.

THE GUNS

OF

THE SAUCY

"TEASER."

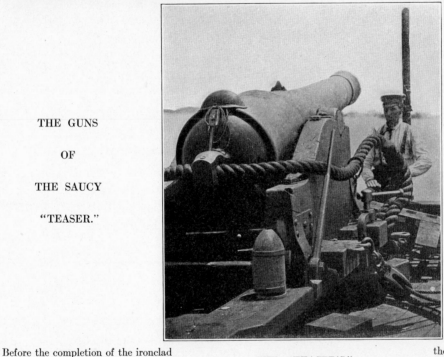

ONE OF

THE FIRST

CONFEDERATE

GUNBOATS

THE "TEASER'S"

32-POUNDER

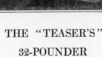

Before the completion of the ironclad "Virginia," ("Merrimac,") the Confederate navy had but five small steamers in the James River to oppose eight of the largest Federal vessels at Hampton Roads. The "Teaser" was a river-tug mounting but one gun at the time, yet in the engagement in which the "Virginia" first appeared the "Teaser," under command of Lieutenant W. A. Webb, C. S. N., boldly used her one gun against the Federal shore battery of sixty. In the upper picture this gun appears, a 12-pounder rifle. Its exposed position is evidence of the courage that was necessary to man it. In the lower picture is seen the 32-pounder that was added to the "Teaser's" armament later. With only these two guns she encountered both the "Maratanza" and the "Monitor," near Haxall's, on the James River, July 4, 1862, and replied valiantly to their fire. The third of the Federal shots, however, pierced her boiler, and her crew were forced to desert her. Many of the vessels procured by the Confederates to piece out its navy were no better built and some not so heavily armed as the "Teaser," yet in river and harbor, in sound and at sea, with few guns they were fought as valiantly as vessels were ever fought against heavy odds.

The Confederate Navy ✦ ✦ ✦ ✦ ✦ ✦

Secretary Mallory had started to build up his organization, undismayed by the conditions that he was forced to contend against. There were many Southerners in the Federal navy whose sympathies were with the new Government, and their resignations were daily being handed to the authorities at Washington, and their services tendered to the Confederate States.

Many of the men who left the Federal service were commanders of ships, and there were instances where they might easily have turned their vessels over to the Confederacy, but, without an exception, they returned the ships entrusted to them to the Federal Government before leaving the service, thus "retiring with clean hands." There were also several officers on coast-line vessels that were in Southern ports after the firing of the first gun, who sailed back to the North with their ships before going south to join the Confederates.

Sixteen captains, thirty-four commanders, and seventy-six lieutenants, together with one hundred and eleven regular and acting midshipmen, resigned from the United States Navy. To make provision for these officers, the Confederate service was increased by the Amendatory Act of April 21, 1862, and made to consist of:

Four admirals, 10 captains, 31 commanders, 100 first lieutenants, 25 second lieutenants, 20 masters, in line of promotion; 12 paymasters, 40 assistant paymasters, 22 surgeons, 15 passed assistant surgeons, 30 assistant surgeons, 1 engineer-in-chief, and 12 engineers.

That all the admirals, 4 of the captains, 5 of the commanders, 22 of the first lieutenants and 5 of the second lieutenants shall be appointed solely for gallant or meritorious conduct during the war. The appointments shall be made from the grade immediately below the one to be filled and without reference to the rank of the officer in such grade, and the service for which the appointment shall be conferred shall be specified in the commission. Provided, that all officers below the grade of second lieutenant may be promoted more than one grade for the same service. . . .

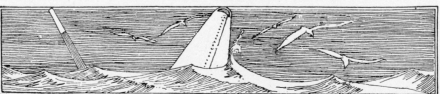

COPYRIGHT, 1911, PATRIOT PUB. CO.

DECK OF C. S. S. "TEASER" AFTER HER CAPTURE BY THE "MARATANZA"

As a consort of the "Virginia" ("Merrimac"), this little converted tug-boat was not afraid in the famous battle in Hampton Roads. Later, no longer under the protecting wing of her huge ironclad leader, she met the "Monitor" and the "Maratanza" near Haxall's, on the James River, July 4, 1862. The little vessel had run aground and was forced to engage her superior antagonists. She opened fire and put a shot into the wheel-house of the "Maratanza," whose answering fire at the third shot exploded a shell in the boiler of the "Teaser." Lieutenant Hunter Davidson and her crew escaped to shore. In the captured vessel were found despatches from which the Federals gleaned valuable information.

THE
"MARATANZA"

AFTER
HER EXPLOIT

The Confederate Navy

One of the first Southern naval men to resign from the Federal Naval Department was Commander Raphael Semmes, who at once went South to enter the service of the new Government. He was sent to the North to secure what arms and ammunition he could, to contract for the delivery of more, and, if possible, to find ships that might serve as a nucleus for the navy of the Confederacy. A large amount of ordnance supplies was delivered or contracted for, but no vessels could be found that would be in the least adapted to service on the high seas, and with this portion of his mission unfulfilled, Semmes returned to Montgomery, twelve days before the firing on Fort Sumter.

Meanwhile, other agents of the Government had been attempting to find suitable ships in the Southern harbors that might be bought. All of these were reported as unsuitable for service as naval vessels, but Commander Semmes, after learning the qualifications of one of them, asked the Secretary of the Navy to secure her, have her altered, give him command, and then allow him to go to sea. The secretary acceded to this request, and the little boat was taken into New Orleans and operations were started to transform her into a gunboat which might fly the Confederate colors and, by harassing the commerce of the North, do her share in the work of warfare. The plans for the reconstruction of the vessel had scarcely been completed when the word was flashed around the world that Fort Sumter had been fired on and had fallen, and the ship, the first of a navy that was to contend against the third largest navy in the world, was christened after the first fort to fall into the hands of the Confederacy, the *Sumter*.

The Navy Department of the South now redoubled its efforts to provide the ships necessary for the defense of its coast and inland rivers. Almost any craft that could be fitted to mount a gun was pressed into service, and as quickly as the means would allow, these boats were prepared for their work, and officers and crews assigned to them.

WORKING ON THE STERN OF THE "INDIANOLA"

After capturing the great ironclad, the Confederates towed their prize over to the east bank of the Mississippi, where she sank, near Jefferson Davis' plantation. Two days later, as they were trying to raise her, they were frightened off by Porter's famous dummy monitor, made of pork-barrels and an old coal-barge, and the next day, although the "harmless monitor" was hard and fast aground, they destroyed the "Indianola" and abandoned her. The "Indianola" had two propellers in addition to her side wheels, and she was worked by seven engines in all. She was heavily armored with 3-inch iron plates. Her clever capture by the Confederates in the darkness was one of the achievements of the Confederate navy; and had it been followed up by the raising of the vessel, the Federals would have had a most formidable antagonist on the Mississippi in the vicinity of Vicksburg, where on the water side they were having things their own way.

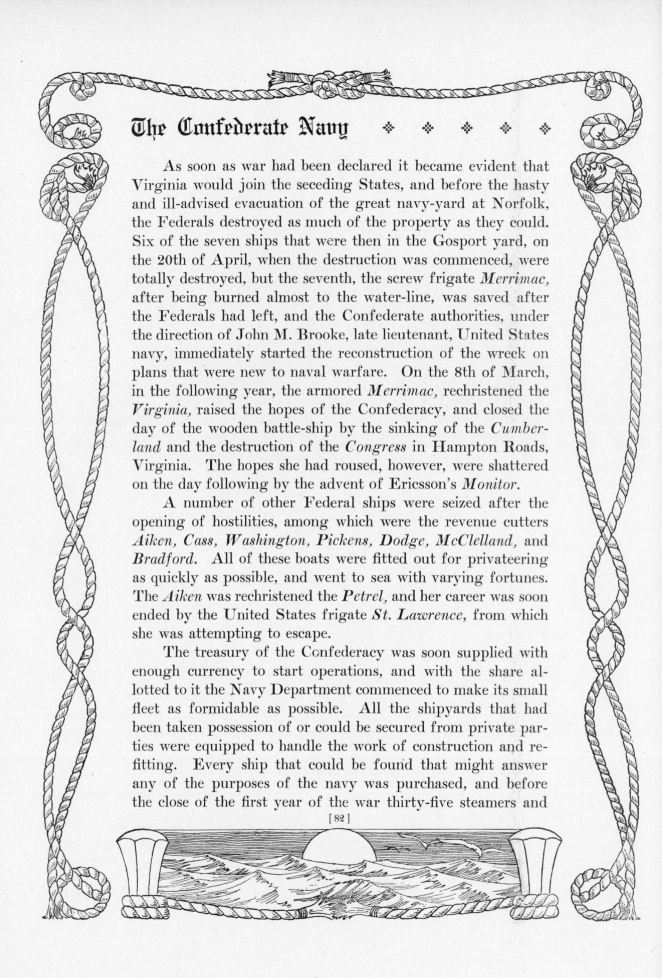

The Confederate Navy ❖ ❖ ❖ ❖ ❖

As soon as war had been declared it became evident that
Virginia would join the seceding States, and before the hasty
and ill-advised evacuation of the great navy-yard at Norfolk,
the Federals destroyed as much of the property as they could.
Six of the seven ships that were then in the Gosport yard, on
the 20th of April, when the destruction was commenced, were
totally destroyed, but the seventh, the screw frigate *Merrimac,*
after being burned almost to the water-line, was saved after
the Federals had left, and the Confederate authorities, under
the direction of John M. Brooke, late lieutenant, United States
navy, immediately started the reconstruction of the wreck on
plans that were new to naval warfare. On the 8th of March,
in the following year, the armored *Merrimac,* rechristened the
Virginia, raised the hopes of the Confederacy, and closed the
day of the wooden battle-ship by the sinking of the *Cumberland* and the destruction of the *Congress* in Hampton Roads,
Virginia. The hopes she had roused, however, were shattered
on the day following by the advent of Ericsson's *Monitor.*

A number of other Federal ships were seized after the
opening of hostilities, among which were the revenue cutters
Aiken, Cass, Washington, Pickens, Dodge, McClelland, and
Bradford. All of these boats were fitted out for privateering
as quickly as possible, and went to sea with varying fortunes.
The *Aiken* was rechristened the *Petrel,* and her career was soon
ended by the United States frigate *St. Lawrence,* from which
she was attempting to escape.

The treasury of the Confederacy was soon supplied with
enough currency to start operations, and with the share al-
lotted to it the Navy Department commenced to make its small
fleet as formidable as possible. All the shipyards that had
been taken possession of or could be secured from private parties were equipped to handle the work of construction and refitting. Every ship that could be found that might answer
any of the purposes of the navy was purchased, and before
the close of the first year of the war thirty-five steamers and

COPYRIGHT, 1911, REVIEW OF REVIEWS CO.

AN EARLY DEFENDER OF THE MISSISSIPPI
THE CONFEDERATE GUNBOAT
"GENERAL BRAGG"

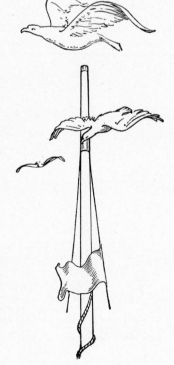

Early in the war, at the suggestion of two Mississippi River steamboat captains, J. E. Montgomery and J. H. Townsend, fourteen river-steamers were seized by the Confederate Government. Their bows were plated with one-inch iron, and pine bulwarks and cotton-bales were used to protect their machinery. They were organized into the river-defense fleet. The "General Bragg," side-wheel steamer, with seven others of these vessels, was stationed below Fort Pillow, under command of J. E. Montgomery, while Flag-Officer Foote was annoying Fort Pillow with his mortar boats. Seizing their opportunity on the hazy morning of May 10, 1862, the Confederate vessels moved up the river, bent on breaking up Foote's mortar-boat parties. The "General Bragg," under command of William H. H. Leonard, steaming far in advance of her con-sorts, surprised the "Cincinnati" before the rest of the Federal fleet could come to her assistance. In the attack the "General Bragg" received a full broadside from the "Cincinnati," which disabled her and put her out of the action, but not until she had rammed the Federal gunboat, tearing a great hole in her side and flooding her shell-room. She was towed to the shore and sank in eleven feet of water. The career of this Confederate river-defense flotilla was brief, however, for on the 6th of June, when Charles Ellet's rams had been added to the fleet of the Federals in the engagement off Memphis, the Confederate fleet was put out of commission. This picture of the "General Bragg" was taken after she had been raised and refitted by the Federals and added to Porter's fleet on the Mississippi, where she served creditably till the war's close.

sailing craft of various dimensions, classes, and armaments had been equipped, while many others were in the process of construction. Of those in commission, twenty-one were steam vessels, most of them small, and chosen for speed rather than power. The armament of all was very light in comparison with the war-ships of the Federal fleets. Several of them carried but one gun, others carried two, and the majority carried less than five.

Quite wonderful was the advance made in other departments than that of shipbuilding. The Navy Department had erected a powder-mill, engine-, boiler-, and machine-shops, and five ordnance workshops. There had been established a rope-walk capable of making all kinds of cordage from a rope-yarn to a 9-inch cable and able to turn out eight thousand yards per month. This was in addition to the eighteen shipbuilding yards already planned and in operation. The ladies of Georgia had presented to the Confederate States a floating battery that was partially finished at the end of the first year of the war. The State of Alabama had turned over an iron-clad ram as a gift to the Confederate service.

Most of the ships that had been completed at the close of the first year of the war were sent to sea as privateers to hamper the Northern merchant marine. Others were used to guard the mouths of the rivers of the Confederacy, while several of them moved on the offensive in the rivers. The *George Page* (renamed the *Richmond*), a small steamer, lightly equipped, soon became well known to the Federals for its continual menacing of the forts on the Occoquan River and Quantico Creek, often advancing close and firing shells into them.

Soon after the commencement of the war, the Confederate privateers became such a menace that President Lincoln issued a proclamation that all the privateers would be regarded as pirates, and that their crews and officers would be subjected to punishment as such. Six months after the issuing of this order the crew of the captured privateer *Savannah* was tried

COPYRIGHT, 1911, REVIEW OF REVIEWS CO.

THE "GENERAL PRICE"—A CONFEDERATE WAR–BOAT THAT CHANGED HANDS

This was one of the fourteen river-steamers condemned and seized for the Confederate Government by General Lovell at New Orleans, January 15, 1862. Converted into a war-boat, she took a bold part in the engagement near Fort Pillow, which resulted in the sinking of the "Cincinnati." She arrived on the scene just as the "General Bragg" was disabled and boldly rammed the Federal gunboat for the second time, when a shot from the "Carondelet" disabled her. In the engagement with the Ellet rams off Memphis, she met the same fate as the "General Bragg" and the other vessels. She and the "General Beauregard," while making a dash from opposite sides upon the "Monarch," both missed that speedy vessel and collided with each other. The "General Price" was so badly injured that her captain ran her upon the Arkansas shore, to be added to the prizes won by the Ellet rams. The action put an end to the river-defense flotilla of the Confederates. Like the Federal river fleet at first, this organization was not under control of the Confederate navy, which, on the Mississippi, was commanded by Flag-Officer George N. Hollins, C. S. N. General Polk and the whole Mississippi delegation had urged upon the Confederate Congress the fitting out of this independent flotilla, which cost more than the million and a half dollars appropriated for it. The Confederate General Lovell at New Orleans had no faith in its efficiency because of his belief that the fleet was not properly officered. He stated emphatically that "fourteen Mississippi captains and pilots would never agree about anything after they once got under way."

for piracy, but the jury disagreed. While awaiting a new trial, the Confederacy imprisoned an equal number of officers of the Federal army, who were held as prisoners of war, and notified the Federals that whatever punishment was inflicted upon the privateersmen would be imposed upon the officers who were held as hostages. The great nations of the world refused to accept the ultimatum of the Union that the privateers were practising piracy, and from that time to the close of the war the men captured on privateers were treated as prisoners of war.

Now took place, on the part of the Confederate Navy Department, a most important move which opened a new chapter in naval history. On the 9th of May, 1861, Secretary Mallory, convinced that the resources of the Confederacy were not sufficient to complete a navy that would be adequate to maintain the defenses of the waterways of the South, commissioned James D. Bulloch to go to England and attempt to have some suitable ships constructed there, informing him at the same time that the necessary funds would be secured and placed at his disposal by the representatives of the Confederacy in England. The matter of building war-vessels in England presented many difficulties, for, under the British policy of neutrality, any ship of either of the warring powers that took on any armament or other equipment that was classed as contraband, was guilty of a breach of the neutrality agreement, and might be taken possession of by the British Government.

Captain Bulloch, a graduate of Annapolis, was well suited to the task, and he at once entered into negotiations for the building of two ships, which were to be delivered to him personally as his property. While built on the general lines of ships that would be suitable for privateering, they were not to be armed or in any way equipped as battle-ships by their makers. In spite, however, of all the precautions taken, the ships were not more than half completed before the suspicions of the Federal agents were aroused. But, though they were

COPYRIGHT, 1911, REVIEW OF REVIEWS CO.

REMARKABLE PHOTOGRAPHS OF CONFEDERATE RAMS—THE "ALBEMARLE"

THE CAPTURED RAMS

These pictures are remarkable as being among the scant remaining photographic evidence of the efforts made by the Confederacy to put a navy into actual existence. The "Albemarle" was built at the suggestion of two men whose experience had been limited to the construction of flat-boats. Under the supervision of Commander James W. Cooke, C. S. N., the vessel was completed; and on April 18, 1864, she started down the river, with the forges and workmen still aboard of her, completing her armor. Next day she sank the "Southfield." In the picture she is in Federal hands, having been raised after

THE CONFEDERATE RAM "LADY DAVIS"

Cushing's famous exploit had put her *hors du combat*. The "Lady Davis," formerly a tug, was purchased in Baltimore and was the first war-vessel to be put afloat by the State of South Carolina, March 13, 1861. She made several captures of Federal vessels around Charleston and was in Tattnall's little fleet on the sounds. In the picture she is in sharp and significant contrast with the huge sailing frigate whose wooden sides and many guns already belong to a past era. The efforts that brought such vessels as the "Albemarle" and the "Lady Davis" into the war marked the beginning of a new American navy. In these pictures both of these formidable vessels have been stripped.

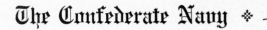

morally certain that the ships were to serve in the Confederate navy, there was no tangible evidence upon which they could be detained, and both boats were completed and sailed out of English waters without any contraband stores aboard them. They were later equipped at other ports from ships that had carried out their arms and ammunition. Bulloch remained in Europe during the greater part of the war, and was a valuable assistant to the Secretary of the Navy of the Confederacy.

During the time in which he was superintending the gathering of this foreign-built force, Secretary Mallory was also organizing his department for efficient work in providing for the needs of all naval forces. He organized a bureau of orders and details, a bureau of ordnance and hydrography, a bureau of provisions and clothing, which also had charge of the paying of the naval forces, and a bureau of medicine and surgery. These bureaus were headed by competent men, and the detailed work of the department was soon being carried on in a thorough, business-like manner.

The matter of securing recruits was easily handled; there was no time when the number of men enlisted was not more than was necessary to man all the ships in the service. The men enlisted in the navy who could not be sent to sea were usually assigned to garrison the forts on the coast and along the rivers, while at times they were called upon to serve in the field with the regular army.

Most of the ships that were built for the Confederacy abroad were manned largely by recruits gathered on foreign shores, some of them being natives of the Confederate States, and others men who sympathized with the cause sufficiently to fight under its colors. The danger in running these boats through the blockading squadrons that lined the Confederate shores and the impossibility of getting men out of the ports on other ships, made it necessary to take what men could be secured. These vessels, however, were always officered by Confederates bearing Government commissions.

COPYRIGHT, 1911 REVIEW OF REVIEWS CO.

APRIL, 1865—ALL THAT WAS LEFT OF THE IRONCLAD RAM "VIRGINIA NO. 2"

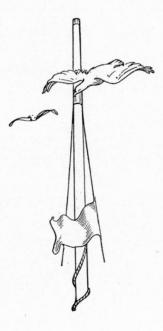

The Confederates had built the "Virginia No. 2" for the defense of the James River. She was commanded by Commodore R. B. Pegram, C. S. N., and was the flagship of Commodore John K. Mitchell, C. S. N., who with two other gunboats opposed the Federal fleet that was attempting to work its way up to Richmond. The pierced and battered smokestack of the "Virginia" shows how bravely she stood up to the fire of the Federal monitors and the Howlett's house batteries. The "Virginia" and her consorts were active in shelling General Butler's Dutch Gap canal. On October 22, 1864, the "Virginia" discovered a new Federal masked battery nearly two miles below Chaffin's Bluff. With her consorts she stood up for two hours against the fire of the 100-pounder Parrott rifles on the shore, at a range of 500 yards. On the night of January 23, 1865, Commodore Mitchell of the "Virginia" and

his fleet attempted to pass below the Federal obstructions in the river, but both the "Virginia" and the "Richmond" grounded and were exposed all the next day to a ruinous fire from the Federal batteries and gunboats. One 15-inch solid shot tore a terrific hole in the "Virginia," killing six and wounding fourteen of her crew. The tide at last floated her and the "Richmond." Nothing daunted, she again led the fleet down the river in a night expedition. The squadron reached Point of Rocks and was discovered by the Federals who, training a calcium light upon the channel, poured a terrific fire from their batteries. The "Virginia's" pilot was driven from the wheel-house. The Confederate gunboats retired. As the Federal lines were drawn more closely around Petersburg and Richmond, the "Virginia" at last was sunk with other vessels in the channel of the James as an obstruction to navigation.

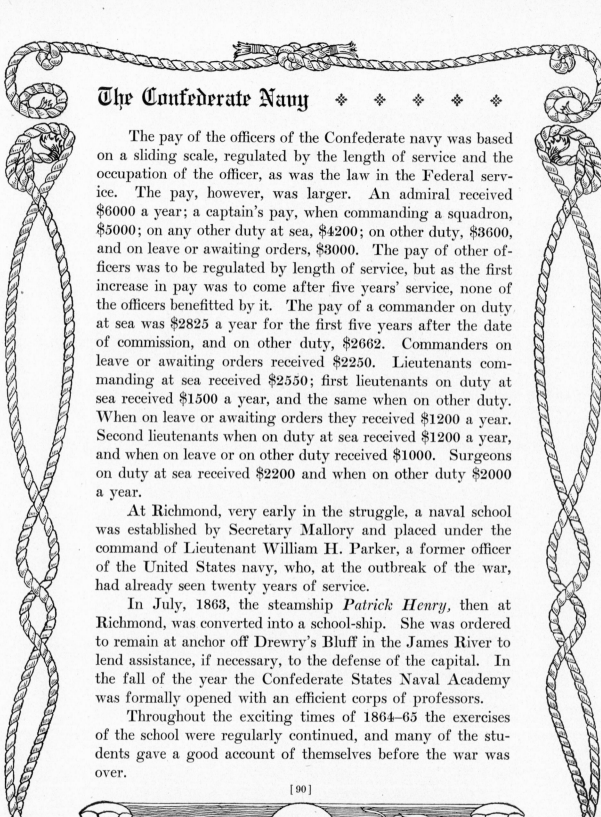

The Confederate Navy ❖ ❖ ❖ ❖ ❖

The pay of the officers of the Confederate navy was based on a sliding scale, regulated by the length of service and the occupation of the officer, as was the law in the Federal service. The pay, however, was larger. An admiral received $6000 a year; a captain's pay, when commanding a squadron, $5000; on any other duty at sea, $4200; on other duty, $3600, and on leave or awaiting orders, $3000. The pay of other officers was to be regulated by length of service, but as the first increase in pay was to come after five years' service, none of the officers benefitted by it. The pay of a commander on duty at sea was $2825 a year for the first five years after the date of commission, and on other duty, $2662. Commanders on leave or awaiting orders received $2250. Lieutenants commanding at sea received $2550; first lieutenants on duty at sea received $1500 a year, and the same when on other duty. When on leave or awaiting orders they received $1200 a year. Second lieutenants when on duty at sea received $1200 a year, and when on leave or on other duty received $1000. Surgeons on duty at sea received $2200 and when on other duty $2000 a year.

At Richmond, very early in the struggle, a naval school was established by Secretary Mallory and placed under the command of Lieutenant William H. Parker, a former officer of the United States navy, who, at the outbreak of the war, had already seen twenty years of service.

In July, 1863, the steamship *Patrick Henry,* then at Richmond, was converted into a school-ship. She was ordered to remain at anchor off Drewry's Bluff in the James River to lend assistance, if necessary, to the defense of the capital. In the fall of the year the Confederate States Naval Academy was formally opened with an efficient corps of professors.

Throughout the exciting times of 1864–65 the exercises of the school were regularly continued, and many of the students gave a good account of themselves before the war was over.

III

FIRST EXPEDITIONS
OF THE
FEDERAL NAVY

THE "PAWNEE"—ONLY 1,289 TONS, BUT THE HEAVIEST FEDERAL VESSEL IN THE POTOMAC
WHEN THE WAR BEGAN—SHE RECEIVED THE SURRENDER OF ALEXANDRIA, VA., IN MAY,
1861, AND FOUGHT GALLANTLY IN THE FIRST EXPEDITION AGAINST HATTERAS, AUGUST, 1861

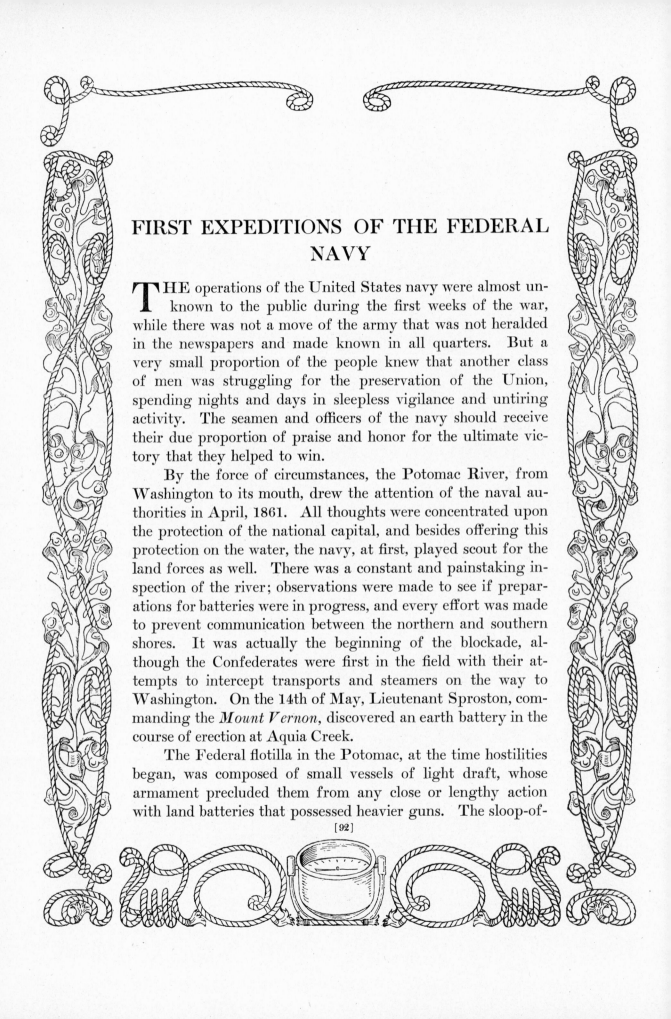

FIRST EXPEDITIONS OF THE FEDERAL NAVY

THE operations of the United States navy were almost unknown to the public during the first weeks of the war, while there was not a move of the army that was not heralded in the newspapers and made known in all quarters. But a very small proportion of the people knew that another class of men was struggling for the preservation of the Union, spending nights and days in sleepless vigilance and untiring activity. The seamen and officers of the navy should receive their due proportion of praise and honor for the ultimate victory that they helped to win.

By the force of circumstances, the Potomac River, from Washington to its mouth, drew the attention of the naval authorities in April, 1861. All thoughts were concentrated upon the protection of the national capital, and besides offering this protection on the water, the navy, at first, played scout for the land forces as well. There was a constant and painstaking inspection of the river; observations were made to see if preparations for batteries were in progress, and every effort was made to prevent communication between the northern and southern shores. It was actually the beginning of the blockade, although the Confederates were first in the field with their attempts to intercept transports and steamers on the way to Washington. On the 14th of May, Lieutenant Sproston, commanding the *Mount Vernon*, discovered an earth battery in the course of erection at Aquia Creek.

The Federal flotilla in the Potomac, at the time hostilities began, was composed of small vessels of light draft, whose armament precluded them from any close or lengthy action with land batteries that possessed heavier guns. The sloop-of-

COPYRIGHT, 1911, REVIEW OF REVIEWS CO.

ON THE "PAWNEE"—THE SHIP THAT SAW SUMTER CAPTURED

The quarterdeck and starboard battery of U. S. S. "Pawnee" appear here from photographs taken in Charleston Harbor. Here on the morning of April 12, 1861, officers and crew watched in an agony of suspense the pitiless iron rain that fell upon Sumter in the bombardment that began the Civil War. The "Pawnee," the "Pocohontas," the "Harriet Lane," and the "Baltic," together with two tugs, had sailed from New York with provisions and reënforcements for Major Anderson's little garrison. As the vessels approached Charleston Harbor, before daylight of April 12th, they heard the boom of shotted guns; and in the gray dawn, smoke rose sullenly in the direction of Sumter. When daylight disclosed the Stars and Stripes still waving over the fort, amid the roar of heavy artillery, Com-

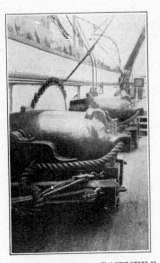

GUNS OF THE "PAWNEE"

mander Stephen Clegg Rowan, of the "Pawnee," immediately volunteered to run his vessel in to the relief of the garrison. Lieutenant Gustavus V. Fox, later Assistant Secretary of the Federal Navy, in command of this expedition, would not consent to such a perilous undertaking, and the fleet lay helplessly by until the surrender of the heroic defenders at four o'clock in the afternoon of the 13th. The next day the garrison was taken off in the "Baltic." The "Pawnee" was next assigned to patrol duty in the Potomac, and on May 24th, in coöperation with the zouaves of the lamented Ellsworth, compelled the Confederates to evacuate Alexandria. Lieutenant Reigart B. Lowry landed and took formal possession of the town, with a detachment of seamen. This was the first Federal foothold in Virginia.

war *Pawnee* was the largest vessel in the river, and she was only of about thirteen hundred tons and carried a battery of fifteen guns. The commander of this vessel, Stephen C. Rowan, co-operating with the ill-fated Colonel Ellsworth and his regiment of Zouaves, took possession of the town of Alexandria, Virginia, May 24, 1861, and it was the navy that hoisted the Stars and Stripes once more over the custom-house.

There was an apparent fruitlessness in a naval force continually contending with shore batteries. If one was silenced and its gunners driven off, the odds were that it would be re-erected the next night, and the work would have to be done all over again. Constantly did the Navy Department request from the Secretary of War that a land force should act with it in the destruction of the Potomac batteries. But General McClellan declared that he could not spare the troops. As a naval writer of that day has pictured the situation, it can be well understood:

"Under such circumstances, the service of the Potomac flotilla was probably among the most fatiguing and discouraging of the war. The crews of the vessels spent a great portion of their nights in rowing up and down the river on picket duty, watching for mail-carriers, smugglers, and spies of all kinds; and in the daytime the ships were often aground on the bars and shoals, in spite of all precaution. They were in hourly danger of being opened upon by masked batteries, which could be constructed unseen in the thick undergrowth of the shores; their quarters in the little steamers were exceedingly uncomfortable; their prizes were rowboats, and small, worthless river craft. . . . For their reward, these hard-working, much-enduring men received too often only the complaints of the country that nothing was done, and sneers at the inefficiency of the Navy Department, and especially of the Potomac flotilla."

As we look back upon these times, when North and South were on tiptoe with excitement, it was remarkable that the Government had not made, before the end of May, any really

COPYRIGHT, 1911 REVIEW OF REVIEWS CO.

ON DANGEROUS DUTY—OFFICERS ON THE "PHILADELPHIA"

This river vessel was early pressed into service for one of the most important and danger-ous performances of the navy in the war. After Virginia seceded, the Confederates promptly removed all lightships and buoys from the Potomac, completely cutting off Wash-ington from the North. Selected by ballot of a board made up of the chiefs of departments at Washington, Lieutenant Thomas Stowell Phelps was entrusted as an officer "skilled in surveying" with the perilous task of resurveying the channel and replacing guiding marks. He was given the armed tender "Anacostia" and the "Philadelphia" for this work. Four 12-pound army field-pieces were mounted at either end of the latter vessel and covered with old canvas to conceal them. The crew and a company of the Seventy-first New York were kept carefully concealed below, while on the deck Phelps stood fearlessly at work. Near Aquia Creek it was particularly important that the river should be surveyed. Phelps ran boldly up under the guns of the Confederate batteries and worked for two hours, with the Confederate gunners, lock-strings in hand, plainly visible. Years afterward Colonel Wm. F. Lynch, C. S. A., who commanded the battery, explained that he had not given the order to fire because the "Philadelphia" seemed to him to be "the property of some poor devil who had lost his way and from her appearance was not worth the powder." The "Philadelphia" was also flagship in the expedition, March 13–14, 1862, to Albemarle Sound, North Carolina, where Commodore S. C. Rowan invaded the Southern inlets.

hostile move except that of occupying Alexandria. But, at the time of this occupation, the Confederates had already erected three strong earthworks at the railway terminus at Aquia Creek, Virginia, and other batteries were protecting the landing, three being mounted in positions on the higher ground, back of the river.

On the 29th of May, the *Thomas Freeborn,* a paddle-wheel steamer of about two hundred and fifty tons, mounting three guns, with the *Anacostia,* a small screw steamer of about two hundred tons, and the *Resolute,* less than half the latter's size, came down the river. Commander James H. Ward was at the head of the little squadron, whose largest guns were but 32-pounders. Upon reaching Aquia Creek, Ward engaged these batteries. Little damage was done, but these were the first shots fired by the navy in the Civil War. On the 1st of June, the action was renewed with great vigor. The *Pawnee* had joined the squadron, every vessel of which had been hit more than once, but although Commander Ward relates that more than a thousand shot had been discharged within range, he had no damage to report, which was, as he wrote, "truly remarkable," and later in the war, when gunnery practice had improved, it would have been impossible. Again, on the 2d of June, the *Pawnee* attacked the batteries, and though struck a number of times, had no casualties to report.

On the 5th, the steamer *Harriet Lane,* of historic memory, attacked the Confederate batteries at Pig Point, near Hampton Roads, and Captain John Faunce, while bearing testimony to the gallant conduct of the officers and men under his command, regretfully announced that he had five casualties on board his little vessel.

On the 27th of June, the navy lost its first officer and it was no other than the gallant Commander Ward, of the *Freeborn,* who was shot and mortally wounded while in the act of sighting the bow gun. A party had been landed in order to clear the ground at Mathias Point, and this had been surprised

COPYRIGHT, 1911, REVIEW OF REVIEWS CO.

ON THE "FREEBORN"

SHOWING HOW WARD, THE FIRST FEDERAL COMMANDER, WAS LOST

This photograph of 1861, long in the possession of the family of Commander James Harman Ward, and here reproduced for the first time, is the only vestige of a visual record of his brave deed on June 27th, the same year. In the picture, taken on the deck of the little improvised gunboat "Freeborn," the man sighting the gun has reverently donned the blouse and straw hat of Commander Ward to show how that brave officer stood when he received his mortal wound. After the firing on Sumter, the lull in the excitement had brought no respite for the navy, and the duty of patrolling the Potomac night and day devolved first upon Commander Ward. In addition to the "Freeborn," a side-wheel steamer carrying but three guns, his squadron consisted of the "Anacostia" and the "Resolute," carrying two guns each. With these vessels, on May 31st, he boldly attacked the Confederate batteries at Aquia Creek and next day, with the assistance of the "Pawnee," the Confederates were driven from their works. Again supported by the "Pawnee," on June 27th, Commander Ward attacked the Confederates at Mathias Point. While a body of sailors from his consort, under command of Lieutenant James C. Chapman, effected a landing, the gunboats kept up a rapid fire. Commander Ward, in his anxiety that this should prove effective, was in the act of sighting a gun himself when he was suddenly wounded in the abdomen and soon expired.

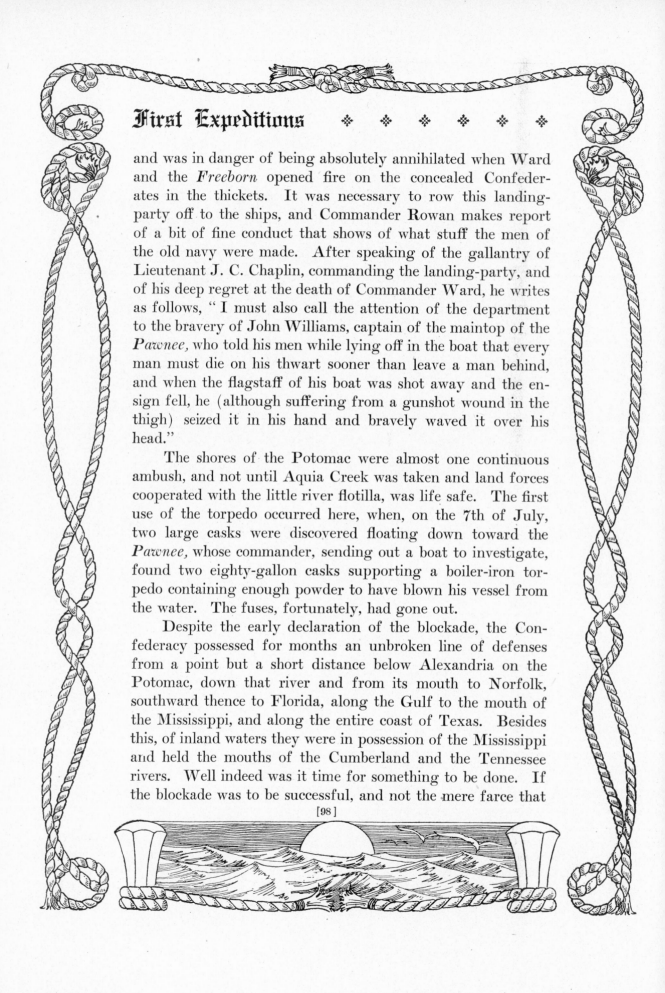

and was in danger of being absolutely annihilated when Ward and the *Freeborn* opened fire on the concealed Confederates in the thickets. It was necessary to row this landing-party off to the ships, and Commander Rowan makes report of a bit of fine conduct that shows of what stuff the men of the old navy were made. After speaking of the gallantry of Lieutenant J. C. Chaplin, commanding the landing-party, and of his deep regret at the death of Commander Ward, he writes as follows, " I must also call the attention of the department to the bravery of John Williams, captain of the maintop of the *Pawnee,* who told his men while lying off in the boat that every man must die on his thwart sooner than leave a man behind, and when the flagstaff of his boat was shot away and the ensign fell, he (although suffering from a gunshot wound in the thigh) seized it in his hand and bravely waved it over his head."

The shores of the Potomac were almost one continuous ambush, and not until Aquia Creek was taken and land forces cooperated with the little river flotilla, was life safe. The first use of the torpedo occurred here, when, on the 7th of July, two large casks were discovered floating down toward the *Pawnee,* whose commander, sending out a boat to investigate, found two eighty-gallon casks supporting a boiler-iron torpedo containing enough powder to have blown his vessel from the water. The fuses, fortunately, had gone out.

Despite the early declaration of the blockade, the Confederacy possessed for months an unbroken line of defenses from a point but a short distance below Alexandria on the Potomac, down that river and from its mouth to Norfolk, southward thence to Florida, along the Gulf to the mouth of the Mississippi, and along the entire coast of Texas. Besides this, of inland waters they were in possession of the Mississippi and held the mouths of the Cumberland and the Tennessee rivers. Well indeed was it time for something to be done. If the blockade was to be successful, and not the mere farce that

AQUIA CREEK LANDING, ON THE POTOMAC—ONE OF THE FIRST FEDERAL NAVY OBJECTIVES

This little landing on the river became at the very outbreak of the war one of the chief objectives of the Federal navy. After the firing upon Sumter, the Confederates seized commanding points from Alexandria southward and mounted batteries of heavy guns as rapidly as possible. Aquia Creek, which was the terminus of the Aquia Creek & Fredericksburg Railroad, was fortified with twenty guns from the captured Norfolk Navy-yard, and was the chief menace to navigation of the Potomac by the Federal vessels. It was the first important duty of the navy to open and maintain the water communications of Washington with the North. If the Confederates could succeed in closing up the Potomac, their boast that the Confederate flag would fly over the National Capitol would not be an idle one, and thus the very first operations of the gunboats in the Potomac were of vital importance to the success of the Federal cause. Under the guns of the two batteries at Aquia Creek, Lieutenant Phelps performed the difficult and dangerous though unsung task of surveying the channel and replacing the buoys in the Potomac. The little flotilla of small vessels in the river carried only a light armament, and until joined by the "Pawnee," a sloop of less than 1,300 tons, was almost powerless against such heavy ordnance as had been mounted by the Confederates. Yet when the "Freeborn" and the "Anacostia" and the "Resolute" boldly advanced to attack Captain W. F. Lynch's batteries at Aquia Creek on May 29, 1861, the guns of the navy spoke out the brave determination which ever characterized that arm of the service throughout the four years of war.

JAMES HARMAN WARD

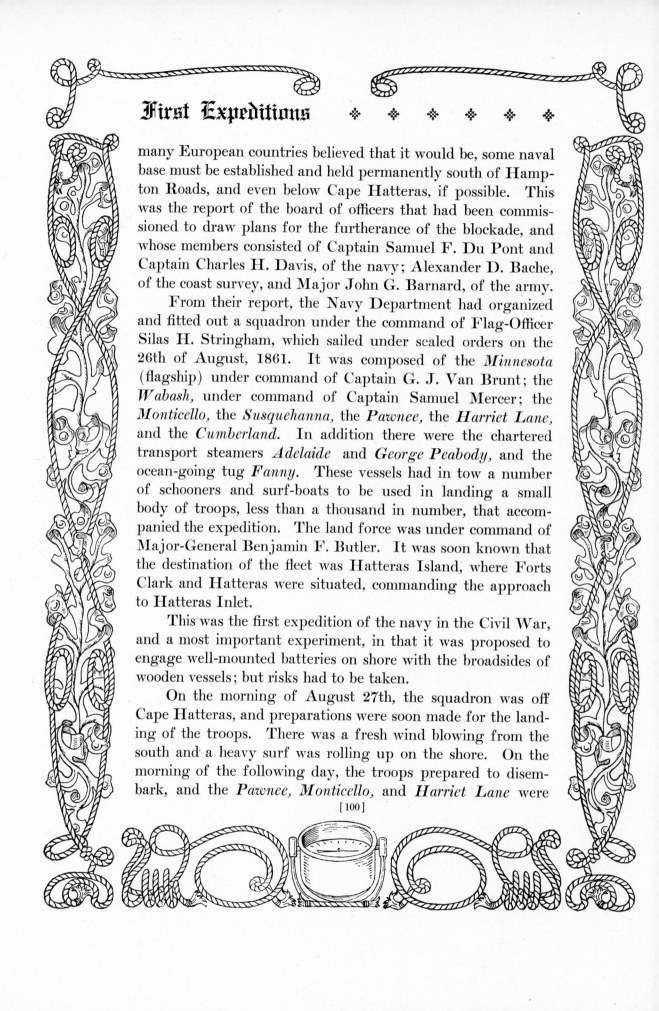

many European countries believed that it would be, some naval base must be established and held permanently south of Hampton Roads, and even below Cape Hatteras, if possible. This was the report of the board of officers that had been commissioned to draw plans for the furtherance of the blockade, and whose members consisted of Captain Samuel F. Du Pont and Captain Charles H. Davis, of the navy; Alexander D. Bache, of the coast survey, and Major John G. Barnard, of the army.

From their report, the Navy Department had organized and fitted out a squadron under the command of Flag-Officer Silas H. Stringham, which sailed under sealed orders on the 26th of August, 1861. It was composed of the *Minnesota* (flagship) under command of Captain G. J. Van Brunt; the *Wabash,* under command of Captain Samuel Mercer; the *Monticello,* the *Susquehanna,* the *Pawnee,* the *Harriet Lane,* and the *Cumberland.* In addition there were the chartered transport steamers *Adelaide* and *George Peabody,* and the ocean-going tug *Fanny.* These vessels had in tow a number of schooners and surf-boats to be used in landing a small body of troops, less than a thousand in number, that accompanied the expedition. The land force was under command of Major-General Benjamin F. Butler. It was soon known that the destination of the fleet was Hatteras Island, where Forts Clark and Hatteras were situated, commanding the approach to Hatteras Inlet.

This was the first expedition of the navy in the Civil War, and a most important experiment, in that it was proposed to engage well-mounted batteries on shore with the broadsides of wooden vessels; but risks had to be taken.

On the morning of August 27th, the squadron was off Cape Hatteras, and preparations were soon made for the landing of the troops. There was a fresh wind blowing from the south and a heavy surf was rolling up on the shore. On the morning of the following day, the troops prepared to disembark, and the *Pawnee, Monticello,* and *Harriet Lane* were

COPYRIGHT, 1911, PATRIOT PUB. CO.

AQUIA CREEK

WHERE THE FIRST SHOTS WERE FIRED BY THE NAVY

The importance of Aquia Creek Landing, on the Potomac, to the navy grew steadily as the advance offensive line which the Confederates had seized upon at the outbreak of the war began to be pushed back into Virginia. As a strategic position the little landing was the scene of many stirring events during the ebb and flow of the military operations. The navy, in coöperating, came to know it as a point of supply. Long before February, 1863, when these pictures were taken, the Potomac flotilla had had its full of the abundance of toil by night and day in the arduous and perilous task of patrolling the great river. Both banks in 1861 were lined with hostile non-combatants; goods were smuggled across constantly by Maryland sympathizers to their fighting friends in Virginia. Federal merchant-vessels were captured in attempting to get up the river to Washington. The suppression of all this fell to the lot of the little flotilla on the Potomac; and the task, which was the real beginning of the blockade, though devoid of glory and fame, was well and thoroughly accomplished and was one of the most praiseworthy achievements of the navy in the war.

ordered to cover their landing. Now the difficulties increased; the iron surf-boats were rolled broadside on the beach, and what men got ashore had to wade through the heavy surf. But three hundred or so succeeded in reaching dry land, a rather forlorn end to the land expedition, as it had no supplies and the ammunition was soaked through. But in the mean time, the *Wabash* got under way, and towing the old *Cumberland* with the *Minnesota* following, led in toward Fort Clark. Soon the battle was on between the land and sea. Flag-Officer Stringham deserves great praise for the way he handled his small squadron; ships were kept in constant movement, and, though well within range, suffered little or no damage from the shots of the fort. The concentrated fire of the vessels upon the little battery, which mounted but five guns, soon bore results. Shortly after noon Fort Clark was abandoned, and the shivering troops that had reached the beach took possession and hoisted the Federal flag.

It was at first thought that Fort Hatteras had surrendered after the short bombardment, but on approaching closer the Confederate batteries once more reopened. The next morning, however, the bombardment being resumed, the fort was seriously damaged, and the powder magazine, having been set on fire, the Confederates hoisted the white flag shortly after eleven o'clock. There was an amusing little note added to the morning's work by the fact that Flag-Officer Barron, who lately had been an officer of the United States navy, refused to surrender the fort to the land forces that now came up from the direction of Fort Clark, the Confederate commander claiming that they had taken no part in the action. Therefore he was rowed off to the flagship, where he gave up his sword to his former friend, Flag-Officer Stringham.

Six hundred and fifteen men and officers were captured at Fort Hatteras, and twenty-five guns, all of which had come from the navy-yard at Norfolk. The moral effect of this easily earned victory was great throughout the North. The real

DU PONT AND OFFICERS ON THE "WABASH"

Here are two groups taken on board the "Wabash," which took part in the first real expedition of the navy —to Hatteras. In the lower picture appears the pivot-gun, one of the largest that at that time was fired from the deck of any vessel—a 200-pounder Parrott rifle. The crew are not at quarters, but the condition of the gun shows it was the pet of the forward watch. This gun was on the

THE FORWARD PIVOT–GUN

topgallant forecastle, and had a sweep in every direction except directly aft. At Fort Fisher this gun's crew showed magnificent practice, as they had at Fort Walker, the first engagement at which the big gun had been fired. In the upper picture the little vine growing out of the flower-pot is an evidence of the sailor's desire to make a cabin as much of a home as is possible.

importance of the conflict had not yet been fully realized, but the spirits of all the Northern people were still drooping after the disastrous defeat at Bull Run. They required some salve for their wounded pride, and the successful conclusion of the first naval expedition gave them this and restored confidence, as well. But the most important features were the realization of the plans of the naval committee, and the fact that the victory had gained a base upon the Southern coast for the support of the blockading squadrons, while, at the same time, a foothold was afforded for military invasion.

Stringham's fleet had now almost complete command of the most important passage to the North Carolina sounds. More than one port of entry of the blockade-runners was closed. The important capture of the Hatteras forts was quickly followed by operations along the coast that extended into the various sounds, and a little fort on Beacon Island, Ocracoke Inlet, some twenty miles further south, was captured. It was in an unfinished condition, and was practically abandoned upon receipt of the news of the fall of Forts Clark and Hatteras. Lieutenant Maxwell landed with a small force on Beacon Island and destroyed the guns found there—four 8-inch navy shell-guns and fourteen 32-pounders; then setting fire to a store-ship that he found a few miles beyond, near the little town of Portsmouth, he regained the fleet.

Thus was secured, from Hatteras Inlet southward to Cape Lookout, virtually the entire possession of the coast to the Cape Fear River; northward the occupation of Hatteras controlled the coast as far as Hampton Roads.

IV

THE
BLOCKADE

THE SPEEDY "RHODE ISLAND"—ONE OF THE FEW FEDERAL CRUISERS SWIFT ENOUGH TO CATCH THE GREYHOUND BLOCKADE-RUNNERS THAT COULD OUTDISTANCE MOST OF THE FLEET

A GREYHOUND CAUGHT—WRECK OF THE BLOCKADE-RUNNER "COLT"

The wreck of this blockade-runner, the "Colt," lies off Sullivan's Island, Charleston Harbor, in 1865. The coast of the Carolinas, before the war was over, was strewn with just such sights as this. The bones of former "greyhounds" became landmarks by which the still uncaptured block-ade-runners could get their bearings and lay a course to safety. If one of these vessels were cut off from making port and surrounded by Federal pursuers, the next best thing was to run her ashore in shallow water, where the gunboats could not follow and where her valuable cargo could be se-cured by the Confederates. A single cargo at war-time prices was enough to pay more than the cost of the vessel. Regular auctions were held in Charleston or Wilmington, where prices for goods not needed by the Confederate Government were run up to fabulous figures. The business of blockade-running was well organized abroad, especially in England. One successful trip was enough to start the enterprise with a handsome profit. A blockade-runner like the "Kate," which made forty trips or more, would enrich her owners almost beyond the dreams of avarice.

COPYRIGHT, 1911, PATRIOT PUB. CO.

THE REMAINS OF THE "RUBY"
SOON AFTER HER CAPTURE BY U. S. S. "PROTEUS," FEBRUARY, 1865

Here on the beach of Morris Island lies all that was left of the swift and doughty blockade-runner "Ruby." She was one of the most successful of her kind. She was busy early in 1862, plying between Nassau and Charleston. Not until February 27, 1865, while trying to get in with an assorted cargo of the type usually denominated "hardware," was she at last entrapped. The Federal screw-steamer "Proteus," Commander R. W. Shufeldt, picked up her scent and gave chase, with the result seen in the picture. It was for taking such risks as these that the captains of the blockade-runners received $5,000 a month instead of the $150 which was the prevailing rate in the merchant service before the war. Officers and crews were paid in like proportion. Coal was worth $20 a ton instead of $4, as formerly. The whole expense of the trip was from three to four times what it would have been in time of peace, and yet a single cargo of cotton was worth from a quarter of a million to a million dollars, and the freight rates in and out ranged from $300 to $1,000 a ton. It was too alluring a business to be deterred by difficulty and danger. As Disraeli remarked, the exploits of the blockade-runners "increase our respect for the energy of human nature."

COPYRIGHT, 1911, PATRIOT PUB. CO.

A LATE CAPTURE—DECEMBER, 1864—FLYING THE BRITISH FLAG

In this blockade-runner is seen the type of vessel in which foreign capital was lavishly invested. She is still flying the British flag, under which she plied her trade, and appears to have been the property of a syndicate of British merchants. In the early stages of the war the Confederacy purchased a number of vessels abroad for use as privateers and blockade-runners. In the beginning the latter were officered by members of the Confederate navy, but later in the war blockade-running became so profitable that the Confederacy could afford to leave it almost entirely to private initiative, rendering such assistance as was needed to enable the vessels to make port or to discharge their cargo in case they were driven on the beach. With the exception of a lighthouse which the Confederates established on the "Mound" near Fort Fisher, there were no guides for blockade-runners at night, except the glow of fires of the ever-busy salt-works and the range lights which were put out in the various channels only after the vessel had exchanged signals with the shore and which were removed immediately after she had made port. It is a remarkable fact that no blockade-runner commanded by an officer of the Confederate navy was ever captured. The famous veteran, the "Robert E. Lee," the best blockade-runner of the Confederacy and long commanded by Lieut.-Commander John Wilkinson, C. S. N., did not meet her fate until October, 1863, on the very first trip she made after Commander Wilkinson had been superseded at Halifax, N. S., by an officer from the merchant marine.

[108]

COPYRIGHT, 1911, PATRIOT PUB. CO.

A FLEET-FOOTED BLOCKADE-RUNNER, WITH TELESCOPING STACKS

This rakish side-wheel steamer was photographed off Norfolk, Va., December, 1864, some time after the boat had been compelled by force of arms to change her occupation from Confederate blockade-running to very useful work with the Federal blockading fleet, under the name of "Fort Donelson." She was of 900 tons burden. Burning anthracite coal, with telescoping smokestacks which could be lowered till almost level with the deck, these vessels left Bermuda and Nassau "on moons"—that is to say, when their arrival off the Southern coast would be attended by as much darkness as possible. Mostly Clyde-built vessels, their first trip would be from some British port with a crew shipped to Bermuda or Nassau "and a market." Little difficulty was experienced in securing recruits willing to take the places of those who did not wish to go the whole cruise. The run-ners would leave Bermuda and Nassau half a dozen at a time at favorable opportunities, with a regularity and despatch that the Northern newspapers of the day were fond of commend-ing to the blockading squadron. Old veterans like the "R. E. Lee" and the "Kate" plied with the precision of regular packets. At Havana the blockade-runners were more fre-quent callers than the regular merchantmen between that city and New York. The "Fort Donelson," while in the Federal navy, on August 15, 1864, under command of Acting Vol. Lieut. T. Pickering, captured a suspicious-looking vessel, the "Dacotah," but she was subsequently released. In January, 1865, the "Fort Donelson," under command of Acting Master G. W. Frost, took part in the expedition against Fort Fisher, which dealt such a heavy blow at blockade-running, the business in which she was formerly engaged.

THE BLOCKADE

THERE are two kinds of blockades—military and commercial. A military blockade is merely the equivalent, on the part of a naval force, of that of a siege upon land, and has been practised from the very earliest times. Commercial blockades are instituted with the principal object of stopping an enemy's imports, crippling his trade, and isolating him from commerce with the outside world. In the old monarchies and the republics of antiquity, trade, even when affecting national interest, was held in contempt; there is no record in the histories of early nations of this commercial form of warfare. When Columbus and Vasco da Gama opened the great ocean routes and provided markets that turned royal minds to the value of commerce, international customs and trade relations were entirely changed—the new weapon of the blockade grew suddenly to be an element in warfare. The Dutch provinces of Spain, in their great fight for independence, were the first to make use of it, when they established the commercial blockade of the Scheldt.

The blockade which the United States proclaimed, and at last succeeded in enforcing, against the ports of the Southern Confederacy was of a twofold character; it was both military and commercial, and was recognized by the Supreme Court of the United States as being valid, and sanctioned by both municipal and international law. By the amended proclamation of President Lincoln on the 27th of April, 1861, the whole seacoast of the South Atlantic and the Gulf of Mexico, from Virginia to the Rio Grande, a stretch of over three thousand miles, was interdicted from commercial relations with any foreign shore. But had the President or his advisers perceived the magnitude of the task or apprehended its difficulties and

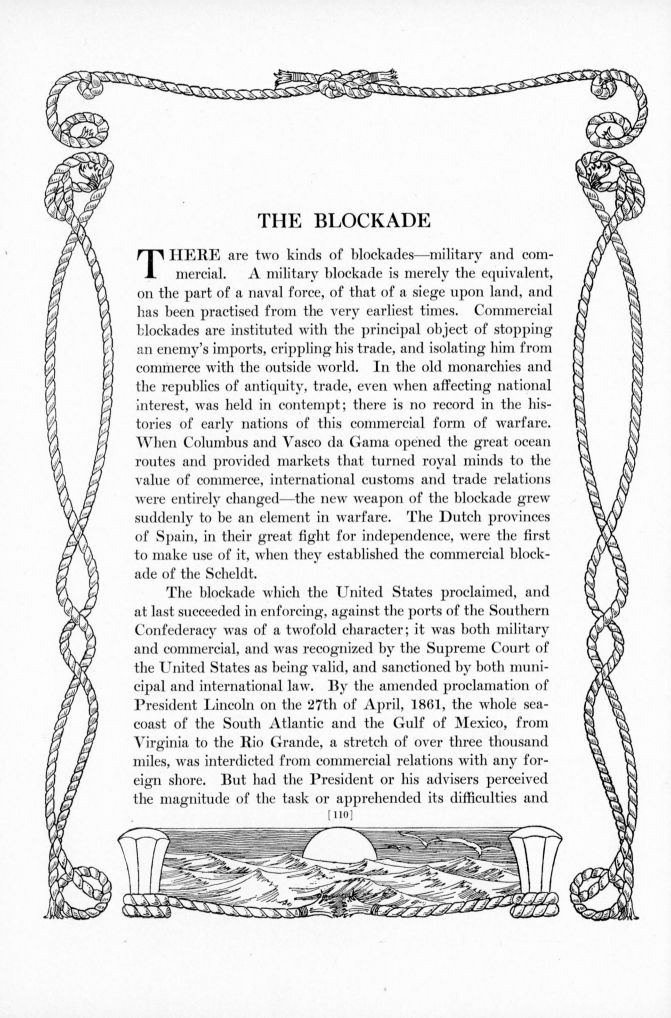

COPYRIGHT 1911 REVIEW OF REVIEWS CO.

THE FIRST FEDERAL BLOCKADING SQUADRON
PHOTOGRAPHED BY A CONFEDERATE IN '61

This dimmed Confederate photograph of early in 1861 ranks as a unique historical document—for it shows, beyond Fort Pickens on the point of Santa Rosa Island, the Federal squadron that began the blockade on the Atlantic coast. Two tiny figures at the lower right gaze across the waters—Confederates who little dream how mighty a part those ships and their sisters will play in the coming struggle. The view was taken from the lighthouse by Edwards of New Orleans. The relief of Fort Pickens was the first dramatic incident of the war in which the navy played a part. In January, 1861, the "Brooklyn," Captain W. S. Walker, was sent with some United States troops on board to reënforce the little garrison at Fort Pickens. But, owing to the conciliatory policy of the Buchanan Administration, a joint-order from the Secretary of War and the Secretary of the Navy was sent to the naval and military commanders on January 29th, instructing them not to land the troops unless Fort Pickens should be attacked. On April 12th Lieutenant John L. Worden, later of "Monitor" fame, arrived with a special message from Secretary Welles, and that night the fort was saved by soldiers landed from the "Brooklyn."

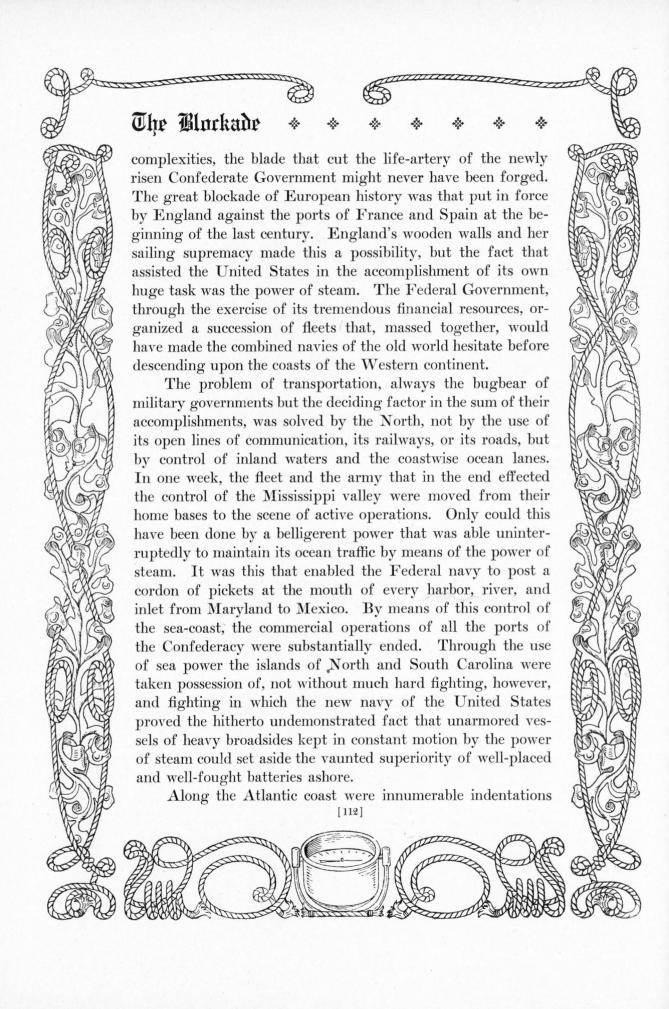

complexities, the blade that cut the life-artery of the newly risen Confederate Government might never have been forged. The great blockade of European history was that put in force by England against the ports of France and Spain at the beginning of the last century. England's wooden walls and her sailing supremacy made this a possibility, but the fact that assisted the United States in the accomplishment of its own huge task was the power of steam. The Federal Government, through the exercise of its tremendous financial resources, organized a succession of fleets that, massed together, would have made the combined navies of the old world hesitate before descending upon the coasts of the Western continent.

The problem of transportation, always the bugbear of military governments but the deciding factor in the sum of their accomplishments, was solved by the North, not by the use of its open lines of communication, its railways, or its roads, but by control of inland waters and the coastwise ocean lanes. In one week, the fleet and the army that in the end effected the control of the Mississippi valley were moved from their home bases to the scene of active operations. Only could this have been done by a belligerent power that was able uninterruptedly to maintain its ocean traffic by means of the power of steam. It was this that enabled the Federal navy to post a cordon of pickets at the mouth of every harbor, river, and inlet from Maryland to Mexico. By means of this control of the sea-coast, the commercial operations of all the ports of the Confederacy were substantially ended. Through the use of sea power the islands of North and South Carolina were taken possession of, not without much hard fighting, however, and fighting in which the new navy of the United States proved the hitherto undemonstrated fact that unarmored vessels of heavy broadsides kept in constant motion by the power of steam could set aside the vaunted superiority of well-placed and well-fought batteries ashore.

Along the Atlantic coast were innumerable indentations

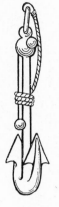

COPYRIGHT 1911, REVIEW OF REVIEWS CO.

OFFICERS ON DECK OF THE U. S. S. "RHODE ISLAND"

This proved to be one of the most useful of the vessels purchased by the Navy Department during the war. Commissioned in May, 1861, she was one of the last of the Federal warships to go out of service, June, 1865. During the entire war she was commanded by Commander (later Rear-Admiral) Stephen Decatur Trenchard. At the time this picture was taken at Cape Haytien, her executive officers were Lieutenant Pennell, Lieutenant Farquhar, and Master Rodney Brown. Other officers were Chief-Engineer McCutcheon, Captain's Clerk F. C. T. Beck, Paymaster R. Hall Douglas, Paymaster's Clerk, Langdon Rodgers. She had first been employed as a special despatch-boat for the rapid transmission of Government orders to all squadron commanders. Her speed proved so great that she was soon converted into a heavily armed cruiser (twelve guns) and sent to West Indian waters to search for Confederate privateers and blockade-runners. She made numerous prizes and was subsequently transferred to Wilkes' flying squadron. She was finally attached to Admiral Porter's South Atlantic squadron and took part in both attacks on Fort Fisher. For his conduct there Commander Trenchard was specially mentioned in orders by his chief.

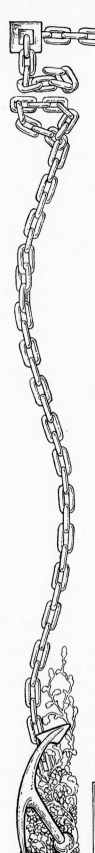

that multiplied a thousand times the difficulties of maintaining a strict blockade. From Cape Henry to Matamoras, every bay, sound, harbor, and inlet offered tempting shelter to any craft inward bound and laden with the contraband of war, and from these hidden nooks vessels loaded with cotton for the idle factories of Europe essayed the hazardous voyage that brought the reward of French and British gold.

Remarkable as it may seem, it was the Confederacy that made the first move in the game of blockade. The State of Virginia attempted to close the Potomac and to prevent egress and ingress to the national capital. A total lack of naval force prevented such accomplishment. But the Federal navy's blockade of the Southern ports became ultimately the determining factor in the downfall of the Confederacy. Vicksburg and Port Hudson surrendered as much to Farragut and to Porter as to Grant. Sherman's march to the sea would never have been undertaken had not the Federal fleets already held possession of Port Royal and so strongly invested the harbors of Savannah, Charleston, and Wilmington. In his campaign against Richmond, McClellan sought shelter under the guns of the navy, and Grant was enabled, through the navy's control of the coast, to maintain his base at City Point.

Had Jefferson Davis a navy at his command, the result of the internecine struggle might have been far different. It was the blockade as much as the battles that brought to every Southern home the horrible reality of want that follows in the track of war. The people of the North knew no deprivations, but the women and children of the South, before the conflict ended, were suffering from the lack of the very things that ships, and ships only, could bring them. The watching cordons spread along the coast ultimately precluded the import of articles, not only of trade but of necessity. It was natural that the ports of Virginia and North Carolina received the first attention of the Federal navy.

Agreeable to the requirements of international law, notice

FEDERALS ON THE WHARF AT PORT ROYAL—1862

In these photographs of March, 1862, Federals are busily at work making the newly captured Port Royal the strong and handy Southern base it remained throughout the war. It had become apparent early in the war that, if the blockade were to be made effective, the Federal Government must repossess itself as quickly as possible of the forts guarding the entrances to the important harbors of the South. From the Rio Grande to the Chesapeake the coast defenses were in the hands of the Confederacy. It was impossible for the navy to prevent the ingress and egress of blockade-runners under friendly guns. President Lincoln, in June, 1861, convened a board including Captain Samuel Francis Du Pont and Captain Charles H. Davis, of the navy, Major John G. Barnard, of the army, and Professor Alexander D. Bache, of the coast survey. After careful study they presented a plan to the President. Its first object was to obtain possession of Hatteras Inlet and thus close the main entrance to Albemarle and Pamlico Sounds, which were veritable havens of

refuge to the blockade-runner. This was to be followed up by the capture of Port Royal for a naval base, where vessels could be coaled and repaired without the necessity of being withdrawn from the blockading squadron for the long period required to reach a Northern port. On August 29th a fleet under Flag-Officer Silas H. Stringham, together with a military force commanded by General Benjamin F. Butler, carried out successfully the first of these plans. This was the first expedition in which the army coöperated with the navy. On November 7th another joint expedition, under Flag-Officer Samuel Francis Du Pont, silenced and captured the forts at Port Royal. Then into the sounds had to be sent light-draft gunboats to drive the Confederates from position after position back toward Charleston and Savannah—the first effective step by the Federal navy toward narrowing the field of the blockade-runners, compelling them to seek harbors where the larger vessels of the old navy could be effectively used against them.

STORES AT THE NEWLY CAPTURED BASE

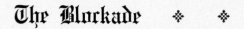

of the blockade was given formally, first at Hampton Roads by Flag-Officer G. J. Pendergast three days after President Lincoln had signed the proclamation declaring it. This was on the 30th of April, 1861. On the 11th of May, Captain W. W. McKean, commanding the frigate *Niagara* which had hastened home from Japanese waters, appeared off Charleston and gave notice to the foreign ships then in that port that the blockading laws would be rigidly enforced. On the 25th of May, he appeared off Pensacola, Florida, and the same day gave notice. Neutral vessels were boarded and warned off the coasts. The steam frigate *Brooklyn,* under Commander C. H. Poor, at the same time proclaimed the blockade at the mouth of the Mississippi, and Lieutenant D. D. Porter, in the *Powhatan,* did the same thing at the entrance to Mobile Bay. The menace had begun. By July, every port had been informed.

Europe, especially England, was at first inclined to laugh at the attempt to close these profitable markets. It was indeed at the outset, in view of the bigness of the task, apparently ludicrous. Here was a coast three thousand five hundred and forty-nine miles long, containing almost two hundred places where anchors could be dropped and cargoes landed. But very soon the shoe began to pinch. As a foreign writer of renown, in reviewing this phase of the war, puts it, " the rapid rise in the prices of all imported commodities in the insurgent States presented the exact measure of the efficiency of the blockade." In December of 1861, when Congress met, the Secretary of the Navy reported that in addition to the regular forces then afloat there had been purchased one hundred and thirty-six vessels; that thirty-four ships had been repaired and put in commission, and that fifty-two vessels were in process of construction, making in all two hundred and sixty-four ships manned, armed, and equipped, and flying the flag of the United States. In the eight months of the war the available navy had been more than trebled.

Engaged in the blockade duty were two separate squad-

COPYRIGHT, 1911, REVIEW OF REVIEWS CO.

THE OUTLYING NAVY-YARD—HILTON HEAD, 1862

These scenes show the activities that sprang up around Hilton Head after the success of the Port Royal expedition. The picture above is of the foundry shop erected by the Federals. Here hundreds of mechanics were kept constantly employed, repairing the iron work needed aboard the gunboats and doing work for which the ships otherwise would have had to go North. The central picture shows the anchor rack, where were kept all sizes of anchors from the small ones used for mooring buoys to those of the largest ships. In the early part of the war hundreds of anchors were

THE ANCHOR RACK

lost to the navy by ships slipping their moorings to stand off-shore in bad weather. Later the employment of long heavy deep-sea cables obviated this necessity, enabling ships to ride out gales. Not a single vessel of the regular navy foundered or was wrecked during the whole war. One of the first things done by the Federal authorities after gaining a foothold at Hilton Head was to replace all buoys and lights. In the lower picture one of the monitors is convoying the new lightship that was sent down from the North to replace the one removed, at the outbreak of hostilities, by the Confederates.

COPYRIGHT, 1911, REVIEW OF REVIEWS CO.

MONITOR AT PORT ROYAL CONVOYING LIGHTSHIP

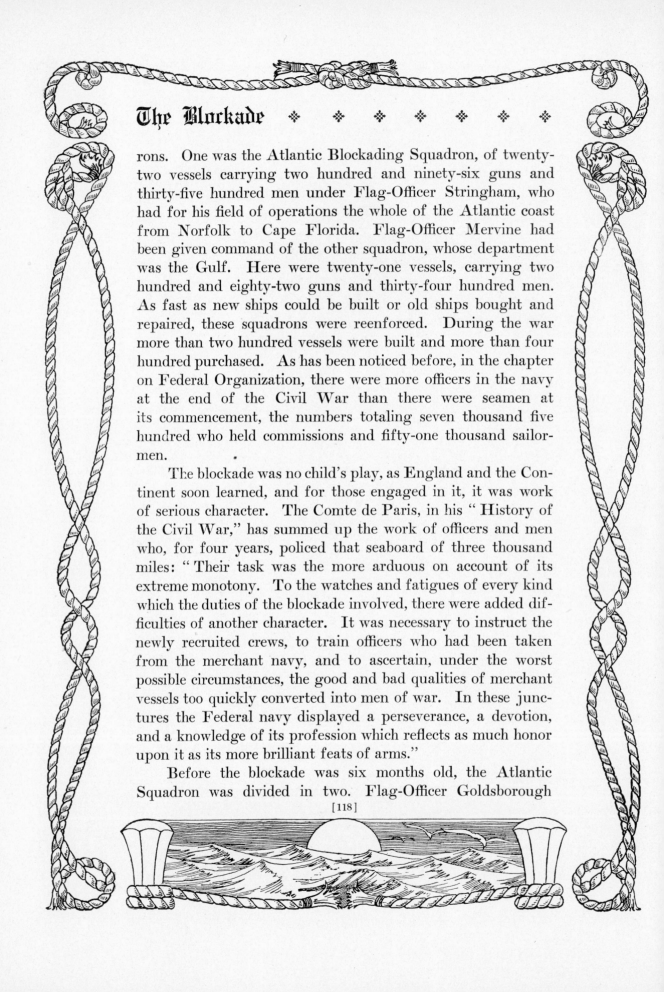

rons. One was the Atlantic Blockading Squadron, of twenty-two vessels carrying two hundred and ninety-six guns and thirty-five hundred men under Flag-Officer Stringham, who had for his field of operations the whole of the Atlantic coast from Norfolk to Cape Florida. Flag-Officer Mervine had been given command of the other squadron, whose department was the Gulf. Here were twenty-one vessels, carrying two hundred and eighty-two guns and thirty-four hundred men. As fast as new ships could be built or old ships bought and repaired, these squadrons were reenforced. During the war more than two hundred vessels were built and more than four hundred purchased. As has been noticed before, in the chapter on Federal Organization, there were more officers in the navy at the end of the Civil War than there were seamen at its commencement, the numbers totaling seven thousand five hundred who held commissions and fifty-one thousand sailor-men.

The blockade was no child's play, as England and the Continent soon learned, and for those engaged in it, it was work of serious character. The Comte de Paris, in his " History of the Civil War," has summed up the work of officers and men who, for four years, policed that seaboard of three thousand miles: " Their task was the more arduous on account of its extreme monotony. To the watches and fatigues of every kind which the duties of the blockade involved, there were added difficulties of another character. It was necessary to instruct the newly recruited crews, to train officers who had been taken from the merchant navy, and to ascertain, under the worst possible circumstances, the good and bad qualities of merchant vessels too quickly converted into men of war. In these junctures the Federal navy displayed a perseverance, a devotion, and a knowledge of its profession which reflects as much honor upon it as its more brilliant feats of arms."

Before the blockade was six months old, the Atlantic Squadron was divided in two. Flag-Officer Goldsborough

When the war broke out, Samuel Phillips Lee, who was born in Virginia in 1811, had already seen twenty-six years of almost continuous service. During the Civil War he was frequently shifted, but everywhere set an example to the service. At the passage of Forts Jackson and St. Phillip he commanded the sloop-of-war "Oneida." He fought conspicuously in the battles of the Mississippi, from New Orleans to Vicksburg. In July of 1862 he was placed in command of the North Atlantic blockading squadron, making the blockade more effective than ever. Late in the war, in the summer of '64, he was transferred to the Mississippi squadron, keeping the Cumberland River open for the army.

The sloop below, attached to the blockading squadron during the war, won quite a name for herself, although not engaged in any of the larger actions, by capturing a number of prizes. In 1861, under Captain C. Green, she caught the blockade-runner "Alvarado" and took the British vessel "Aigburth" at sea laden with contraband intended for the Confederacy. On December 15th, of the following year, she captured the ship "Havelock" and a large brig that was trying to make the coast, laden with cloth and percussion-caps. The "Jamestown" was ordered to the East Indies September 11, 1862, where she remained till after the war's close. She had a roving commission full of adventure.

ADMIRAL S. P. LEE

NORTH ATLANTIC BLOCKADING

SQUADRON, 1862

A FAST SAILER

THE SLOOP–OF–WAR

"JAMESTOWN"

COPYRIGHT, 1911, REVIEW OF REVIEWS CO.

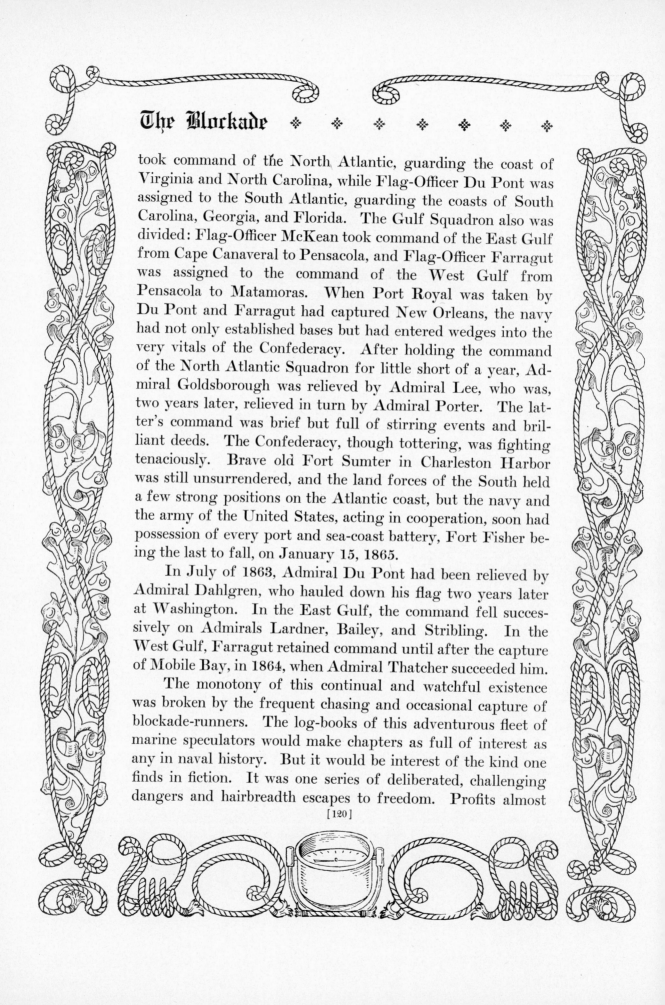

took command of the North Atlantic, guarding the coast of Virginia and North Carolina, while Flag-Officer Du Pont was assigned to the South Atlantic, guarding the coasts of South Carolina, Georgia, and Florida. The Gulf Squadron also was divided: Flag-Officer McKean took command of the East Gulf from Cape Canaveral to Pensacola, and Flag-Officer Farragut was assigned to the command of the West Gulf from Pensacola to Matamoras. When Port Royal was taken by Du Pont and Farragut had captured New Orleans, the navy had not only established bases but had entered wedges into the very vitals of the Confederacy. After holding the command of the North Atlantic Squadron for little short of a year, Admiral Goldsborough was relieved by Admiral Lee, who was, two years later, relieved in turn by Admiral Porter. The latter's command was brief but full of stirring events and brilliant deeds. The Confederacy, though tottering, was fighting tenaciously. Brave old Fort Sumter in Charleston Harbor was still unsurrendered, and the land forces of the South held a few strong positions on the Atlantic coast, but the navy and the army of the United States, acting in cooperation, soon had possession of every port and sea-coast battery, Fort Fisher being the last to fall, on January 15, 1865.

In July of 1863, Admiral Du Pont had been relieved by Admiral Dahlgren, who hauled down his flag two years later at Washington. In the East Gulf, the command fell successively on Admirals Lardner, Bailey, and Stribling. In the West Gulf, Farragut retained command until after the capture of Mobile Bay, in 1864, when Admiral Thatcher succeeded him.

The monotony of this continual and watchful existence was broken by the frequent chasing and occasional capture of blockade-runners. The log-books of this adventurous fleet of marine speculators would make chapters as full of interest as any in naval history. But it would be interest of the kind one finds in fiction. It was one series of deliberated, challenging dangers and hairbreadth escapes to freedom. Profits almost

COPYRIGHT, 1911, REVIEW OF REVIEWS CO.

BOLD BLOCKADERS—THE "PAUL JONES"

This fast side-wheel steamer under Commander C. Steedman saw her first active service in the war in following up the advantages gained by the Federal navy at Port Royal. July 29, 1862, she led three other gunboats up the Ogeechee River to the first attack upon Fort McAllister. The following October she led the expedition to Florida which captured the Confederate batteries on St. John's Bluff. The following year, under Commander A. C. Rhind, she was with the fleet of Rear-Admiral Dahlgren, which captured Fort Wagner on Morris Island in Charleston Harbor, July 18th. Of her seven guns, two were 50-pounder rifles and one a 100-pounder, which made her a very efficient blockader. The trim little gunboat "Marblehead" (shown below), rating something over five hundred tons, was active throughout the war. In April, 1862, under the command of Lieutenant S. Nicholson, she was in the Chesapeake aiding McClellan in his operations before Yorktown. In February, 1863, she joined the blockading squadron, and under Lieutenant-Commanders R. W. Scott and R. W. Meade, Jr., she participated in the operations in the vicinity of Charleston, supporting the movements up the Stono River and the attacks on Morris Island.

COPYRIGHT, 1911, REVIEW OF REVIEWS CO.

THE TRIM GUNBOAT "MARBLEHEAD"

beyond belief were made by the owners of these vessels which were mostly built in Great Britain and were the fastest steaming craft of their day. They were loaded with arms, ammunition, and other supplies needed by the Confederacy, and departed on the return voyage loaded down to their gunwales with cotton. It is a question whether, in the main, the traffic was successful, for so many of these greyhounds were captured by the blockading fleets, and destroyed or wrecked, that in figuring up profit and loss the totals must have almost equaled. During the war the number of blockade-runners destroyed or captured was one thousand five hundred and four. The gross proceeds of the property condemned as lawful captures at sea and prizes to the vessels who took them, before November 1, 1864, amounted to $21,840,000. Subsequently this sum was increased by new decisions of the prize-courts, and actually the total loss to owners who ventured in the business and who principally resided in Great Britain, was in the neighborhood of $30,000,000. The damage paid in the Alabama Claims decision was very little more than half this sum.

The first prize captured off Charleston was the ship *General Parkhill* that was taken by the *Niagara*. The second of Charleston's prizes was the schooner *Savannah* that was taken by the United States brig *Perry* on June 3, 1861. She had been a pilot-boat before the war, and was not in any sense a blockade-runner except for the fact that she had escaped from Charleston and made the open sea. It was intended that she should intercept American merchant vessels, and she was practically a privateer. She had already made one or two prizes when, mistaking the *Perry* for a merchantman, she suffered the consequences. The blockade had more to do with the blockade-runners than with the privateers; the history of these latter vessels, daring as any adventurers in the days of Drake or Frobisher, is of the greatest interest. The careers of the *Sumter* and the brig *Jefferson Davis*, the *Amelia*, the *Dixie*, the *Petrel*, the *Bonita*, the *James Gray*, and many others would

COPYRIGHT, 1911, PATRIOT PUB. CO.

A PURSUER OF MANY PRIZES—THE "SANTIAGO DE CUBA"

This vigilant blockader was one of the first to see active service. As early as December 3, 1861, Commander D. B. Ridgely brought her ten guns to bear upon the schooner "Victoria" and captured her off Point Isabel on her way to the West Indies with a cargo of cotton. In February of the next year, the "Santiago" caught the sloop "O. K." off Cedar Keys, Florida. The next month she drove a blockade-runner ashore. On April 23, 1862, she captured two schooners and (two days later) a steamer, all on their way from Charleston loaded with cotton. On April 30th she added to her prizes the schooner "Maria," and on May 27th the schooner "Lucy C. Holmes," both with more cotton; on August 3, 1862, at sea, the steamer "Columbia," loaded with munitions of war, and on August 27th the schooner "Lavinia" with a cargo of turpentine. In 1863 the side-wheel steamer "Britannia" and the blockade-runner "Lizzie" were her captures, the former loaded heavily with cotton. Cotton was so valuable at this stage of the war that if a blockade-runner attempted to lighten herself by throwing over a part of her cargo, volunteers were called for from the crew of the closest vessel pursuing to swim out and climb up on the cotton-bales until they could be recovered for their own particular ship after the prize was made. In 1864, after capturing the famous blockade-runner "A. D. Vance" and the "Lucy," the "Santiago de Cuba" served with distinction at Fort Fisher.

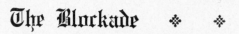

make exciting reading. Their careers, however, were all short; many of the blockade-runners kept at sea much longer. The *Robert E. Lee,* under the command of Captain John Wilkinson, C.S.N., ran the blockade no less than twenty-one times, and carried out from six thousand to seven thousand bales of cotton worth two million dollars in gold, at the same time bringing back return cargoes of equal value.

On November 9, 1863, she attempted to run in once more from the island of Bermuda, but Wilkinson and his luck had deserted her; she was under the command of another captain, and was captured off Cape Lookout shoals by the steamer *James Adger* and taken to Boston as a prize. As many of these captured blockade-runners were added to the squadrons off the coast, the hare became a member of the pack of hounds, and not a few of them, like the *Bat, A. D. Vance* and others, helped chase their sister vessels to their death. Over three hundred piled their bones along the shore—in fact, every harbor-mouth of the South was dotted with them.

On the 31st of January, 1863, there took place a brilliant and famous attempt on the part of the Confederate naval forces in Charleston to break the blockade, when the ironclads *Palmetto State* and *Chicora* actually put out from their harbor and steamed some distance out to sea, these rams having engaged several strong Federal gunboats, capturing one and putting the others to flight. Flag-Officer Ingraham, the senior officer of the attack, was fully persuaded that he had broken the blockade, and upon his return to Charleston so reported to General Beauregard. The latter did everything in his power to force this claim upon the attention of foreign governments, for if the consuls of European nations at Charleston would have acted upon such representation, it would have been necessary for the Federal Government to have established a fresh blockade in accordance with the laws of nations. However, to put it briefly, although this intrepid exploit came as a thunderclap to the North, the great Federal armada had

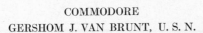

COMMODORE
GERSHOM J. VAN BRUNT, U. S. N.

The gallant commander of the "Minnesota." He and his ship were early in the thick of things and served under Rear-Admiral Goldsborough at Hatteras Inlet. Made commodore July 16, 1862, Van Brunt was actively engaged in blockade duty during the rest of the war.

REAR-ADMIRAL
JAMES L. LARDNER, U. S. N.

In command of the steam frigate "Susquehanna," he formed an active part of Admiral Du Pont's "circle of fire" at Port Royal, November 7, 1861. In 1862-3 he was in command of the East Gulf blockading squadron and in 1864 of the West Indian squadron.

REAR-ADMIRAL
CHARLES WILKES, U. S. N.

A nephew of the celebrated John Wilkes of London, this officer in 1838-42 led the exploring expedition that discovered the Antarctic continent. In 1861 he obtained fame of another kind by seizing Mason and Slidell aboard the British steamer "Trent" and conveying them to Boston in his ship, the "San Jacinto." He had been cruising in the West Indies, looking for the Confederate cruiser

"Sumter," and seized the opportunity for what appeared to be bigger game. Wilkes was thanked by Congress and applauded by the people of the North, but his act nearly brought on a war with England. On August 28, 1862, in command of a flotilla, he destroyed City Point, which was later to become the army base in the closing operations in Virginia. Wilkes afterward did excellent service with his famous "flying squadron," capturing blockade-runners in the West Indian waters.

COPYRIGHT, 1911, REVIEW OF REVIEWS CO.

THE COMMANDER WHO CLOSED IN ON CHARLESTON—DAHLGREN AND HIS STAFF

The South Atlantic blockading squadron was fortunate in being commanded by the best brains of the navy throughout the war. Admiral Du Pont, whose genius had helped to organize the Naval Academy at Annapolis, guided the fortunes of the squadron until July 6, 1863, when he was succeeded by Admiral Dahlgren (seen in the center of picture, his thumb thrust in his coat), who remained in command until after both Savannah and Charles-ton had fallen. He was chosen by the Administration to recapture Fort Sumter and secure possession of Charleston. The task proved an impossible one. But Dahlgren in coöperation with the military forces captured Morris Island and drew the cordon of the blockade closer about Charleston. Admiral Dahlgren was the inventor of a new form of cannon. He also introduced the light boat-howitzers which proved so useful in the blockading service.

COPYRIGHT, 1911, REVIEW OF REVIEWS CO.

ADMIRAL DU PONT AND STAFF, ON BOARD THE "WABASH," OFF SAVANNAH, 1863

From left to right: Capt. C. R. P. Rodgers, fleet captain; Rear-Adm. S. F. Du Pont, commanding fleet; Commander Thomas G. Corbin, commanding "Wabash"; Lieutenant Samuel W. Preston, flag-lieutenant; Admiral's Secretary McKinley; Paymaster John S. Cunningham; Lieut. Alexander Slidell McKenzie; Fleet Surgeon George Clymer; Lieut. James P. Robertson; Ensign Lloyd Phenix; Commander William Reynolds, Store-Ship "Vermont"; Lieut.-Com. John S. Barnes, Executive Officer. Rear-Admiral Samuel Francis Du Pont was the man who first made the blockade a fact. To his naval genius the Federal arms owed their first victory in the war. His plan for the capture of Port Royal on the Southern coast was brilliantly carried out. Forming his fleet in a long line, he, in the "Wabash," boldly led it in an elliptical course past first one fort and then the other, completing this "terrible circle of fire" three times till the Confederate guns were silenced. Du Pont's plan of battle became a much followed precedent for the navy during the war, for by it he had won his victory with a loss of but eight killed and twenty-three wounded. A midshipman at the age of twelve, he had got his training in the old navy.

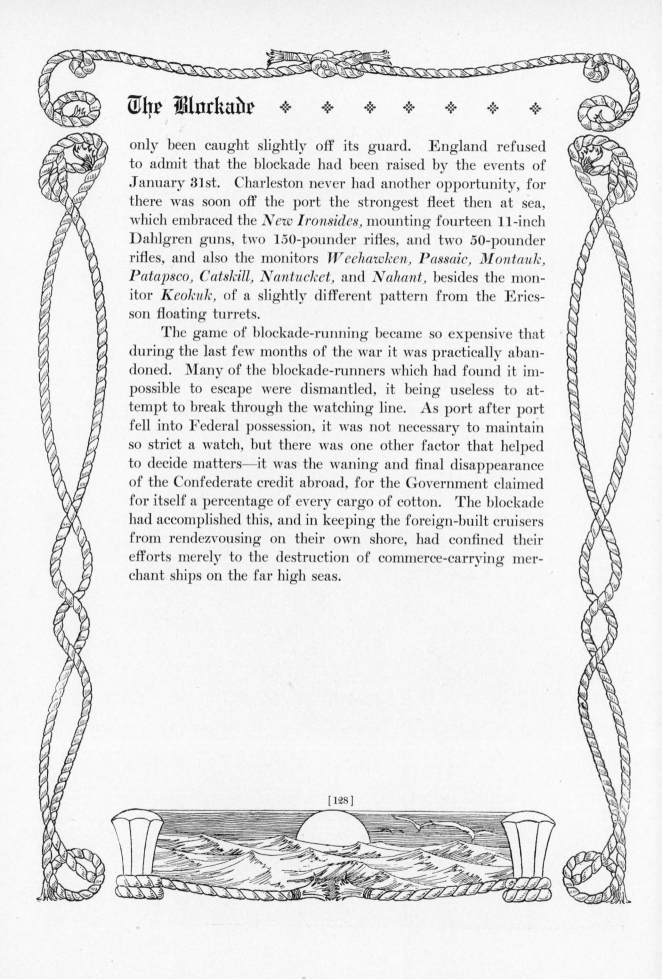

only been caught slightly off its guard. England refused to admit that the blockade had been raised by the events of January 31st. Charleston never had another opportunity, for there was soon off the port the strongest fleet then at sea, which embraced the *New Ironsides,* mounting fourteen 11-inch Dahlgren guns, two 150-pounder rifles, and two 50-pounder rifles, and also the monitors *Weehawken, Passaic, Montauk, Patapsco, Catskill, Nantucket,* and *Nahant,* besides the monitor *Keokuk,* of a slightly different pattern from the Ericsson floating turrets.

The game of blockade-running became so expensive that during the last few months of the war it was practically abandoned. Many of the blockade-runners which had found it impossible to escape were dismantled, it being useless to attempt to break through the watching line. As port after port fell into Federal possession, it was not necessary to maintain so strict a watch, but there was one other factor that helped to decide matters—it was the waning and final disappearance of the Confederate credit abroad, for the Government claimed for itself a percentage of every cargo of cotton. The blockade had accomplished this, and in keeping the foreign-built cruisers from rendezvousing on their own shore, had confined their efforts merely to the destruction of commerce-carrying merchant ships on the far high seas.

V

THE BIRTH OF THE

IRONCLADS

THE RIVER IRONCLAD "ESSEX"

ONE OF JAMES B. EADS' MISSISSIPPI MONSTERS, CONVERTED BY HIM FROM
A SNAG-BOAT, AND COMPLETED IN JANUARY, 1862

THE TYPE FAVORED BY ERICSSON

This splendid picture of the vessel lying at anchor in the James, off Bermuda Hundred, shows clearly the details of the type of perfected monitor most favored by Ericsson. Only a few months after the duel of the "Monitor" and the "Merrimac" in Hampton Roads, no less than thirty-five ironclads of the monitor type were being constructed for the Federal navy. The old Continental Iron Works in New York, that had built the original monitor, were busy turning out six vessels of the "Passaic" class, while others were being rushed up by shipbuilders in the East, and on the Ohio and the Mississippi. Ericsson was already at work upon the huge "Dictator" and "Puritan," each nearly five times as large as the first monitor. These were destined not to be completed till after the close of the war. But the navy-yards at New York, Philadelphia, and Boston were at work upon the four double-turreted monitors of the "Miantonomoh" class. Not satisfied with all this activity, the Navy Department, in September, 1862, let the contracts for nine more monitors similar to the "Passaic" class, but slightly larger. Among these was the "Saugus";

COPYRIGHT, 1911, REVIEW OF REVIEWS CO.

THE SINGLE TURRETED U. S. MONITOR "SAUGUS"

and one of her sister-ships, the "Canonicus," gave her name to the class. The most famous of the nine was the "Tecumseh." Her bold commander, T. A. N. Craven, in an effort to grapple with the Confederate ram "Tennessee" in Mobile Bay, ran through the line of torpedoes and lost his ship, which had fired the first two guns in Farragut's brilliant battle. Ericsson did not approve of the principle of the double-turreted monitor. In the "Saugus" is well exemplified his principle of mounting guns in such a manner that they could be brought to bear in any direction. This object was defeated somewhat in the double-turreted type, since each turret masked a considerable angle of fire of the other. The "Saugus," together with the "Tecumseh" and "Canonicus" and the "Onondaga," served in the six-hour action with Battery Dantzler and the Confederate vessels in the James River, June 21, 1864. Again on August 13th she locked horns with the Confederate fleet at Dutch Gap. She was actively engaged on the James and the Appomattox and took part in the fall of Fort Fisher, the event that marked the beginning of the last year of the war.

THE LATEST TYPE OF "IRON SEA–ELEPHANT" IN 1864

After having steadily planned and built monitors of increasing efficiency during the war, the Navy Department finally turned its attention to the production of a double-turreted ocean cruiser of this type. The "Onondaga" was one of the first to be completed. In the picture she is seen lying in the James River. There, near Howlett's, she had steamed into her first action, June 21, 1864, with other Federal vessels engaging Battery Dantzler, the ram "Virginia," and the other Confederate vessels that were guarding Richmond. The "Onondaga" continued to participate in the closing operations of the navy on the James. Of this class of double-turreted monitors the "Monadnock" and the "Miantonomoh" startled the world after the war was over. Foreign and domestic skeptics maintained that Gustavus Vasa Fox, Assistant Secretary of the Navy, who had earnestly advocated the construction of monitors while the type

COPYRIGHT, 1911, REVIEW OF REVIEWS CO.

THE DOUBLE–TURRETED MONITOR "ONONDAGA"

was still an experiment, had merely succeeded in adding so many "iron coffins" to the navy. It was asserted that no monitor would prove seaworthy in heavy weather, to say nothing of being able to cross the ocean. In the spring of 1866, therefore, the Navy Department determined to despatch the "Miantonomoh" across the Atlantic; and, to show his faith in the "iron coffins" he had advocated, Assistant Secretary Fox embarked on her at St. John, N. B., on June 5th. Meanwhile the "Monadnock" had been despatched around the Horn to San Francisco; her progress was watched with far greater enthusiasm than that of the "Oregon" during the Spanish War. The "Miantonomoh" reached Queenstown in safety, after a passage of ten days and eighteen hours, and about the same time the "Monadnock" arrived at her destination, thus proving beyond cavil both the speed and seaworthiness of the American monitor.

THE BIRTH OF THE IRONCLADS

AN EPOCH IN NAVAL WARFARE

UNDER the date of July 4, 1861, the Secretary of the Navy of the United States, the Honorable Gideon Welles, in his report, explained very clearly the exact position of the iron-clad vessel of war during its period of inception. Caution, and doubt as to the feasibility of such construction are clearly expressed here, and also a certain temerity in the way of expending the departmental allowance:

> Much attention has been given within the last few years to the subject of floating batteries, or iron-clad steamers. Other governments, and particularly France and England, have made it a special object in connection with naval improvements; and the ingenuity and inventive faculties of our own countrymen have also been stimulated by recent occurrences toward the construction of this class of vessel. The period is, perhaps, not one best adapted to heavy expenditures by way of experiment, and the time and attention of some of those who are most competent to investigate and form correct conclusions on this subject are otherwise employed. I would, however, recommend the appointment of a proper and competent board to inquire into and report in regard to a measure so important; and it is for Congress to decide whether, on a favorable report, they will order one or more iron-clad steamers, or floating batteries, to be constructed, with a view to perfect protection from the effects of present ordnance at short range, and make an appropriation for that purpose.

For a long time the armored vessel had been the pet of the inventor, and the building of iron ships of war had been contemplated. To go into the history of such attempts would be to review, in a measure, all the records of the past, for iron-protected ships had been constructed for many years, and as far back as 1583 the Dutch had built a flat-bottomed sailing

JOHN ERICSSON, LL.D.—THE PRECURSOR OF A NEW NAVAL ERA

The battle of Ericsson's "Monitor" with the "Merrimac" settled the question of wooden navies for the world. Born in Sweden in 1803, Ericsson was given a cadetship in the corps of engineers at the age of eleven. In 1839, with several notable inventions already to his credit, he came to America and laid before the Navy Department his new arrangement of the steam machinery in warships. It had been regarded with indifference in England, yet it was destined to revolutionize the navies of the world. In 1841 Ericsson was engaged in constructing the U. S. S. "Princeton." She was the first steamship ever built with the propelling machinery below the water-line, and embodied a number of Ericsson's inventions—among them a new method of managing guns. At the time Ericsson laid his plans for the "Monitor" before the Navy Department, there existed a strong prejudice against him throughout the bureaus because his name had been unjustly associated with the bursting of the "Princeton's" 12-inch gun, February 28, 1844, by which the Secretary of State, the Secretary of the Navy, Cap- tain Kennon, and Colonel Gard- iner were killed. The Naval Board nevertheless had the cour- age to recommend the "Moni- tor," and this last great invention of Ericsson brought him immor- tal fame. He died in New York in 1889. His body was sent back to his native land on board the U. S. S. "Baltimore" as a mark of the navy's high esteem.

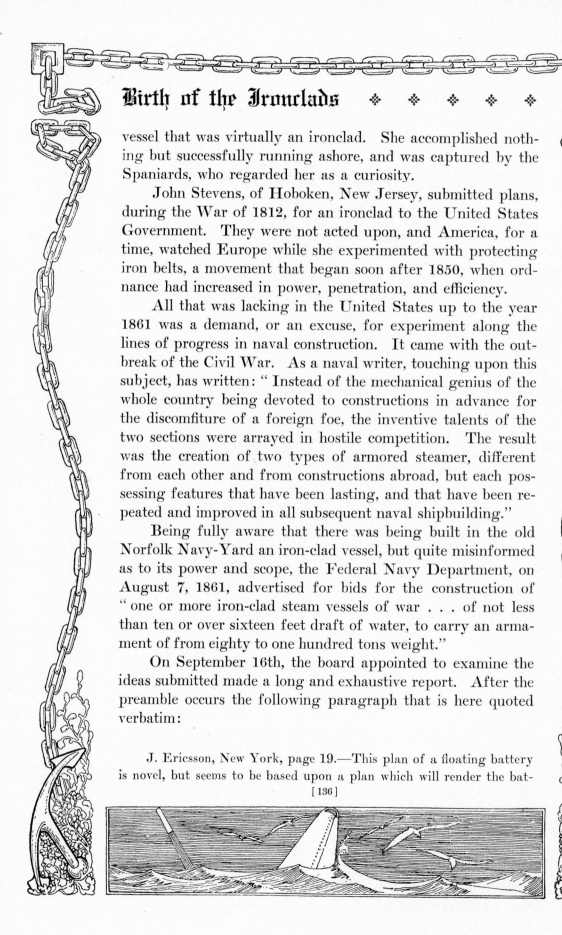

vessel that was virtually an ironclad. She accomplished nothing but successfully running ashore, and was captured by the Spaniards, who regarded her as a curiosity.

John Stevens, of Hoboken, New Jersey, submitted plans, during the War of 1812, for an ironclad to the United States Government. They were not acted upon, and America, for a time, watched Europe while she experimented with protecting iron belts, a movement that began soon after 1850, when ordnance had increased in power, penetration, and efficiency.

All that was lacking in the United States up to the year 1861 was a demand, or an excuse, for experiment along the lines of progress in naval construction. It came with the outbreak of the Civil War. As a naval writer, touching upon this subject, has written: " Instead of the mechanical genius of the whole country being devoted to constructions in advance for the discomfiture of a foreign foe, the inventive talents of the two sections were arrayed in hostile competition. The result was the creation of two types of armored steamer, different from each other and from constructions abroad, but each possessing features that have been lasting, and that have been repeated and improved in all subsequent naval shipbuilding."

Being fully aware that there was being built in the old Norfolk Navy-Yard an iron-clad vessel, but quite misinformed as to its power and scope, the Federal Navy Department, on August 7, 1861, advertised for bids for the construction of " one or more iron-clad steam vessels of war . . . of not less than ten or over sixteen feet draft of water, to carry an armament of from eighty to one hundred tons weight."

On September 16th, the board appointed to examine the ideas submitted made a long and exhaustive report. After the preamble occurs the following paragraph that is here quoted verbatim:

J. Ericsson, New York, page 19.—This plan of a floating battery is novel, but seems to be based upon a plan which will render the bat-

COPYRIGHT, 1911, PATRIOT PUB. CO.

U. S. S. "GALENA"—ONE OF THE THREE FIRST EXPERIMENTS IN FEDERAL IRONCLADS

The Civil War in America solved for the world the question of the utility of armor plate in the construction of war vessels. This problem had been vexing the naval authorities of Europe. France and England were vying with each other at building iron-belted vessels that differed only from the old wooden line-of-battle ships in the addition of this new protection. Following this foreign precedent, Lieutenant John M. Brooke, C. S. N., planned to raise the hull of the "Merrimac" and convert her into an ironclad of original design, which became the standard for all subsequent efforts by the naval constructors of the Confederacy. It was not till October 4, 1861, four months after the Confederacy had raised the "Merrimac," that the first contracts for ironclad vessels were let by the Navy Department. For two months a naval board, appointed by President Lincoln, had been poring over various plans submitted, and finally recommended the adoption of three. A vessel of the foreign type, to be called the "New Ironsides," was to be in effect a floating battery, mounting fourteen 9-inch smooth-bores in her broadsides and two 150-pounder rifles. She proved one of the most formidable vessels of her class. A small corvette, to be called the "Galena," was also ordered, her sides to be plated with three-inch iron. The third was Ericsson's "Monitor."

tery shot- and shell-proof. We are somewhat apprehensive that her properties for sea are not such as a sea-going vessel should possess. But she may be moved from one place to another on the coast in smooth water. We recommend that an experiment be made with one battery of this description on the terms proposed, with a guarantee and forfeiture in case of failure in any of the properties and points of the vessel as proposed.

Price, $275,000; length of vessel, 172 feet; breadth of beam, 41 feet; depth of hold, $11\frac{1}{2}$ feet; time, 100 days; draft of water, 10 feet; displacement, 1255 tons; speed per hour, 9 statute miles.

This was the first notice of the famous *Monitor*. The idea of her construction was not exactly new, but no vessel of this class had ever been launched. She resembled, in a measure, the suggested floating battery of Stevens, but still more that proposed in the plans of Theodore R. Timby, of New York, and submitted to the War Department by him in the year 1841. This included specifications and drawings for a revolving iron battery, and practically was the foreshadowing of the *Monitor*. In fact, when the backers of Ericsson came to look into the matter, it was considered advisable to purchase Timby's patents.

There were also built at this time two heavily and almost completely armored ships, both more or less experimental, one, the *Galena,* destined to be a failure, while the other, named the *New Ironsides* and built by contract with Merrick and Sons, of Philadelphia, became, with the addition of the turret principle, the war-ship of future years. She was 232 feet long, 58 feet in beam, and 4120 tons displacement, a large size for that day. Her battery consisted of sixteen 11-inch Dahlgren guns, two 200-pounder Parrott rifles, and four 24-pound howitzers. She was the most formidable ship afloat. Although containing powerful engines, traditions of the older navy still prevailed, and the *New Ironsides* was at first fully rigged as a bark. Soon, however, the cumbersome masts were taken out and replaced with light poles that gave her a still closer appearance

COPYRIGHT, 1911, PATRIOT PUB. CO.

INADEQUATE ARMOR—DECK OF THE "GALENA" AFTER HER GREAT FIGHT

The "Galena" early proved incapable of the work for which she had been planned. It was the belief that her armor would enable her to stand up against the powerful land-batteries of the Confederates. This the "New Ironsides" could do; her sixteen guns could pour in such a hail of missiles that it was difficult for cannoneers on land to stand to their posts. The "Galena," with but six guns, found this condition exactly reversed, and on May 15, 1862, she was found wanting in the attack on Fort Darling, at Drewry's Bluff, the Federal navy's first attempt to reach Richmond. There, under Commander John Rodgers, she came into direct competition with Ericsson's "Monitor." Both vessels were rated in the same class, and their tonnage was nearly equal. The engagement lasted three hours and twenty minutes. The two ironclads, anchored within six hundred yards of the fort, sprung their broadsides upon it, eight guns in all against fourteen. In the action the "Galena" lost thirteen men killed and eleven wounded. A single 10-inch shot broke through her armor and shattered her hull almost beyond repair. The "Monitor" remained entirely uninjured, without the loss of a single man. After the engagement the "Galena" was found to be so cut up that her armor plate was removed and she was converted into a wooden gunboat, thus continuing in service through the war.

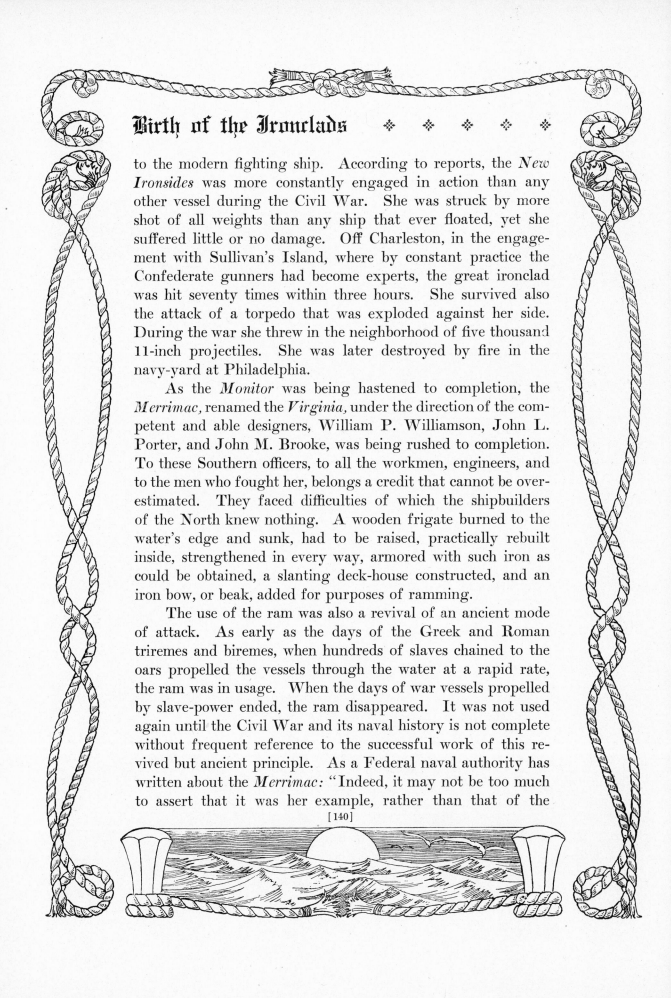

to the modern fighting ship.   According to reports, the *New Ironsides* was more constantly engaged in action than any other vessel during the Civil War.   She was struck by more shot of all weights than any ship that ever floated, yet she suffered little or no damage.   Off Charleston, in the engagement with Sullivan's Island, where by constant practice the Confederate gunners had become experts, the great ironclad was hit seventy times within three hours.   She survived also the attack of a torpedo that was exploded against her side. During the war she threw in the neighborhood of five thousand 11-inch projectiles.   She was later destroyed by fire in the navy-yard at Philadelphia.

As the *Monitor* was being hastened to completion, the *Merrimac,* renamed the *Virginia,* under the direction of the competent and able designers, William P. Williamson, John L. Porter, and John M. Brooke, was being rushed to completion. To these Southern officers, to all the workmen, engineers, and to the men who fought her, belongs a credit that cannot be overestimated.   They faced difficulties of which the shipbuilders of the North knew nothing.   A wooden frigate burned to the water's edge and sunk, had to be raised, practically rebuilt inside, strengthened in every way, armored with such iron as could be obtained, a slanting deck-house constructed, and an iron bow, or beak, added for purposes of ramming.

The use of the ram was also a revival of an ancient mode of attack.   As early as the days of the Greek and Roman triremes and biremes, when hundreds of slaves chained to the oars propelled the vessels through the water at a rapid rate, the ram was in usage.   When the days of war vessels propelled by slave-power ended, the ram disappeared.   It was not used again until the Civil War and its naval history is not complete without frequent reference to the successful work of this revived but ancient principle.   As a Federal naval authority has written about the *Merrimac:* "Indeed, it may not be too much to assert that it was her example, rather than that of the

COPYRIGHT. 1911. REVIEW OF REVIEWS CO.

THE FIRST INLAND MONITOR—THE "OZARK"

This hybrid-looking vessel was the first of the Federal attempts to adapt the monitor type of construction to the needs of the navy on the Western rivers. She was a cross between the Ericsson design (which she resembled in her turret and pilot-house) and the early type of river gunboat, apparent in her hull, stacks, and upper works. Her armament consisted of two 11-inch smooth-bores in the turret and a 12-pounder pivot-gun at the stern. Having joined Porter's Mississippi squadron early in 1864, she was the last of the entrapped vessels to get free above the Falls at Alexandria, in the Red River expedition. Porter pronounced her turret all right but considered her hull too high out of water, and declared that she lacked three inches of iron plating on her fifteen inches of oak. Porter had discovered, in running the batteries at Vicksburg, that heavy logs, hung perpendicularly on the sides of his gunboats, prevented shot of heavy size from doing more than slightly indenting the iron plating. He recommended that the three-inch plating of the "Ozark" would be adequate if it were covered on the outside with a facing of wood in addition to the wooden backing within.

COPYRIGHT, 1911 REVIEW OF REVIEWS CO.

THE "OZARK'S" PIVOT-GUN

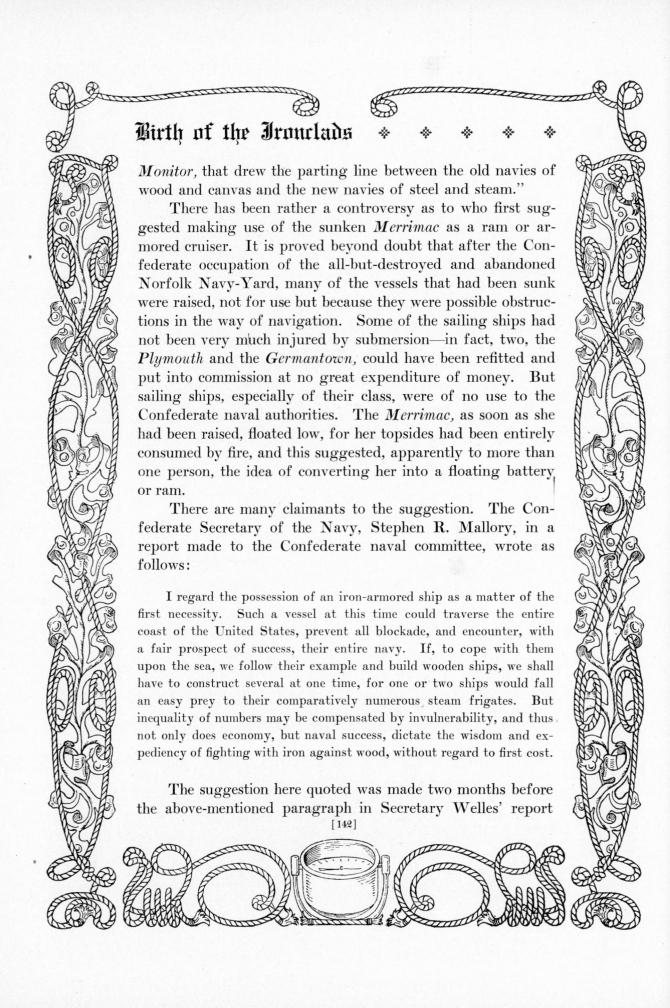

Monitor, that drew the parting line between the old navies of wood and canvas and the new navies of steel and steam."

There has been rather a controversy as to who first suggested making use of the sunken *Merrimac* as a ram or armored cruiser. It is proved beyond doubt that after the Confederate occupation of the all-but-destroyed and abandoned Norfolk Navy-Yard, many of the vessels that had been sunk were raised, not for use but because they were possible obstructions in the way of navigation. Some of the sailing ships had not been very much injured by submersion—in fact, two, the *Plymouth* and the *Germantown,* could have been refitted and put into commission at no great expenditure of money. But sailing ships, especially of their class, were of no use to the Confederate naval authorities. The *Merrimac,* as soon as she had been raised, floated low, for her topsides had been entirely consumed by fire, and this suggested, apparently to more than one person, the idea of converting her into a floating battery or ram.

There are many claimants to the suggestion. The Confederate Secretary of the Navy, Stephen R. Mallory, in a report made to the Confederate naval committee, wrote as follows:

I regard the possession of an iron-armored ship as a matter of the first necessity. Such a vessel at this time could traverse the entire coast of the United States, prevent all blockade, and encounter, with a fair prospect of success, their entire navy. If, to cope with them upon the sea, we follow their example and build wooden ships, we shall have to construct several at one time, for one or two ships would fall an easy prey to their comparatively numerous steam frigates. But inequality of numbers may be compensated by invulnerability, and thus not only does economy, but naval success, dictate the wisdom and expediency of fighting with iron against wood, without regard to first cost.

The suggestion here quoted was made two months before the above-mentioned paragraph in Secretary Welles' report

COPYRIGHT, 1911, REVIEW OF REVIEWS CO.

THE HEYDAY OF THE MONITOR
A FLEET OF FIVE IN '64

On the Appomattox River, in 1864, lie five of the then latest type of Federal ironclad—all built on the improved Ericsson plan, doing away with the objectionable "overhang" of the deck, dispensed with in order to give greater speed and seaworthiness. By this time the Federal navy had found abundant opportunity to try out the qualities of the monitor type. A monitor presented less than a third as much target area as any one of the old broadside ships that could possibly compete with her armament. Her movable turret enabled her to train her guns almost instantly on an adversary and bring them to bear constantly as fast as they could be loaded, no matter what the position or course of either vessel. If a monitor went aground, she remained a revolving fort irrespective of the position of her hull. A shot to do serious damage must strike the heavy armor of the monitor squarely. The percentage of shots that could be so placed from the deck of a rolling ship was very small, most of them glancing off from the circular turret and pilot-house or skidding harmlessly along the deck. Only the most powerful land batteries could make any impression on these "iron sea-elephants" which the Federals had learned how to use. Their only vulnerable spot was below the water-line. The boom across the river in the picture, as well as the torpedo-nets, arranged at the bows of the vessels, indicates that the Confederates strove constantly to seize the advantage of this one weakness. The monitors in the James and Appomatox were too vigilant to be thus caught, although hundreds of floating mines were launched in the current or planted in the channel. The fleet, ever on the watch for these, was kept busy raking them up and rendering them harmless for passing ships.

was written, and before the *Merrimac* had been raised. Secretary Mallory had had good training for his position. For several years he had been chairman of the Committee on Naval Affairs of the United States Senate, and had been foremost in his interest in the navy and in the changes that were taking place in naval methods. Although many people of inventive mind and constructive imagination had worked along the lines that were now to be seriously adopted, Secretary Mallory was the first one in a position of authority to take the initiative in a change which abruptly ended the past eras of naval ship building, and inaugurated that of the new.

It was in June, 1861, that a board was appointed to make a survey of the *Merrimac,* draw plans, and estimate the cost of the conversion of that vessel into an iron-clad battery. The board consisted of Lieutenant John M. Brooke, inventor of the Brooke rifled gun, Chief Engineer William P. Williamson, and Lieutenant John L. Porter, chief constructor of the Confederate navy. All of these gentlemen were officers who had seen long service in the navy of the United States. In a letter from Mallory, addressed to Flag-Officer Forrest, Porter and Williamson are mentioned as being the constructor and engineer of the *Merrimac.* John M. Brooke, however, had much to do with her completion. He supervised the placing of the battery inside the armored citadel, which consisted of one 7-inch pivoted Brooke rifle at each end, and eight guns, four in a broadside, six of which were 9-inch Dahlgrens, and two 32-pounder Brooke rifles. In appearance, the *Merrimac,* when completed, resembled very much the Eads ironclads which had appeared on the Mississippi River. An odd coincidence was that the *Monitor* was commissioned as a ship of war on the 25th of February, 1862, and only the day before the *Merrimac,* henceforth known in Confederate annals as the *Virginia,* had received her first commander, Flag-Officer Franklin Buchanan. In the orders issued to him by Secretary Mallory, occur some prophetic paragraphs:

[144]

THE "MAHOPAC" ON ACTIVE SERVICE

The monitor "Mahopac," as she floated in the James near Bermuda Hundred in 1864, illustrates one of the newer types completed in 1864. The lower picture gives a good idea of her deck. The gun-ports of her turret are open. The coffin-like hatchway in the foreground was the only means of entrance. In action or rough weather this was tightly closed. Air-holes with their gratings are seen at intervals about the deck, but these too had to be closed during a storm. It was almost a submarine life led by the officers and crew in active service. Every opportunity was seized to get above deck for a breathing space. The "Mahopac" had a crew of 92 men. Her first engagement was with Battery Dantzler in the James River, Nov. 29, 1864. In December, 1864, and January, 1865, the "Mahopac" was in the first line of the ironclads that bombarded Fort Fisher. Her men declared that she silenced every gun on the sea-face of that fort.

COPYRIGHT, 1911, REVIEW OF REVIEWS CO

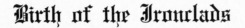

Birth of the Ironclads

You will hoist your flag on the *Virginia*, or any other vessel of your squadron, which will, for the present, embrace the *Virginia, Patrick Henry, Jamestown, Teaser, Raleigh*, and *Beaufort*.

The *Virginia* is a novelty in naval construction, is untried, and her powers unknown, and the department will not give specific orders as to her attack upon the enemy. Her powers as a ram are regarded as very formidable, and it is hoped that you may be able to test them.

Like the bayonet charge of infantry, this mode of attack, while the most destructive, will commend itself to you in the present scarcity of ammunition. It is one, also, that may be rendered destructive at night against the enemy at anchor.

Even without guns, the ship would be formidable as a ram.

Could you pass Old Point and make a dashing cruise on the Potomac as far as Washington, its effect upon the public mind would be important to the cause.

The reason that the *Merrimac* did not pass Old Point Comfort, or proceed to New York, is told in another place, when she and the little Ericsson *Monitor* met. However, as far as her anticipated work was done, it was successful. With the wooden vessels she had it all her own way. But as of the *Monitor* herself, after the engagement, too high hopes were formed, so, of her antagonist, before she had been tried out, too much was expected.

The monitors failed signally against well-protected shore batteries. As more and more of these turreted vessels were ordered to be constructed during the war, they were divided into classes that differed but slightly from the original type. There were two-turreted, and, even at the last, three-turreted monitors; although the low free-board was maintained, the protecting overhang had disappeared, and this added greatly to their seaworthiness. The tragic loss on the 31st of December, 1862, of the original little vessel, which became a coffin for sixteen of her crew in a gale off Cape Hatteras, had taught ship-designers more than a little. A war-ship must first be seaworthy, and beside having defensive and offensive qualities,

COPYRIGHT, 1911, REVIEW OF REVIEWS CO.

THE "OSAGE" IN 1864

ONE OF THE NEW LEVIATHANS OF THE RIVER

The low, rotating monitor-turret of this ironclad and her great guns saved both herself and the transport "Black Hawk" from capture during the return of the Red River expedition. The "Osage" was a later addition to the squadron; she and her sister ironclad, the "Neosho," were among the most powerful on the rivers. Porter took both with him up the Red River. On the return the "Osage" was making the descent with great difficulty, in tow of the "Black Hawk," when on April 12th she ran aground opposite Blair's plantation. A Confederate force twelve hundred strong, under General Thomas Green, soon appeared on the west bank and, planting four field-pieces, advanced to attack the stranded ironclad. The brisk enfilading fire of the "Lexington" and the "Neosho" did not deter them. Lieutenant-Commander T. O. Selfridge waited till the heads of the Confederates appeared above the river bank. Then he let drive at them with his two big guns, pouring upon them a rain of grape, canister, and shrapnel. General Green, who behaved with the greatest gallantry, had his head blown off. After an hour and a half the Confederates withdrew from the unequal contest, with a loss of over four hundred dead and wounded. The "Osage" was sent to Mobile Bay in the spring of 1865 and was there sunk by a submarine torpedo on March 29th.

COPYRIGHT, 1911, REVIEW OF REVIEWS CO

A VETERAN OF THE RIVERS—THE "PITTSBURG"

The "Pittsburg" was one of the seven ironclads that Eads completed in a hundred days. She first went into action at Fort Donelson, where she was struck forty times. Two shots from the Confederates pierced her below the guards. She began shipping water so fast that it was feared that she would sink. In turning around to get out of range, she fouled the "Carondelet's" stern, breaking one of her rudders. In going ahead to clear the "Carondelet" from the "Pittsburg," Commander Walke was forced to approach within 350 yards of the fort, which immediately concentrated the fire of the batteries upon that single vessel, whose consorts were all drifting out of action in a disabled condition. It was only by great coolness and courage that the "Carondelet" was extricated after being exposed to a terrific fire for some time. The "Pittsburg" was conspicuous in the fight with the Confederate flotilla at Fort Pillow. She was sent by Admiral Porter on the famous "land cruise" up the Yazoo, which nearly cost him the flotilla. She ran the batteries at Vicksburg and helped to silence the batteries at Grand Gulf, Mississippi. In May, 1863, she was with Admiral Porter on the first Red River expedition and distinguished herself in the action with Fort Beauregard. The next year she was in the second Red River expedition and shared with the other vessels the dangers of the return. She was one of the most serviceable of the first Eads ironclads.

COPYRIGHT, 1911, REVIEW OF REVIEWS CO.

THE "CINCINNATI," A SALVAGED GUNBOAT

The "Cincinnati" was one of the first seven Eads ironclads to be built and was the second to meet disaster. She was Foote's flagship at Fort Henry and in the engagement she was struck thirty-one times. Two of her guns and one of her paddle-wheels were disabled, and her smokestacks, after-cabin, and boats were riddled with shot. She was soon in commission again and joined the flotilla above Island No. 10. In the sudden attack by which the Confederate gunboats surprised the Federal squadron above Fort Pillow, the "Cincinnati" again met disaster and was towed to shallow water, where she sank. Again she was repaired in time to take part in the bombardment of Vicksburg, May 27, 1863, under Lieutenant George D. Bache. Here she gallantly engaged single-handed the batteries on Fort Hill to the north of the town. The terrific hail of grape-shot from the Confederate guns compelled her to close her bow ports. In endeavoring to get away, she was so badly hit that she could barely be gotten into shoal-water before she sank. The Confederates set fire to her a few days later, but even that was not to be the end of the gallant ironclad. After the occupation of Vicksburg, she was raised and found to be not so badly damaged as had been supposed. The next year she was on duty in the Missis- sippi between Fort Adams and Natchez. In 1865 she was sent by Admiral Lee to take part in the final naval operations that led to the fall of Mobile.

COPYRIGHT, 1911, REVIEW OF REVIEWS CO.

MONARCHS OF THE FLOTILLA—THE "LOUISVILLE," ONE OF THE ORIGINAL EADS IRONCLADS

Below appears the Federal ironclad "Benton." As James B. Eads went on constructing gunboats for the Mississippi squadron, he kept improving on his own ideas. The "Benton" was his masterpiece. She was finished soon after the original seven ironclads ordered by the army. Though her engines were slow, she proved to be the most powerful fighting vessel in the Federal Mississippi squadron. She held that distinction till late in 1864, when the river monitors began to appear. The "Benton" was Foote's flagship in the operations around Island No. 10; and when the gallant old officer retired, it was on her deck that he bade good-bye to his officers and men. The "Benton" then became the flagship of Captain Charles Henry Davis, who in her directed the famous battle off Memphis where the Ellet rams proved their prowess. The first commander of the "Benton" was Lieutenant S. Ledyard Phelps. He fought the gunboat in both of the above engagements. The "Benton" was hit twenty-five times while supporting Sherman's unsuccessful assault on Vicksburg from the north, and she was Admiral Porter's flagship when he ran by the batteries at the beginning of the maneuver by which Grant approached and invested Vicksburg from the southward, thus accomplishing the fall of "the key to the Mississippi."

U S. GUNBOAT "BENTON," TUG "FERN"

COPYRIGHT 1911, REVIEW OF REVIEWS CO.

THE "GENERAL PRICE," A CAPTIVE BY THE ELLET RAMS

After the "General Price" became a Federal gunboat, the pilot-house was protected and moved forward and other alterations were made. The Ellet rams continued their useful work. Charles Rivers Ellet took the first vessel past the batteries at Vicksburg after Grant had determined upon his venturesome movement upon the city from the south. Admiral Farragut, who had come up from the Red River, requested General Alfred W. Ellet to let him have two of the ram fleet to run the batteries in order to augment the blockade of the Red River. On March 25, 1863, Lieutenant-Colonel J. A. Ellet, in command of the "Lancaster," with his nephew, Charles Rivers Ellet, in command of the "Switzerland," chose a time near daylight for the attempt. "These Ellets were all brave fellows and were full of the spirit of adventure," said Admiral Porter. Scorning the cover of darkness, they got abreast of the batteries, which promptly opened on them in a thundering chorus. A shell exploded the boilers of the "Lancaster" and she went to pieces and sank almost immediately. The "Switzerland" had her boilers perforated by a plunging shot and received other injuries, but she got through; and in her and in other of the Ellet rams, Charles Rivers Ellet performed other distinguished services.

CHARLES RIVERS ELLET

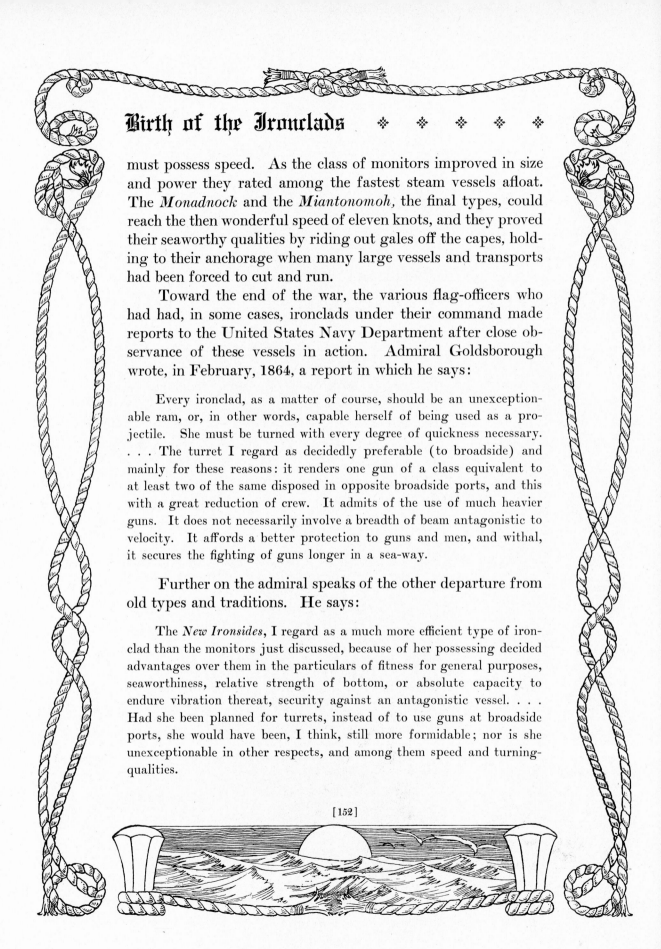

must possess speed. As the class of monitors improved in size and power they rated among the fastest steam vessels afloat. The *Monadnock* and the *Miantonomoh,* the final types, could reach the then wonderful speed of eleven knots, and they proved their seaworthy qualities by riding out gales off the capes, holding to their anchorage when many large vessels and transports had been forced to cut and run.

Toward the end of the war, the various flag-officers who had had, in some cases, ironclads under their command made reports to the United States Navy Department after close observance of these vessels in action. Admiral Goldsborough wrote, in February, 1864, a report in which he says:

Every ironclad, as a matter of course, should be an unexceptionable ram, or, in other words, capable herself of being used as a projectile. She must be turned with every degree of quickness necessary. . . . The turret I regard as decidedly preferable (to broadside) and mainly for these reasons: it renders one gun of a class equivalent to at least two of the same disposed in opposite broadside ports, and this with a great reduction of crew. It admits of the use of much heavier guns. It does not necessarily involve a breadth of beam antagonistic to velocity. It affords a better protection to guns and men, and withal, it secures the fighting of guns longer in a sea-way.

Further on the admiral speaks of the other departure from old types and traditions. He says:

The *New Ironsides,* I regard as a much more efficient type of ironclad than the monitors just discussed, because of her possessing decided advantages over them in the particulars of fitness for general purposes, seaworthiness, relative strength of bottom, or absolute capacity to endure vibration thereat, security against an antagonistic vessel. . . . Had she been planned for turrets, instead of to use guns at broadside ports, she would have been, I think, still more formidable; nor is she unexceptionable in other respects, and among them speed and turning-qualities.

[152]

CHAPTER
VI

THE MOST FAMOUS
AMERICAN
NAVAL BATTLE

COPYRIGHT, 1911, PATRIOT PUB. CO.

THE "MONITOR'S" SECOND COMMANDER
A PHOTOGRAPH FOUR MONTHS AFTER "THE MOST FAMOUS FIGHT"

LIEUTENANT W. N. JEFFERS, WHO SUCCEEDED THE GALLANT AND WOUNDED WORDEN
AFTER THE CONTEST, AND COMMANDED THE IRONCLAD " THROUGH MOST OF HER CAREER"

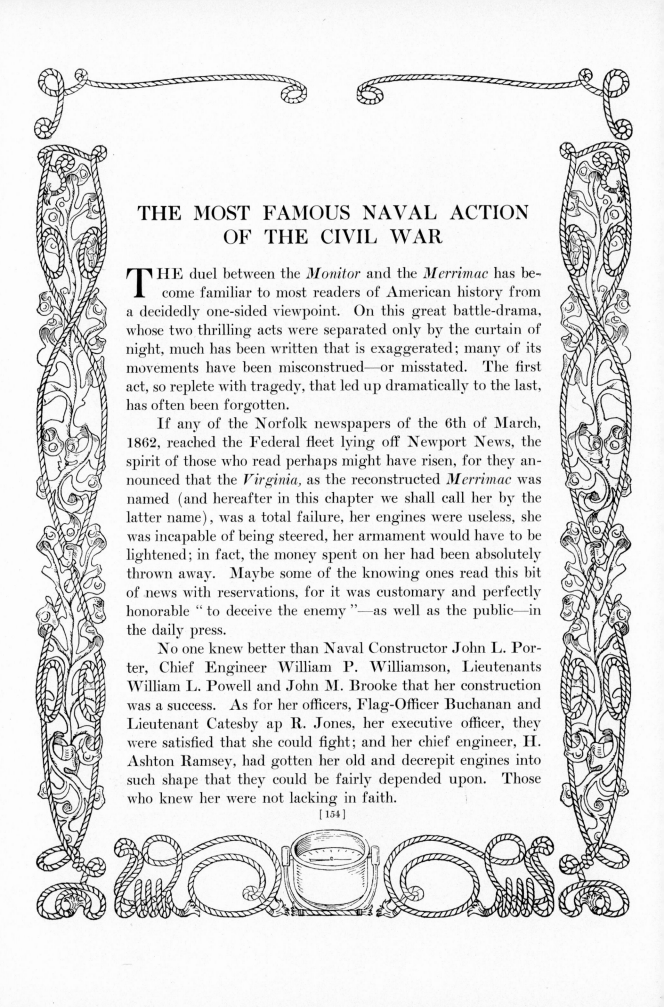

THE MOST FAMOUS NAVAL ACTION
OF THE CIVIL WAR

THE duel between the *Monitor* and the *Merrimac* has become familiar to most readers of American history from a decidedly one-sided viewpoint. On this great battle-drama, whose two thrilling acts were separated only by the curtain of night, much has been written that is exaggerated; many of its movements have been misconstrued—or misstated. The first act, so replete with tragedy, that led up dramatically to the last, has often been forgotten.

If any of the Norfolk newspapers of the 6th of March, 1862, reached the Federal fleet lying off Newport News, the spirit of those who read perhaps might have risen, for they announced that the *Virginia,* as the reconstructed *Merrimac* was named (and hereafter in this chapter we shall call her by the latter name), was a total failure, her engines were useless, she was incapable of being steered, her armament would have to be lightened; in fact, the money spent on her had been absolutely thrown away. Maybe some of the knowing ones read this bit of news with reservations, for it was customary and perfectly honorable " to deceive the enemy "—as well as the public—in the daily press.

No one knew better than Naval Constructor John L. Porter, Chief Engineer William P. Williamson, Lieutenants William L. Powell and John M. Brooke that her construction was a success. As for her officers, Flag-Officer Buchanan and Lieutenant Catesby ap R. Jones, her executive officer, they were satisfied that she could fight; and her chief engineer, H. Ashton Ramsey, had gotten her old and decrepit engines into such shape that they could be fairly depended upon. Those who knew her were not lacking in faith.

COPYRIGHT, 1911, REVIEW OF REVIEWS CO.

THE NORFOLK NAVY-YARD

WHERE THE "VIRGINIA" WAS BUILT

When those two queer-looking craft—the "Monitor" and the "Virginia" ("Merrimac")—approached each other in Hampton Roads on Sunday morning, March 9, 1862, much more hung in the balance to be decided than the mere question of which should win. These were no foreign foes that opposed each other, but men of the same race, and the fighting-machines which they brought into action epitomized the best judgment of men that had been trained in the same navy. The fact that ironclad vessels were to engage for the first time in a momentous conflict was of minor significance. Europe had already taken a long step toward the employment of armor plate; not its place in naval warfare, but the manner in which it was to be given effectiveness by American brains, was at stake. Of these two new armored knights of the sea, the "Virginia"

JOHN M. BROOKE, C. S. N.
DESIGNER OF THE "VIRGINIA'S"
ARMAMENT

(the first to be begun) was the more directly the result of native thought and circumstance. Her hull was all that was left of one of the gallant old fighting frigates built soon after the United States became a nation. The men who planned and superintended her construction were skilled officers of the old navy—John L. Porter and William P. Williamson. Her armament was prepared by another veteran, John M. Brooke, and consisted in part of his own invention, the Brooke rifled gun. She was built at a national navy-yard at Norfolk; and had this not fallen into the hands of the Confederates at the beginning of the war, the remodeled "Merrimac" would never have appeared in Hampton Roads to teach the wooden ships of the old navy the bitter lesson that their usefulness was on the wane and soon to be at an end. The era of the modern warship had come.

With everything on board and steam up, the " total failure " was ready to make her first attack on the 8th of March, 1862. People had crowded down to the water's edge to study her much-heralded " imperfections." What they chiefly noted was that she was very slow, and indeed her speed was not above five knots an hour. Captain William H. Parker, C. S. N., has left so vivid a description of this new departure in naval construction in his " Recollections of a Naval Officer," that the mind's eye can see her perfectly:

The appearance of the *Merrimac* was that of the roof of a house. Saw off the top of a house at the eaves (supposing it to be an ordinary gable-ended, shelving-sided roof), pass a plane parallel to the first through the roof some feet beneath the ridge, incline the gable ends, put it in the water, and you have the *Merrimac* as she appeared. When she was not in action her people stood on top of this roof which was, in fact, her spar-deck.

The Norfolk papers, however, were not so far from wrong. Captain Buchanan commanded her for three days and a little over; Lieutenant Jones, for about the same time, and Flag-Officer Tattnall for forty-five days, yet out of the two months that she was supposed to be in commission and ready to fight, there were actually only about fifteen days that she was not in dock, or laid up in the hands of the navy-yard mechanics.

But to return to the moment of expectation—the morning of the 8th of March. Off Newport News, in Hampton Roads, only six and a half miles from Old Point Comfort and some twelve miles from Norfolk, lay the Federal squadron: the old *Congress* and the *Cumberland* well out in the stream, and farther down toward Fortress Monroe the splendid steam frigates *Minnesota* and *Roanoke,* and the sailing frigate *St. Lawrence.* There were some nondescript vessels and a few decrepit storeships that never counted in the succeeding crowded moments, but certainly six months before it would have been suicide for

CAPTAIN FRANKLIN BUCHANAN, C. S. N., AND CAPTAIN JOSIAH TATTNALL, C. S. N.,
COMMANDING THE "VIRGINIA" ("MERRIMAC")

It was a task of surpassing difficulty and danger that confronted Captain Buchanan when the "Virginia" shipped her anchors on March 8, 1862, and steamed down Elizabeth River to fight a fleet of the most powerful line-of-battle ships in the Federal navy, lying under the guns of formidable land batteries. The "Virginia's" trial trip was this voyage into imminent battle; not one of her guns had been fired; her crew, volunteers from the Confederate army, were strangers to one another and to their officers; they had never even had a practice drill together. The vessel lay too low in the water, and her faulty engines gave her a speed of but five knots, making maneuvering in the narrow channel exceedingly difficult. But Captain Buchanan, who had risen from a sick-bed to take his command, flinched for none of this—nor for the fact that his own brother, McKean, was paymaster on the "Congress." It was one of the most hazardous experiments in all warfare that Captain Buchanan was about to make, and its result revolutionized the American navy. Captain Tattnall, another experienced officer of the old navy, relieved Buchanan on April 11, 1862, and diligently sought a second battle with the "Monitor," but it was not accepted. On May 11th the "Virginia" was destroyed by Tattnall's order.

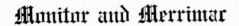

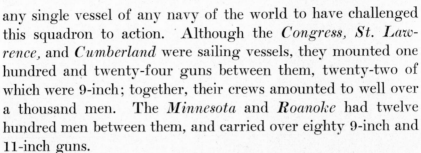

any single vessel of any navy of the world to have challenged this squadron to action. Although the *Congress, St. Lawrence,* and *Cumberland* were sailing vessels, they mounted one hundred and twenty-four guns between them, twenty-two of which were 9-inch; together, their crews amounted to well over a thousand men. The *Minnesota* and *Roanoke* had twelve hundred men between them, and carried over eighty 9-inch and 11-inch guns.

There is no question that the appearance of the *Merrimac,* as she hove in sight accompanied by her consorts, *Beaufort* and *Raleigh,* small river steamers mounting rifled 32-pounders in the bow and carrying crews of about forty men, was a surprise. The *Merrimac,* as she came down the Elizabeth River from Norfolk, had steered very badly. It was necessary for the *Beaufort,* under command of Lieutenant Parker, to pass her a line in order to keep her head straight. Owing to her deep draft, the great ironclad required over twenty-two feet of water to float her clear of the bottom.

About one o'clock in the afternoon the little squadron had swept into the James and turned up-stream. Lying to the last of the flood-tide, the great wooden frigates *Congress* and *Cumberland,* with their washed clothes on the line, were totally unaware of the approach of their nemesis. The *Congress* was just off the point, and the *Cumberland* a short distance above it. It was soon seen that the vessels had at last noticed their untried foe. Down came the lines of washing, signals flashed, and shortly after two o'clock the little *Beaufort,* which was steaming along at the port bow of the *Merrimac,* fired the first shot. Up the flagstaff of the *Merrimac* climbed the signals that spelled the order for close action.

The *Congress* and the *Cumberland,* though taken by surprise, had cast loose, served their guns in marvelous haste, and soon opened a tremendous fire, assisted by the batteries on the shore. The *Merrimac* swept by the *Congress* and made for the latter's consort. The *Cumberland's* broadside was across the

COPYRIGHT, 1911, PATRIOT PUB. CO.

THE "CHEESE BOX" THAT MADE HISTORY
AS IT APPEARED FOUR MONTHS LATER

In this remarkable view of the "Monitor's" turret, taken in July, 1862, is seen as clearly as on the day after the great battle the effect of the Confederate fire upon Ericsson's novel craft. As the two vessels approached each other about half-past eight on that immortal Sunday morning, the men within the turret waited anxiously for the first shot of their antagonist. It soon came from her bow gun and went wide of the mark. The "Virginia" no longer had the broadside of a wooden ship at which to aim. Not until the "Monitor" was alongside the big ironclad at close range came the order "Begin firing" to the men in the "cheese box." Then the gun-ports of the turret were triced back, and it began to revolve for the first time in battle. As soon as the guns were brought to bear, two 11-inch solid shot struck the "Virginia's" armor; almost immediately she replied with her broadside, and Lieutenant Greene and his gunners listened anxiously to the shells bursting against their citadel. They made no more impression than is apparent in the picture. Confident in the protection of their armor, the Federals reloaded with a will and came again and again to close quarters with their adversary, hurling two great projectiles about every eight minutes.

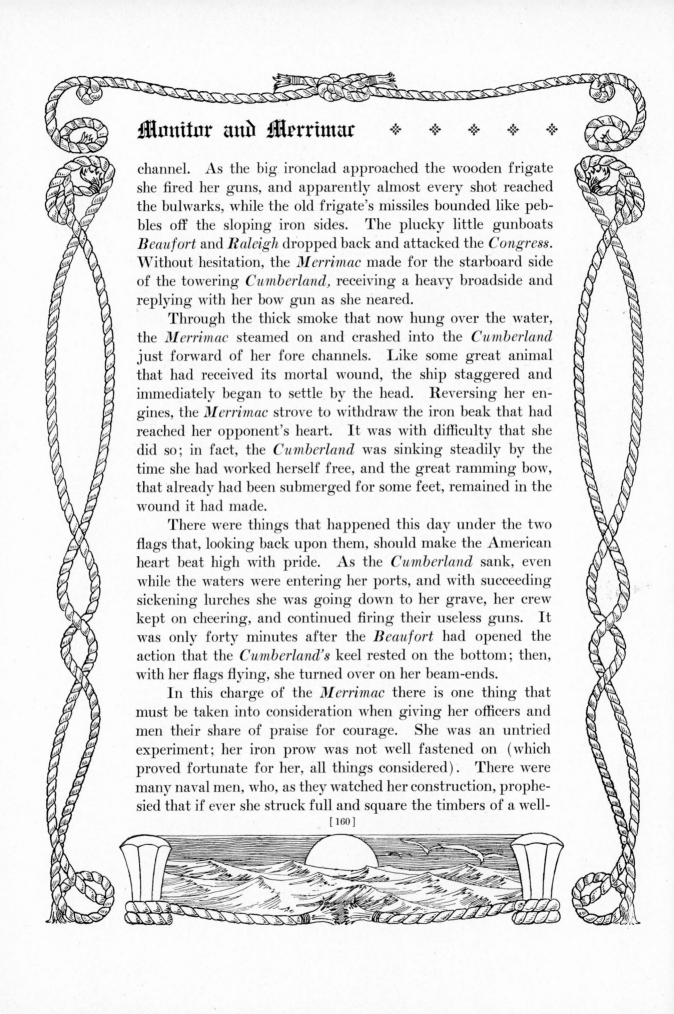

channel. As the big ironclad approached the wooden frigate she fired her guns, and apparently almost every shot reached the bulwarks, while the old frigate's missiles bounded like pebbles off the sloping iron sides. The plucky little gunboats *Beaufort* and *Raleigh* dropped back and attacked the *Congress.* Without hesitation, the *Merrimac* made for the starboard side of the towering *Cumberland,* receiving a heavy broadside and replying with her bow gun as she neared.

Through the thick smoke that now hung over the water, the *Merrimac* steamed on and crashed into the *Cumberland* just forward of her fore channels. Like some great animal that had received its mortal wound, the ship staggered and immediately began to settle by the head. Reversing her engines, the *Merrimac* strove to withdraw the iron beak that had reached her opponent's heart. It was with difficulty that she did so; in fact, the *Cumberland* was sinking steadily by the time she had worked herself free, and the great ramming bow, that already had been submerged for some feet, remained in the wound it had made.

There were things that happened this day under the two flags that, looking back upon them, should make the American heart beat high with pride. As the *Cumberland* sank, even while the waters were entering her ports, and with succeeding sickening lurches she was going down to her grave, her crew kept on cheering, and continued firing their useless guns. It was only forty minutes after the *Beaufort* had opened the action that the *Cumberland's* keel rested on the bottom; then, with her flags flying, she turned over on her beam-ends.

In this charge of the *Merrimac* there is one thing that must be taken into consideration when giving her officers and men their share of praise for courage. She was an untried experiment; her iron prow was not well fastened on (which proved fortunate for her, all things considered). There were many naval men, who, as they watched her construction, prophesied that if ever she struck full and square the timbers of a well-

COPYRIGHT, 1911, PATRIOT PUB. CO.

MEN ON THE "MONITOR" WHO FOUGHT WITH WORDEN

Here on the deck of the "Monitor" sit some of the men who held up the hands of Lieutenant Worden in the great fight with the "Virginia." In the picture, taken in July, 1862, only four months afterward, one of the nine famous dents on the turret are visible. It required courage not only to fight in the "Monitor" for the first time but to embark on her at all, for she was a strange and untried invention at which many high authorities shook their heads. But during the battle, amid all the difficulties of breakdowns by the new untried machinery, Lieutenant S. Dana Greene coolly directed his men, who kept up a fire of remarkable accuracy. Twenty of the forty-one 11-inch shot fired from the "Monitor" took effect, more or less, on the iron plates of the "Virginia." The

ADMIRAL J. L. WORDEN

"Monitor" was struck nine times on her turret, twice on the pilot-house, thrice on the deck, and eight times on the side. While Greene was fighting nobly in the turret, Worden with the helmsman in the pilot-house was bravely maneuvering his vessel and seeking to ram his huge antagonist. Twice he almost succeeded and both times Greene's guns were used on the "Virginia" at point-blank range with telling effect. Toward the close of the action Worden was blinded by a shell striking near one of the peep-holes in the pilot-house and the command devolved upon Greene. Worden, even in his agony of pain while the doctor was attending his injuries, asked constantly about the progress of the battle; and when told that the "Minnesota" was safe, he said, "Then I can die happy."

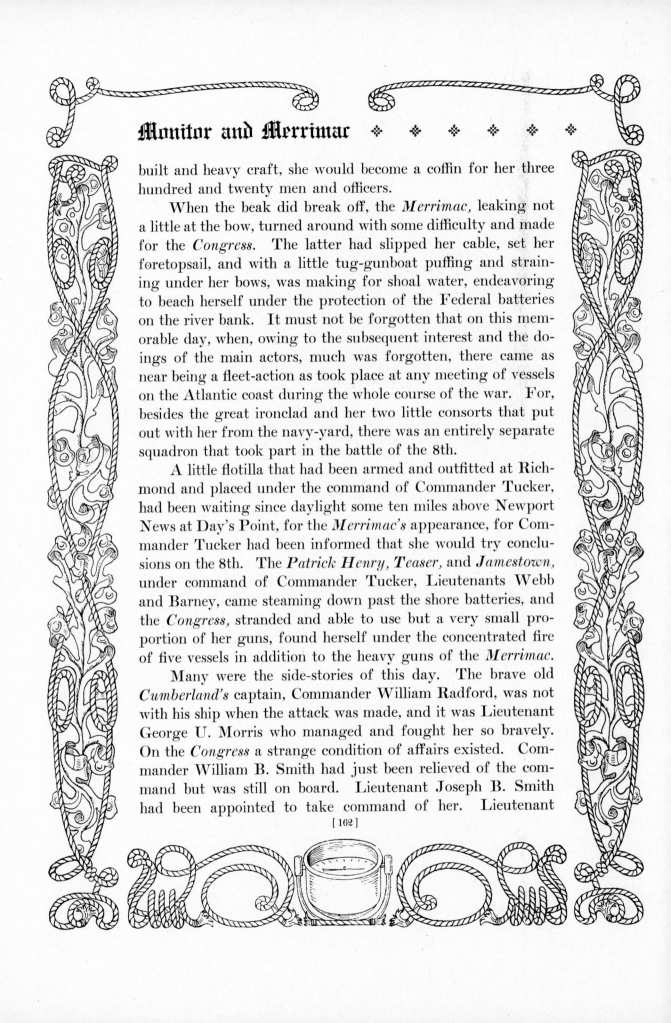

built and heavy craft, she would become a coffin for her three hundred and twenty men and officers.

When the beak did break off, the *Merrimac,* leaking not a little at the bow, turned around with some difficulty and made for the *Congress.* The latter had slipped her cable, set her foretopsail, and with a little tug-gunboat puffing and straining under her bows, was making for shoal water, endeavoring to beach herself under the protection of the Federal batteries on the river bank. It must not be forgotten that on this memorable day, when, owing to the subsequent interest and the doings of the main actors, much was forgotten, there came as near being a fleet-action as took place at any meeting of vessels on the Atlantic coast during the whole course of the war. For, besides the great ironclad and her two little consorts that put out with her from the navy-yard, there was an entirely separate squadron that took part in the battle of the 8th.

A little flotilla that had been armed and outfitted at Richmond and placed under the command of Commander Tucker, had been waiting since daylight some ten miles above Newport News at Day's Point, for the *Merrimac's* appearance, for Commander Tucker had been informed that she would try conclusions on the 8th. The *Patrick Henry, Teaser,* and *Jamestown,* under command of Commander Tucker, Lieutenants Webb and Barney, came steaming down past the shore batteries, and the *Congress,* stranded and able to use but a very small proportion of her guns, found herself under the concentrated fire of five vessels in addition to the heavy guns of the *Merrimac.*

Many were the side-stories of this day. The brave old *Cumberland's* captain, Commander William Radford, was not with his ship when the attack was made, and it was Lieutenant George U. Morris who managed and fought her so bravely. On the *Congress* a strange condition of affairs existed. Commander William B. Smith had just been relieved of the command but was still on board. Lieutenant Joseph B. Smith had been appointed to take command of her. Lieutenant

COPYRIGHT, 1911, PATRIOT PUB. CO.

THE FIRST FIGHTERS OF THE TURRET—THEIR TOUCHING LETTER

In this picture of the " Monitor's" crew taken in July, 1862, are seen the faces of old sailors from the famous old sailing frigate " Sabine," mingled with those of young recruits from the receiving ship " North Carolina." As volunteers these brave fellows had manned the new fighting machine that was to revolutionize the Federal navy.   They had weathered the perilous voyage from New York to Hampton Roads in constant danger of foundering.   With no rest from the anxiety and exhaustion of that voyage, they had fought the greatest naval battle of modern times under conditions that might well make the stoutest heart quail.   Here in a brief respite they have escaped from their murky quarters below deck and are playing checkers and idling about in the sunshine.   There were to be but few more glimpses of the sun for some of them, for on December 31st the " Monitor" met the fate which had threatened her on her first voyage, and she became an "iron coffin" in fact as well as in name.   Sixteen of her company of sixty-five went down with her off Hatteras. After the famous battle the "Monitor's" crew, still waiting for another opportunity to engage the "Merrimac," had sent the touching letter to Lieutenant Worden of which the following is a portion: " To our Dear and honered Captain:—Dear Sir: These few lines is from your own Crew of the ' Monitor,' Hoping to God that they will have the pleasure of Welcoming you Back to us again Soon, for we are all Ready, able, and willing to meet Death or any thing else, only give us Back our own Captain again.   Dear Captain we have got your Pilot-house fixed and all Ready for you when you get well again. . . . But we all join in with our Kindest Love to you hoping that God will Restore you to us again and hoping that your Sufferings is at an end now and we are all so glad to hear that your eye Sight will be Spaired to you again. . . We Remain untill death, your Affectionate Crew, the ' Monitor ' Boys."   Halting words from brave hearts!

Monitor and Merrimac ✦ ✦ ✦ ✦ ✦

Austin Pendergrast was executive officer. As soon as the *Merrimac* was recognized, the ex-captain volunteered his services, which were accepted, and he was assigned to duty under the two officers whom formerly he had ranked. When the news was brought to Washington that the *Congress* had surrendered, the father of Joseph B. Smith, himself an old officer of the navy, made but one comment. "The *Congress* surrendered!" he exclaimed. "Then Joe's dead!" And so it was.

It must not be presumed that the Federal vessels down at Old Point Comfort lay idly by. As soon as the dreaded *Merrimac* hove in sight, everything had been commotion on board of them. The *Minnesota* and *Roanoke* were endeavoring to get up steam, and the *St. Lawrence,* as well as both of the former vessels, at last had summoned tugs that had made fast towing lines, and they were making every effort to gain the scene of active fighting. Near Sewell's Point, at the south of the James where the Elizabeth River flows into it, was a heavy Confederate battery, mounting, among its other pieces of ordnance, the only 11-inch gun the Confederacy possessed.

It was necessary for these three approaching vessels to come into range of this battery, and the *Minnesota* received a shot through her mainmast, while the others succeeded in passing without material damage. It may have been due to the eagerness of all three to get into the fight, or it may have been due to the mist of smoke that came drifting down the stream, that first the *Minnesota,* then the *St. Lawrence,* and lastly the *Roanoke* went aground, although the two last-named were soon afloat.

While the *Congress* and the shore batteries maintained a long and bitter fight of over an hour, the *Minnesota* fired a few broadsides at the *Merrimac* and the Confederate gunboats, and was replied to; the *St. Lawrence,* almost out of range, also endeavored to bring her guns to bear. But it was at the *Congress* that all the Confederate efforts were now directed. The *Merrimac* could not pursue the same tactics against her that

COPYRIGHT, 1911 REVIEW OF REVIEWS CO.

OFFICERS ON DECK OF THE ORIGINAL "MONITOR"—THE NEWLY FLEDGED FIGHTER OF THE NAVY

After the brilliant battle in Hampton Roads, high hopes centered in the 'Monitor" for still greater achievements. On May 9, 1862, under Lieutenant-Commander W. N. Jeffers, she led a squadron against the Confederate works at Sewell's Point, and as she engaged them the "Virginia" ("Merrimac") came down the river, but the two antagonists did not give battle to each other. On May 11th the "Virginia" was destroyed by the Confederates and it was determined to send the "Monitor" and several vessels up the James River in an effort to capture Richmond. On May 15th, the Federal vessels were confronted by the hastily constructed Fort Darling at Drewry's Bluff. These works were all that stood between the Federals and the Confederate Capital, but behind them were the former gunners of the "Virginia" ("Merrimac") and the "Monitor" again found them formidable foemen. Although she herself was not seriously injured by their fire, the "Galena" and other of her consorts were so cut up that the attempt to take Richmond by the water route had to be abandoned.

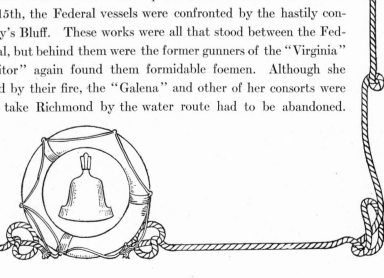

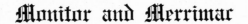

she had against the *Cumberland* for two reasons: there would be no sense in ramming a beached vessel, and even if she had been lying in the deep channel, no such tactics could be employed, owing to the condition of the *Merrimac's* twisted and leaking bow. The *Congress* had been assisted to the place where she ran ashore, between the Middle Ground and Newport News Point, by the tug-gunboat *Zouave,* under Acting Master Henry Reaney, who had passed a line to her, and thus she was dragged to the protection of the Federal batteries.

The decks of the *Congress* were soon littered with the wounded and running with blood; she was afire in the main hold, in the sick-bay, and under the wardroom near the after magazine. No vessel could come to her assistance; the shore batteries under the circumstances offered her little or no protection, and about four o'clock in the afternoon the colors were hauled down. Midshipman Mallory, son of the Confederate Secretary of the Navy, turning to Lieutenant Parker, on the *Beaufort,* pointed to the descending flag, at the same time exclaiming, " I'll swear we fired the last gun." It was true. The little gunboat that had rendered such good account of herself under the same officers in the early actions in North Carolina waters, had fired the first and the last shot of the day.

A strange condition of affairs now followed, and they gave rise to subsequent bitter controversy. Suffice it that when the *Beaufort* and one or two of the other Confederate gunboats, under orders from the flagship to take off the officers and wounded as prisoners and let the crew escape ashore, came alongside the stranded vessel, they were fired upon with both musketry and artillery at close range from the shore. The *Beaufort* was driven off, and the *Merrimac* again opened on the *Congress,* although a white flag had been hoisted to show that she was out of action. Many of the Federal wounded were hit a second time; some were killed; the casualties among the Confederate gunboats, and even on the *Merrimac,* were considerably increased. Lieutenant Pendergrast and Commander

COPYRIGHT, 1911, REVIEW OF REVIEWS CO.

THE LESSON OF THE IRONCLAD—SOME OF THE FIRST TESTS AT THE NAVY-YARD

Here in the Washington Navy-yard, as it appeared on Independence Day, 1866, are the evidences of what the American Civil War had taught not only the United States navy but the world's designers of warships. In four short years of experimentation in the throes of an internecine struggle, the Navy Department had not only evolved the most powerful fighting fleet on the seas of the world, but had stamped it with distinct-ively American ideas.   In the picture, a year after the war, can be seen how the navy had begun to im-prove the experience it had gained.   Already the tests of piercing power of projectiles upon armor plate lie all about, precursors of the steel battleships and big guns that are the marvel of the present day.   The wooden hulls of the early monitors rotted away, and as they did so steel construction was gradually evolved. The monitor principle was finally abandoned in its entirety but the turret still remained.   Likewise the turtle-back construction of the decks of these same vessels remains in the swift and powerful torpedo-boat destroyers.

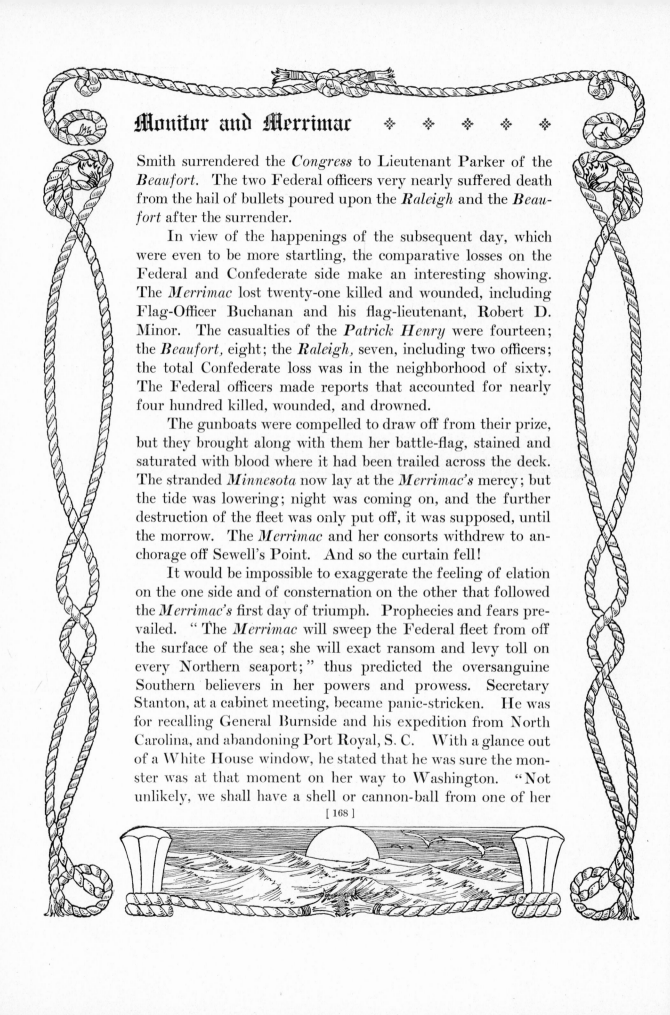

Smith surrendered the *Congress* to Lieutenant Parker of the *Beaufort*. The two Federal officers very nearly suffered death from the hail of bullets poured upon the *Raleigh* and the *Beaufort* after the surrender.

In view of the happenings of the subsequent day, which were even to be more startling, the comparative losses on the Federal and Confederate side make an interesting showing. The *Merrimac* lost twenty-one killed and wounded, including Flag-Officer Buchanan and his flag-lieutenant, Robert D. Minor. The casualties of the *Patrick Henry* were fourteen; the *Beaufort,* eight; the *Raleigh,* seven, including two officers; the total Confederate loss was in the neighborhood of sixty. The Federal officers made reports that accounted for nearly four hundred killed, wounded, and drowned.

The gunboats were compelled to draw off from their prize, but they brought along with them her battle-flag, stained and saturated with blood where it had been trailed across the deck. The stranded *Minnesota* now lay at the *Merrimac's* mercy; but the tide was lowering; night was coming on, and the further destruction of the fleet was only put off, it was supposed, until the morrow. The *Merrimac* and her consorts withdrew to anchorage off Sewell's Point. And so the curtain fell!

It would be impossible to exaggerate the feeling of elation on the one side and of consternation on the other that followed the *Merrimac's* first day of triumph. Prophecies and fears prevailed. " The *Merrimac* will sweep the Federal fleet from off the surface of the sea; she will exact ransom and levy toll on every Northern seaport; " thus predicted the oversanguine Southern believers in her powers and prowess. Secretary Stanton, at a cabinet meeting, became panic-stricken. He was for recalling General Burnside and his expedition from North Carolina, and abandoning Port Royal, S. C. With a glance out of a White House window, he stated that he was sure the monster was at that moment on her way to Washington. "Not unlikely, we shall have a shell or cannon-ball from one of her

COPYRIGHT, 1911, REVIEW OF REVIEWS CO.

ONE OF THE "FIGHTING RAFTS"—1864

This fine figure of a monitor lying in the James in 1864 shows clearly the two great principles Ericsson embodied in his plan. Skeptics said that the "Monitor" would never be able to keep an even keel with the waves washing over her low freeboard. Ericsson, who had seen the huge lumber-rafts in his native Sweden riding steadily though almost submerged, knew better. Again it was objected that the discharge of the guns would kill every man in the turret. But as an officer in the Swedish army, Ericsson had learned, by firing heavy guns from little huts, that if the muzzles protruded the concussion within was inconsiderable. Upon these two ideas he built his model that proved so momentous to the American navy. When C. S. Bushnell took the model to Washington, he was referred to Commander C. H. Davis by the other two members of the Naval Board. Davis, upon examining the model closely, told Bushnell that he could "take the little thing home and worship it, as it would not be idolatry, because it was in the image of nothing 'in the heaven above or on the earth beneath or in the waters under the earth.'" It was not long, however, before the completed monitor became the idol of the Federal navy.

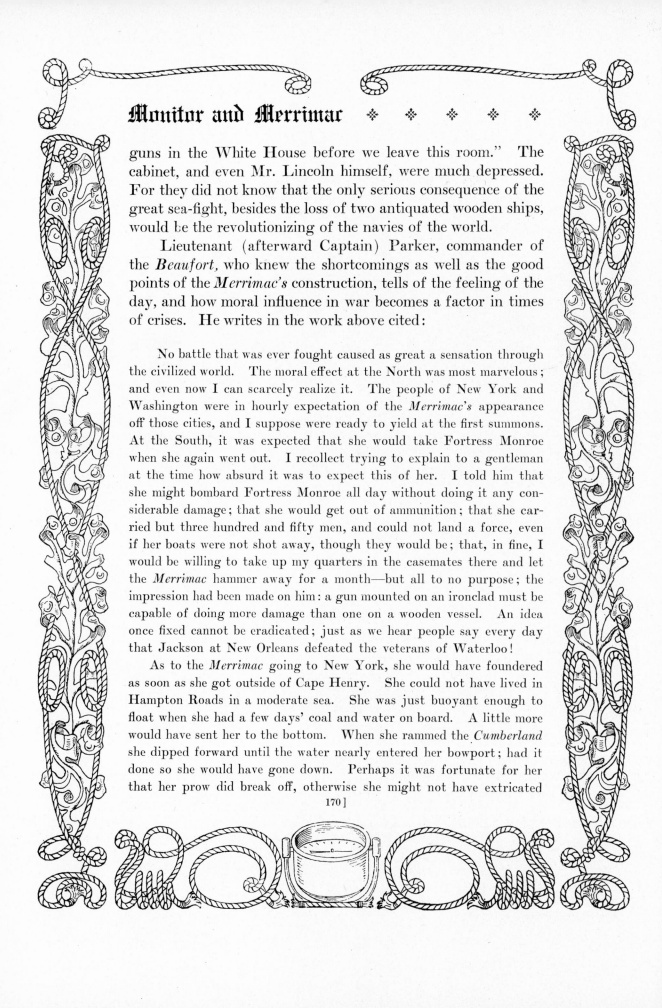

guns in the White House before we leave this room." The cabinet, and even Mr. Lincoln himself, were much depressed. For they did not know that the only serious consequence of the great sea-fight, besides the loss of two antiquated wooden ships, would be the revolutionizing of the navies of the world.

Lieutenant (afterward Captain) Parker, commander of the *Beaufort,* who knew the shortcomings as well as the good points of the *Merrimac's* construction, tells of the feeling of the day, and how moral influence in war becomes a factor in times of crises. He writes in the work above cited:

No battle that was ever fought caused as great a sensation through the civilized world. The moral effect at the North was most marvelous; and even now I can scarcely realize it. The people of New York and Washington were in hourly expectation of the *Merrimac's* appearance off those cities, and I suppose were ready to yield at the first summons. At the South, it was expected that she would take Fortress Monroe when she again went out. I recollect trying to explain to a gentleman at the time how absurd it was to expect this of her. I told him that she might bombard Fortress Monroe all day without doing it any considerable damage; that she would get out of ammunition; that she carried but three hundred and fifty men, and could not land a force, even if her boats were not shot away, though they would be; that, in fine, I would be willing to take up my quarters in the casemates there and let the *Merrimac* hammer away for a month—but all to no purpose; the impression had been made on him: a gun mounted on an ironclad must be capable of doing more damage than one on a wooden vessel. An idea once fixed cannot be eradicated; just as we hear people say every day that Jackson at New Orleans defeated the veterans of Waterloo!

As to the *Merrimac* going to New York, she would have foundered as soon as she got outside of Cape Henry. She could not have lived in Hampton Roads in a moderate sea. She was just buoyant enough to float when she had a few days' coal and water on board. A little more would have sent her to the bottom. When she rammed the *Cumberland* she dipped forward until the water nearly entered her bowport; had it done so she would have gone down. Perhaps it was fortunate for her that her prow did break off, otherwise she might not have extricated

COPYRIGHT, 1911, REVIEW OF REVIEWS CO.

THE FIRST PRIZE OF A MONITOR—FEDERAL OFFICERS ON DECK OF THE CAPTURED CONFEDERATE RAM "ATLANTA"

The honor of the first decisive engagement with one of the formidable ironclads that were constructed by the Confederacy was denied to the original "Monitor." It fell to the monitor "Weehawken," one of seven similar vessels designed by Ericsson for the navy. Under Captain John Rodgers, she, with her sister-vessels, ran first under fire in the attack made upon Fort Sumter and the batteries in Charleston Harbor by Rear-Admiral Du Pont in April, 1863. In June, she and the "Nahant" were blockading the mouth of Wilmington River, Georgia. Early on the morning of the 17th, Captain Rodgers was apprised that the huge Confederate ram, into which the old blockade-runner "Fingal" had been converted, was coming down to raise the blockade. Clearing for action, the "Weehawken" steamed slowly toward the northeastern end of Wassaw Sound, followed by the "Nahant." When about a mile and a half from the "Weehawken," the "Atlanta," which was aground, fired a rifle-shot at her. The "Weehawken," without replying, approached to within three hundred yards of the ram and opened fire. The first shot broke through the armor and wood backing of the "Atlanta," strewing her deck with splinters and prostrating about forty of her crew by the concussion. The second shot broke only a couple of plates, but the third knocked off the top of the pilot-house, wounding the pilots and stunning the man at the wheel. The fourth shot struck a port-stopper in the center, breaking it in two and driving the fragments through the port. Five shots in all were fired by the "Weehawken" in fifteen minutes. Then the colors of the "Atlanta" were hauled down, a white flag was hoisted, and Commander William A. Webb, C. S. N., put off in a boat to the "Weehawken," where he delivered his sword to Captain Rodgers. The fight was over before the "Nahant" could become engaged. The "Atlanta" was not seriously damaged and was added to the Federal navy, where she did good service.

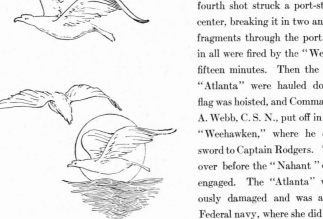

herself. I served afterward in the *Palmetto State*, a vessel of similar construction to the *Merrimac*, but much more buoyant; yet I have seen the time when we were glad to get under a lee, even in Charleston Harbor. The *Merrimac*, with but a few days' stores on board, drew twenty-two and one-half feet of water. She could not have gone to Baltimore or Washington without lightening her very much. This would have brought her unarmored hull out of the water, and then she would no longer have been an ironclad!

I was not so much surprised at the extravagant expectations of the Southern people, who necessarily knew but little of such matters; but I must say I could not have imagined the extent of the demoralization which existed at Fortress Monroe and in the Federal fleet on the 8th and 9th of March. I have been told by an officer of high rank, who was present in the fort, that if the *Merrimac* had fired a shot at it on the 8th, the general in command would have surrendered it; and, if I am not very much mistaken, I have seen a despatch from that general to the effect that if the *Merrimac* passed Fortress Monroe it must necessarily fall! After this, one can well understand what Napoleon has said in reference to the moral as compared to the physical effect in war.

But John Taylor Wood, C. S. N., a lieutenant on the *Merrimac,* speaks in " Battles and Leaders of the Civil War " of the vessel's condition as she lay at anchor off Sewell's Point:

The armor was hardly damaged, though at one time our ship was the focus on which were directed at least one hundred heavy guns, afloat and ashore. But nothing outside escaped. Two guns were disabled by having their muzzles shot off. The ram was left in the side of the *Cumberland*. One anchor, the smoke-stack, and the steampipes were shot away. Railings, stanchions, boat-davits, everything was swept clean. The flagstaff was repeatedly knocked over, and finally a boarding-pike was used. Commodore Buchanan and the other wounded were sent to the Naval Hospital, and after making preparations for the next day's fight, we slept at our guns, dreaming of other victories in the morning."

Shortly after breakfast-time on the 9th, the *Merrimac,* followed by the Confederate squadron, got under way under a

COPYR'GHT, 1911, REVIEW OF REVIEWS CO.

DECK OF THE "CATSKILL"—THE LEADER OF THE GREAT BOMBARDMENT

On July 10, 1863, under Commander George W. Rodgers, and with Rear-Admiral Dahlgren's flag floating above her, the "Catskill" steamed across the bar into Charleston Harbor and opened fire on Fort Wagner on Morris Island. She was followed by the "Montauk," "Nahant," and "Weehawken," and immediately all the Confederate batteries in Charleston Harbor spoke out their terrific thunder. The "Catskill" was no stranger to that battle-ground; she had seen her first service in Admiral Du Pont's squadron that had failed to silence the defenses of Charleston the preceding April. Now came her supreme test under Admiral Dahlgren. As his flagship she became the especial target. A large percentage of the sixty hits were very severe. Yet the brave men in the turret coolly fired their guns, almost oblivious to the heavy shot that was raining upon their armor. Her pilot-house was broken entirely through by one shot, while her side armor and deck-plates were pierced in many places, making the entrance of the water troublesome. But the " Catskill," after firing 128 rounds, came out of action in good working order. On August 17th Commander Rodgers, while maneuvering for a closer berth in the attack on Fort Wagner, was killed in the pilot-house.

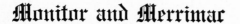

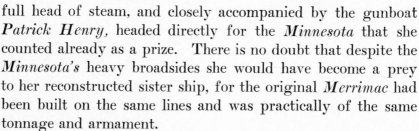

full head of steam, and closely accompanied by the gunboat *Patrick Henry,* headed directly for the *Minnesota* that she counted already as a prize. There is no doubt that despite the *Minnesota's* heavy broadsides she would have become a prey to her reconstructed sister ship, for the original *Merrimac* had been built on the same lines and was practically of the same tonnage and armament.

Only one thing prevented the carrying out of the program, and that was the sudden appearance of the strange little craft that, with her volunteer crew of old sailors, had started from New York on Thursday, the 6th of March, under the command of officers who were not sure whether they would ever reach their destination or not. No power of imagination could invent a more dramatic moment for the arrival of a rescuer than that of the *Monitor's* appearance in Hampton Roads. Late in the afternoon of Saturday, March 8th, as she entered the waters of Chesapeake Bay, there was heard the sound of heavy firing, and Lieutenant John L. Worden, then in command, as he listened intently, estimated the distance to be full twenty miles and correctly guessed that it was the *Merrimac* in conflict with the Federal fleet. While she steamed ahead the *Monitor* was made ready for action, although such preparations were of the simplest character. Before long the flames and smoke from the burning *Congress* could be easily distinguished. At 9 P.M. the *Monitor* was alongside the *Roanoke,* whose commander, Captain Marston, suggested that she should go at once to the assistance of the *Minnesota,* which was still aground.

It was midnight before Lieutenant S. Dana Greene, sent by Worden, reached the *Minnesota* and reported to Captain Van Brunt. While the two officers were talking there came a succession of loud reports, and the *Congress* blew up, as if warning her sisters of the fleet of the fate in store for them. There was little sleep for anyone that night. At seven o'clock in the morning the crew were called to quarters.

COPYRIGHT 1911, PATRIOT PUB. CO.

THE ARMY'S CHIEF RELIANCE ON THE RIVER—THE DOUBLE-TURRETED MONITOR "ONONDAGA"

While Admiral Porter and his squadron were absent on the Fort Fisher expedition, it was of the greatest importance that an adequate flotilla should be left in the James to preclude the possibility of the Confederate gunboats getting down past the obstructions and making a bold and disastrous attack on City Point, the army base. Having left this huge ironclad fighting-vessel behind, Admiral Porter felt at ease. But the undaunted Confederate Flag-Officer J. K. Mitchell was not to be deterred from making one last attempt to strike a telling blow with the "Virginia" and her consorts. On the night of January 23, 1865, he came down to the Federal obstructions and attempted to get by. When the movement was discovered, contrary to all expectations the great "Onondaga" retreated down the river. The moment might well have been one of the greatest anxiety for the Federals, but in maneuvering, the "Virginia" and the "Richmond" both got aground and the "Onondaga," returning with the "Hunchback" and the "Massasoit," inflicted some telling shots upon them. It was found later by a court-martial that Commander William A. Parker, commanding the division on the James, had made an "error of judgment" in handling the "Onondaga."

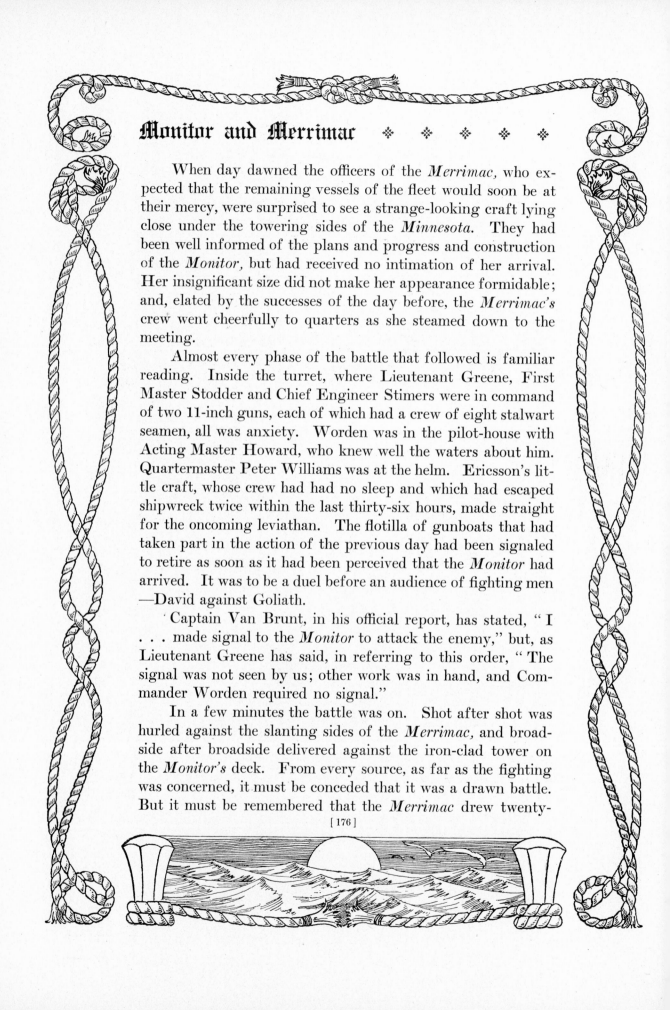

Monitor and Merrimac ❖ ❖ ❖ ❖ ❖

When day dawned the officers of the *Merrimac,* who expected that the remaining vessels of the fleet would soon be at their mercy, were surprised to see a strange-looking craft lying close under the towering sides of the *Minnesota.* They had been well informed of the plans and progress and construction of the *Monitor,* but had received no intimation of her arrival. Her insignificant size did not make her appearance formidable; and, elated by the successes of the day before, the *Merrimac's* crew went cheerfully to quarters as she steamed down to the meeting.

Almost every phase of the battle that followed is familiar reading. Inside the turret, where Lieutenant Greene, First Master Stodder and Chief Engineer Stimers were in command of two 11-inch guns, each of which had a crew of eight stalwart seamen, all was anxiety. Worden was in the pilot-house with Acting Master Howard, who knew well the waters about him. Quartermaster Peter Williams was at the helm. Ericsson's little craft, whose crew had had no sleep and which had escaped shipwreck twice within the last thirty-six hours, made straight for the oncoming leviathan. The flotilla of gunboats that had taken part in the action of the previous day had been signaled to retire as soon as it had been perceived that the *Monitor* had arrived. It was to be a duel before an audience of fighting men —David against Goliath.

Captain Van Brunt, in his official report, has stated, " I . . . made signal to the *Monitor* to attack the enemy," but, as Lieutenant Greene has said, in referring to this order, " The signal was not seen by us; other work was in hand, and Commander Worden required no signal."

In a few minutes the battle was on. Shot after shot was hurled against the slanting sides of the *Merrimac,* and broadside after broadside delivered against the iron-clad tower on the *Monitor's* deck. From every source, as far as the fighting was concerned, it must be conceded that it was a drawn battle. But it must be remembered that the *Merrimac* drew twenty-

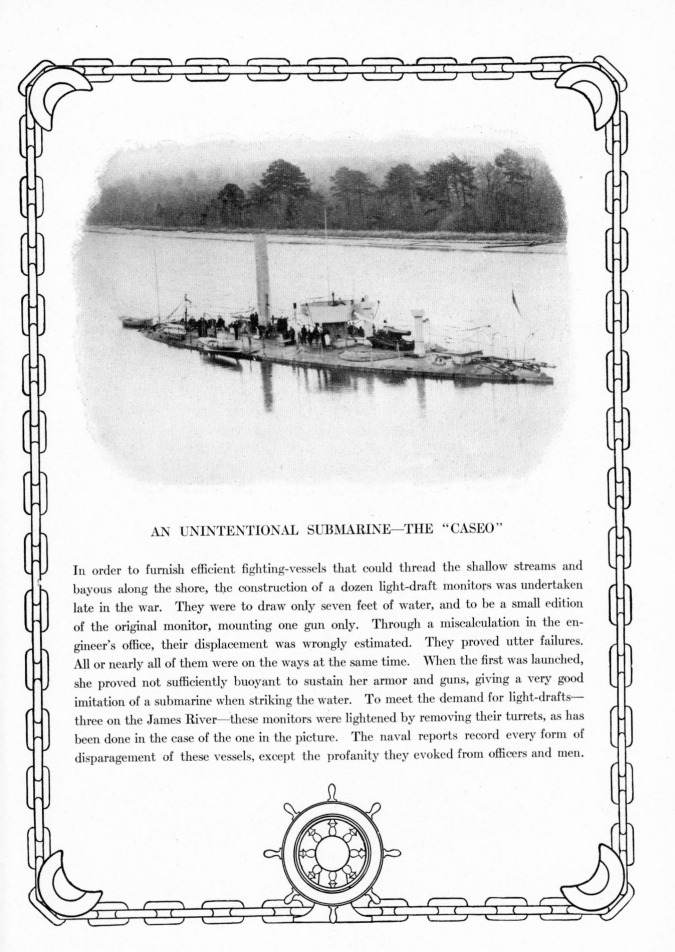

AN UNINTENTIONAL SUBMARINE—THE "CASEO"

In order to furnish efficient fighting-vessels that could thread the shallow streams and bayous along the shore, the construction of a dozen light-draft monitors was undertaken late in the war. They were to draw only seven feet of water, and to be a small edition of the original monitor, mounting one gun only. Through a miscalculation in the engineer's office, their displacement was wrongly estimated. They proved utter failures. All or nearly all of them were on the ways at the same time. When the first was launched, she proved not sufficiently buoyant to sustain her armor and guns, giving a very good imitation of a submarine when striking the water. To meet the demand for light-drafts— three on the James River—these monitors were lightened by removing their turrets, as has been done in the case of the one in the picture. The naval reports record every form of disparagement of these vessels, except the profanity they evoked from officers and men.

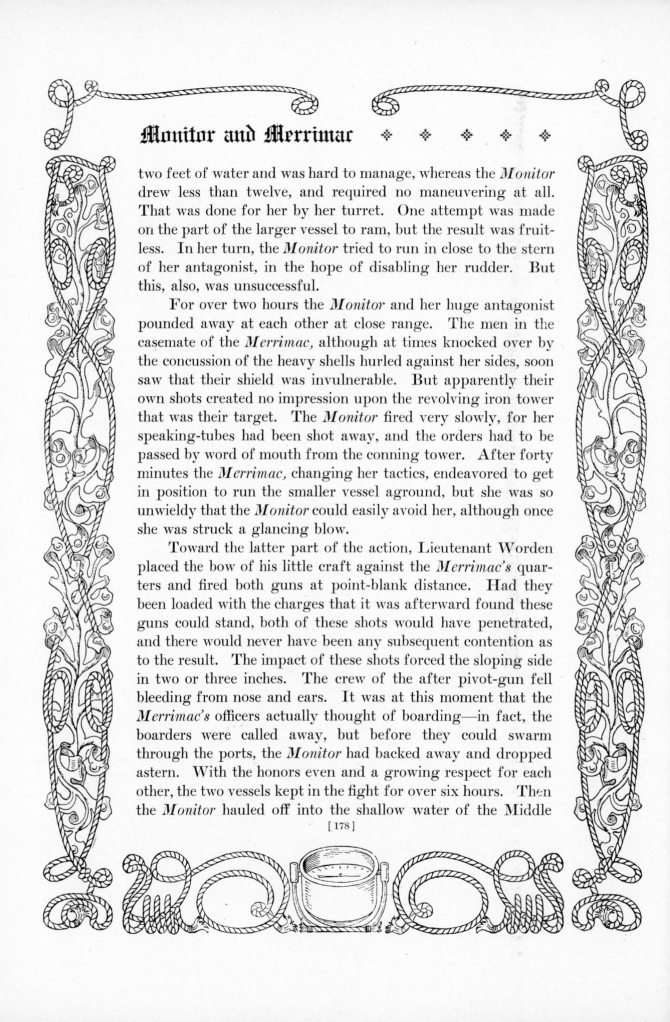

two feet of water and was hard to manage, whereas the *Monitor* drew less than twelve, and required no maneuvering at all. That was done for her by her turret. One attempt was made on the part of the larger vessel to ram, but the result was fruitless. In her turn, the *Monitor* tried to run in close to the stern of her antagonist, in the hope of disabling her rudder. But this, also, was unsuccessful.

For over two hours the *Monitor* and her huge antagonist pounded away at each other at close range. The men in the casemate of the *Merrimac,* although at times knocked over by the concussion of the heavy shells hurled against her sides, soon saw that their shield was invulnerable. But apparently their own shots created no impression upon the revolving iron tower that was their target. The *Monitor* fired very slowly, for her speaking-tubes had been shot away, and the orders had to be passed by word of mouth from the conning tower. After forty minutes the *Merrimac,* changing her tactics, endeavored to get in position to run the smaller vessel aground, but she was so unwieldy that the *Monitor* could easily avoid her, although once she was struck a glancing blow.

Toward the latter part of the action, Lieutenant Worden placed the bow of his little craft against the *Merrimac's* quarters and fired both guns at point-blank distance. Had they been loaded with the charges that it was afterward found these guns could stand, both of these shots would have penetrated, and there would never have been any subsequent contention as to the result. The impact of these shots forced the sloping side in two or three inches. The crew of the after pivot-gun fell bleeding from nose and ears. It was at this moment that the *Merrimac's* officers actually thought of boarding—in fact, the boarders were called away, but before they could swarm through the ports, the *Monitor* had backed away and dropped astern. With the honors even and a growing respect for each other, the two vessels kept in the fight for over six hours. Then the *Monitor* hauled off into the shallow water of the Middle

THE NEW "SEA–ELEPHANT" OF THE NAVY—THE "LEHIGH" IN '64

A naval historian has compared the monitor type of vessel "to the elephant, who swims beneath the surface . . . and communicates through his uplifted trunk with the upper air." In action and in rough weather, the monitor's only means of communication with the upper air are her turret and pilot-house, and from this fact alone it was argued that the monitor type of construction would prove to be an elephant on the hands of the Federal navy. Indeed, on her trial trip Ericsson's "Monitor" came near foundering, and thus she finally met her end in a storm off Cape Hatteras, December 31, 1862. But before this, her faults of construction had been recognized and the Federal Navy Department had undertaken the construction of nine bigger and better monitors. In Charleston Harbor the monitors were hit an aggregate of 738 times, and proved conclusively their superior endurance. The "Lehigh" first made her appearance in the James on an expedition and demonstration made up that river by Acting Rear-Admiral S. P. Lee in July, 1863. In September she was attached to Admiral Dahlgren's fleet. From October 26th to November 4th, under Commander A. Bryson, she and the "Patapsco" were assigned to the special duty of hammering Fort Sumter. On November 16, 1863, she ran aground on Sullivan's Island and was dangerously exposed to the guns of Fort Moultrie for five hours before she could be gotten off.

COPYRIGHT, 1911, REVIEW OF REVIEWS CO.

Ground, but always keeping herself between the *Minnesota* and the vessel that had counted her as prey. In fear of running aground, the *Merrimac* did not follow, and at about two o'clock, turned her bow toward Sewell's Point.

It was a few minutes after noon when the *Monitor* made for the shallow water, and Lieutenant Worden had been stunned and almost blinded by the result of a shell striking the pilot-house. The *Monitor* did not run away, as Confederate papers of the time averred, but as a Southern eye-witness put it:

Much has been written and more said about this celebrated fight— the first encounter between ironclads in the world's history. Viewing it, as I did, at a distance of more than a mile, I will state that my impression at the time was that, after hammering away at each other for three hours, and finding that the men were wearied out without making much impression on either side, both vessels had simultaneously drawn off and decided to call it a drawn battle.

In Captain Van Brunt's report of the engagement he says: "For some time after this the rebels concentrated their whole battery upon the tower and pilot-house of the *Monitor,* and soon after the latter stood down for Fortress Monroe, and we thought it probable she had exhausted her supply of ammunition or sustained some injury. Soon after, the *Merrimac* and two other steamers headed for my ship, and I then felt to the fullest extent my condition. . . . On ascending the poop-deck, I observed that the enemy's vessels had changed their course and were heading for Craney Island."

Captain Parker's candid and unprejudiced review of this action states: "Why the *Merrimac* did not persist in destroying the *Minnesota,* I never exactly understood. . . . Whatever the cause, candor compels me to say that the *Merrimac* failed to reap the fruits of her victory. She went out to destroy the *Minnesota,* and do what further damage to the enemy she could. The *Monitor* was there to save the *Minnesota.* The *Merrimac* did not accomplish her purpose. The *Monitor* did. She did it

THE DETACHED BLOCKADERS—JAMES GORDON BENNETT'S YACHT

While Admiral Porter with the fleet was waiting impatiently at Hampton Roads for the start of the much-delayed expedition against Fort Fisher, there was work a-plenty along the coast to keep up the blockade and circumvent the attempts of such Confederate vessels as the "Roanoke" to raise it. The upper picture is of especial popular interest; lying to the right of the despatch-boat and monitor off Port Royal is James Gordon Bennett's yacht "Rebecca," one of the fastest sailing yachts of her time. When she swept into Port Royal flying the Stars and Stripes, she was taken for a blockade-runner until her identity was learned. The officers of the blockading squadron were handsomely entertained aboard her during her stay, and were glad to get the news she brought from the North. On her way back to New York she was frequently mistaken for a blockade-runner and chased. In the lower picture is seen one of the monitors stationed in Ossabaw Sound. Awnings are stretched in the almost tropical sunshine. Yet the vessel is ready for any emergency.

COPYRIGHT, 1911, REVIEW OF REVIEWS CO.

by resisting the *Merrimac* as long as she did, even if she did have to withdraw. The *Minnesota* was gotten afloat that night and towed below Old Point. I suspect the *Merrimac* was making more water from the leak in her bow than her officers were willing to admit." This last statement is borne out by the testimony of Boatswain Hasker of the *Merrimac,* who states that they reached Norfolk just in time to get into dry dock by high water.

But there is no use in fighting all the contested points of this battle over again. It was a drawn fight, bravely fought, and there is honor enough for both. The thrill of the meeting between these two armored ships was in its novelty. The results were in the reconstruction of the navies of the world.

Neither vessel long survived their famous encounter, and the *Merrimac* was the first to finish her days. Owing to Flag-Officer Buchanan's injuries, the command on that memorable 9th of March had fallen on Lieutenant Jones, and he was relieved before the end of the month by Flag-Officer Josiah Tatnall. Though the *Monitor* stayed close at hand, there was no further meeting after her valiant foe was released from the drydock on April 4th.

When Norfolk was evacuated by the Confederates, on the 10th of May, the further disposition of the *Merrimac* became a grave problem. Tatnall had her lightened three feet in order to take her up the James, but the pilots refused to attempt this in the face of a westerly breeze, and now every officer agreed with Tatnall that she must be blown up. This was done on the 11th. The indignation throughout the South was great, but Tatnall was completely exonerated by a court of inquiry.

After the destruction of the *Merrimac,* the *Monitor* went up the James with Commander Rodgers' squadron in the attack on the entrenchments at Drewry's Bluff. Finally on the 31st of December the *Monitor* was sunk in a gale, while on the way to Beaufort, North Carolina, and sixteen of her officers and crew went to the bottom with her.

VII

THE
MOST DARING
FEAT

THE "PORTSMOUTH"

THIS GALLANT OLD SAILING SLOOP PLAYED HER PART IN
FARRAGUT'S PASSAGE OF THE NEW ORLEANS FORTS BY
BROADSIDES ENFILADING THE CONFEDERATE WATER BATTERY,
PROTECTING THE APPROACH OF PORTER'S MORTAR SCHOONERS

THE MOST DARING FEAT—PASSING
THE FORTS AT NEW ORLEANS

DAVID GLASGOW FARRAGUT made a sudden leap into fame. Late in the year 1861, he was a member of a retiring-board created by the Navy Department under a new law in order to get rid of superannuated officers. From this position he was suddenly promoted to the command of a fleet, and in a little over three months his name was echoing not only through the country but round the world.

It was Commander David D. Porter, in charge of the steamer *Powhatan* in the Gulf Blockading Squadron, who conceived the idea of running by the powerful forts at the mouth of the Mississippi and capturing the city of New Orleans. His plan was approved by the Secretary of the Navy and the President, and strongly endorsed by Commodore, afterward Rear-Admiral, Joseph Smith. After a consultation in which Commander Porter had a voice, Captain Farragut was selected as the leader of the expedition, and it was Porter who brought to him the first notice of his appointment. This was before the official notification of the Navy Department, for in Farragut's private papers was found an abrupt and mysterious note, dated December 21, 1861, which concludes thus: " I am to have a flag in the Gulf, and the rest depends upon myself. Keep calm and silent. I shall sail in three weeks."

The official notification, addressed to Farragut at Hastings-on-Hudson, New York, where he was stopping with his family, informed him that he was appointed to the West Gulf Blockading Squadron, and that the *Hartford* had been designated as his flagship. Within a fortnight, he received from Secretary of the Navy Gideon Welles the following official orders, dated

U. S. S. "HARTFORD"—FARRAGUT'S PET SHIP
PHOTOGRAPHED IN 1862, AFTER HER PASSAGE OF THE FORTS AT NEW ORLEANS

The flagship "Hartford" lies on the placid bosom of the Mississippi, whose waters reflect her masts and spars as if in a polished mirror. This photograph was taken in 1862 by the Confederate photographer Lytle, who, with his camera set up on the levee, took many of the ships that had survived the fiery ordeal of the forts below. It is evidently but a short time since the "Hartford" had passed through that night of death and terror; her top-gallant masts are housed and everything aloft sent down on deck except her fore, main, and mizzen topsail yards, on which the clewed-up sails are hanging to dry. Her spankers, half-trailed up, are drying out also, as is her flying-jib. Her fore, main, and cross-jack yards are up in place; and not only are the awnings spread above the spar-deck, but the boat awnings are out also, showing that although it is early in the year it must have been a scorching day. Of this beautiful vessel Farragut has written that she "was all that the heart could desire." He trusted himself to her in another memorable engagement when, lashed to her shrouds, he steamed past the forts in Mobile Bay on August 5, 1864, recking not of the Confederate torpedoes liberally planted in the harbor.

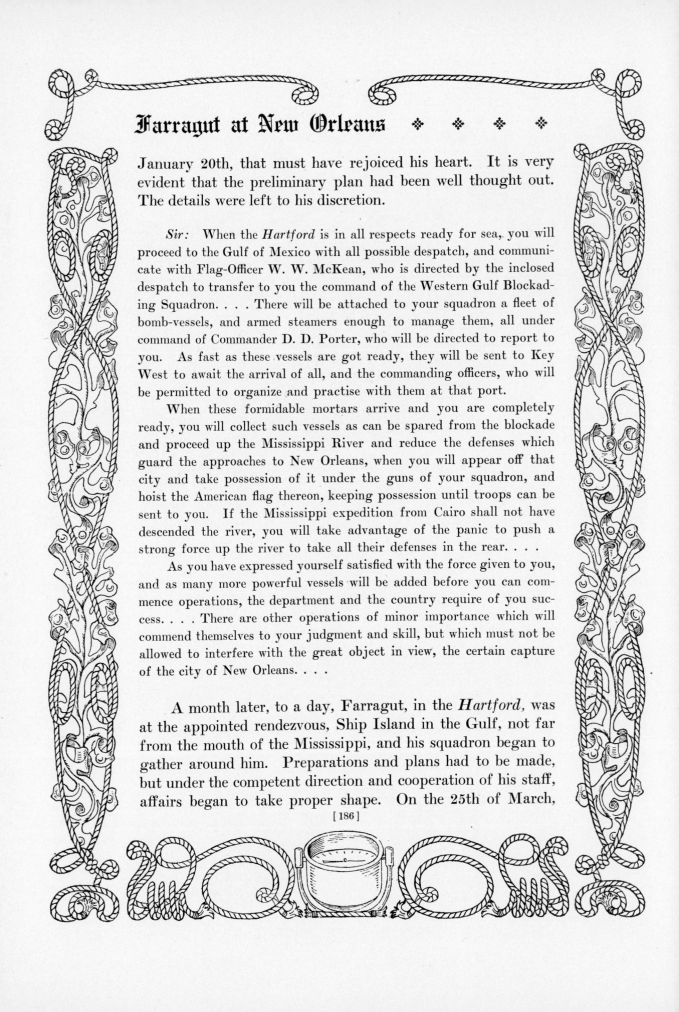

Farragut at New Orleans ✦ ✦ ✦ ✦

January 20th, that must have rejoiced his heart. It is very evident that the preliminary plan had been well thought out. The details were left to his discretion.

Sir: When the *Hartford* is in all respects ready for sea, you will proceed to the Gulf of Mexico with all possible despatch, and communicate with Flag-Officer W. W. McKean, who is directed by the inclosed despatch to transfer to you the command of the Western Gulf Blockading Squadron. . . . There will be attached to your squadron a fleet of bomb-vessels, and armed steamers enough to manage them, all under command of Commander D. D. Porter, who will be directed to report to you. As fast as these vessels are got ready, they will be sent to Key West to await the arrival of all, and the commanding officers, who will be permitted to organize and practise with them at that port.

When these formidable mortars arrive and you are completely ready, you will collect such vessels as can be spared from the blockade and proceed up the Mississippi River and reduce the defenses which guard the approaches to New Orleans, when you will appear off that city and take possession of it under the guns of your squadron, and hoist the American flag thereon, keeping possession until troops can be sent to you. If the Mississippi expedition from Cairo shall not have descended the river, you will take advantage of the panic to push a strong force up the river to take all their defenses in the rear. . . .

As you have expressed yourself satisfied with the force given to you, and as many more powerful vessels will be added before you can commence operations, the department and the country require of you success. . . . There are other operations of minor importance which will commend themselves to your judgment and skill, but which must not be allowed to interfere with the great object in view, the certain capture of the city of New Orleans. . . .

A month later, to a day, Farragut, in the *Hartford,* was at the appointed rendezvous, Ship Island in the Gulf, not far from the mouth of the Mississippi, and his squadron began to gather around him. Preparations and plans had to be made, but under the competent direction and cooperation of his staff, affairs began to take proper shape. On the 25th of March,

COPYRIGHT, 1911, REVIEW OF REVIEWS CO.

THE MEN WHO DARED—SAILORS ON THE "HARTFORD" AFTER PASSING THE NEW ORLEANS FORTS

On this page of unwritten history McPherson and Oliver, the New Orleans war-time photographers, have caught the crew of the staunch old "Hartford" as they relaxed after their fiery test. In unconscious picturesqueness grouped about the spar-deck, the men are gossiping or telling over again their versions of the great deeds done aboard the flagship. Some have seized the opportunity for a little plain sewing, while all are interested in the new and unfamiliar process of "having their pictures taken." The notable thing about the picture is the number of young faces. Only a few of the old salts whose bearded and weather-beaten faces give evidence of service in the old navy still remain. After the great triumph in Mobile Bay, Farragut said of these men: "I have never seen a crew come up like ours. They are ahead of the old set in small arms, and fully equal to them at the great guns. They arrived here a mere lot of boys and young men, and have now

SPAR–DECK OF THE "HARTFORD"

fattened up and knocked the nine-inch guns about like twenty-four pounders, to the astonishment of everybody. There was but one man who showed fear and he was allowed to resign. This was the most desperate battle I ever fought since the days of the old 'Essex.'" "It was the anxious night of my life," wrote Farragut later. The spar-deck shown below recalls another speech. "Don't flinch from that fire, boys! There is a hotter fire for those who don't do their duty!" So shouted Farragut with his ship fast aground and a huge fire-raft held hard against her wooden side by the little Confederate tug "Mosher." The ship seemed all ablaze and the men, "breathing fire," were driven from their guns. Farragut, calmly pacing the poop-deck, called out his orders, caring nothing for the rain of shot from Fort St. Philip. The men, inspired by such coolness, leaped to their stations again and soon a shot pierced the boiler of the plucky "Mosher" and sank her.

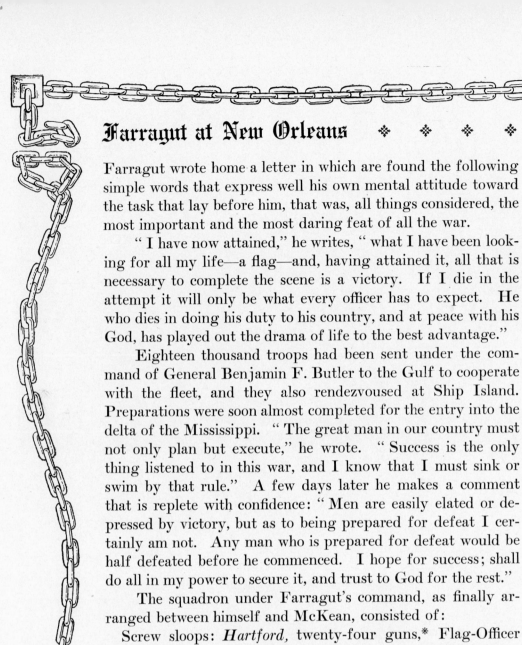

Farragut at New Orleans ✦ ✦ ✦ ✦

Farragut wrote home a letter in which are found the following simple words that express well his own mental attitude toward the task that lay before him, that was, all things considered, the most important and the most daring feat of all the war.

"I have now attained," he writes, "what I have been looking for all my life—a flag—and, having attained it, all that is necessary to complete the scene is a victory. If I die in the attempt it will only be what every officer has to expect. He who dies in doing his duty to his country, and at peace with his God, has played out the drama of life to the best advantage."

Eighteen thousand troops had been sent under the command of General Benjamin F. Butler to the Gulf to cooperate with the fleet, and they also rendezvoused at Ship Island. Preparations were soon almost completed for the entry into the delta of the Mississippi. "The great man in our country must not only plan but execute," he wrote. "Success is the only thing listened to in this war, and I know that I must sink or swim by that rule." A few days later he makes a comment that is replete with confidence: "Men are easily elated or depressed by victory, but as to being prepared for defeat I certainly am not. Any man who is prepared for defeat would be half defeated before he commenced. I hope for success; shall do all in my power to secure it, and trust to God for the rest."

The squadron under Farragut's command, as finally arranged between himself and McKean, consisted of:

Screw sloops: *Hartford,* twenty-four guns,* Flag-Officer David G. Farragut, Fleet-Captain Henry H. Bell, Commander Richard Wainwright; *Pensacola,* twenty-three guns,

* The statistics here given as to the guns of Farragut's squadron do not include howitzers or the guns removed from the steam frigate *Colorado,* a member of the squadron, which on account of her draft was unable to cross the bar. Nineteen guns and one howitzer were removed from the *Colorado* and distributed among the fleet. The *Hartford* received two guns, the *Iroquois* two, the *Miami* one, and the *Mississippi* fourteen. The *Iroquois* also received one gun from the army, not included here.

[188]

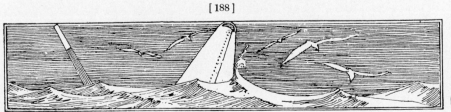

COPYRIGHT, 1911, REVIEW OF REVIEWS CO.

DECK OF THE U. S. S. "RICHMOND" AFTER SHE PASSED THE FORTS
THE MEN AT QUARTERS
COMMANDER JAMES ALDEN ON THE BRIDGE

Thus the crew was assembled the morning after that terrible night of fighting past Forts Jackson and St. Philip. The "Richmond" was the third vessel in line in the center division led by Farragut himself. Only two of her crew were killed and four injured, for Commander Alden had carefully prepared a splinter netting which caught the death-dealing pieces of plank and scantling, and prevented them from sweeping the gun-deck. Early in October, 1861, the "Richmond," under Captain John Pope, led the blockading vessels up the delta of the Mississippi to the Head of the Passes, where the stream broadens into a deep bay two miles wide, giving ample room for maneuvers. The Federal vessels were not to remain here long unmolested. In the dim dawn of Oct. 12th, Captain George Nicholas Hollins, C. S. N., stole upon the fleet unobserved. With his ironclad "Ma-

COMMANDER JAMES ALDEN

nassas" he rammed the "Richmond." A coal barge alongside the Federal vessel saved her from serious injury; the "Manassas," whose boilers were damaged by the collision, limped off up-stream. Soon after, three immense fire-rafts were sighted coming down-stream, and Captain Pope gave the signal for retreat. Both the "Richmond" and the "Vincennes" grounded on the bar at the outlet of Southwest Pass and the Confederate vessels again advanced to attack them. But they were driven off by the heavy broadsides and the guns of the plucky little "Water Witch." In command of Lieutenant Francis Winslow, she had not retreated with the other vessels, but had come down to beg Captain Pope to return. After this inglorious affair no further attempt was made to hold the Head of the Passes. A Federal vessel was then stationed off the mouth of each pass.

Captain Henry W. Morris; *Brooklyn,* twenty-four guns, Captain Thomas T. Craven; *Richmond,* twenty-two guns, Commander James Alden.

Side-wheel steamer: *Mississippi,* seven guns, Commander Melancton Smith.

Screw corvettes: *Oneida,* nine guns, Commander Samuel Phillips Lee; *Varuna,* ten guns, Commander Charles S. Boggs; *Iroquois,* seven guns, Commander John De Camp.

Screw gunboats: *Cayuga,* two guns, Lieutenant Napoleon B. Harrison; *Itasca,* four guns, Lieutenant C. H. B. Caldwell; *Katahdin,* two guns, Lieutenant George H. Preble; *Kennebec,* two guns, Lieutenant John H. Russell; *Kineo,* two guns, Lieutenant George M. Ransom; *Pinola,* three guns, Lieutenant Pierce Crosby; *Sciota,* two guns, Lieutenant Edward Donaldson; *Winona,* two guns, Lieutenant Edward T. Nichols; *Wissahickon,* two guns, Lieutenant Albert N. Smith.

In the final plan of action the fleet was divided into three divisions. The first was to be led by Captain Theodorus Bailey, who had transferred his flag from the old *Colorado* to the little gunboat *Cayuga,* and was to be made up of the *Pensacola, Mississippi, Oneida, Varuna, Katahdin, Kineo,* and *Wissahickon;* Farragut led the second, or center, division, composed of the *Hartford, Brooklyn,* and *Richmond,* and Captain Bell, in the *Sciota,* headed the third, having under his command the *Iroquois, Kennebec, Pinola, Itasca,* and *Winona.* Commander Porter, with his little squadron of six armed steamers, the *Harriet Lane, Owasco, Clifton, John P. Jackson, Westfield, Miami,* and *Portsmouth,* was to stay back with the nineteen mortar schooners that continued to pour their great shells into the forts during the passage of the fleet.

General Lovell, in command of the defenses of New Orleans, did not depend entirely upon Colonel Higgins' gunners in Forts St. Philip and Jackson to keep Farragut away from the city. A considerable fleet of war vessels, some belonging to the Government and some to the State, were in the river, and

HUGER, COMMANDER OF THE "McREA" IN THE FEARLESS CONFEDERATE FLOTILLA

Never were braver deeds done by men afloat in ships than were performed by the Southern officers and sailors of the little flotilla of gunboats and river craft that joined with the great forts ashore in disputing the passage of Farragut's fleet up the river. The ram "Manassas," whose thin plating was pierced through and through, charged again and again at the towering wooden walls of the oncoming ships. She struck the "Mississippi," wounding her badly, and all but sank the "Brooklyn." The men on the little tug "Mosher," which pushed the fire-raft against the "Hartford," sank with their vessel. Desperate deeds of courage were performed by every Confederate gunboat engaged in the battle. Commander Kennon, of the "Governor Moore," in his duel with the "Varuna," fired through the bows of his own ship. On board the "McRea," a little sea-going steam barkentine but lightly armed, Commander Thomas B. Huger was killed. It was a remarkable coincidence that, only a few months before, this splendid and gallant officer had been first-lieutenant of the "Iroquois," the very ship from which he received his death-wound. There had been hardly a change in the personnel of the vessel. All of the officers and men on board of her had once obeyed his orders. Not all of the Confederate river-defense fleet took part in the action, but those that were under the command of ex-officers of the navy plunged in almost with mad reck-lessness, disdaining the odds arrayed against them. Had the two power-ful ironclads, the "Mississippi" and the "Louisiana," been finished and in commission, declared the Con-federates. Farragut's fleet would never have reached New Orleans.

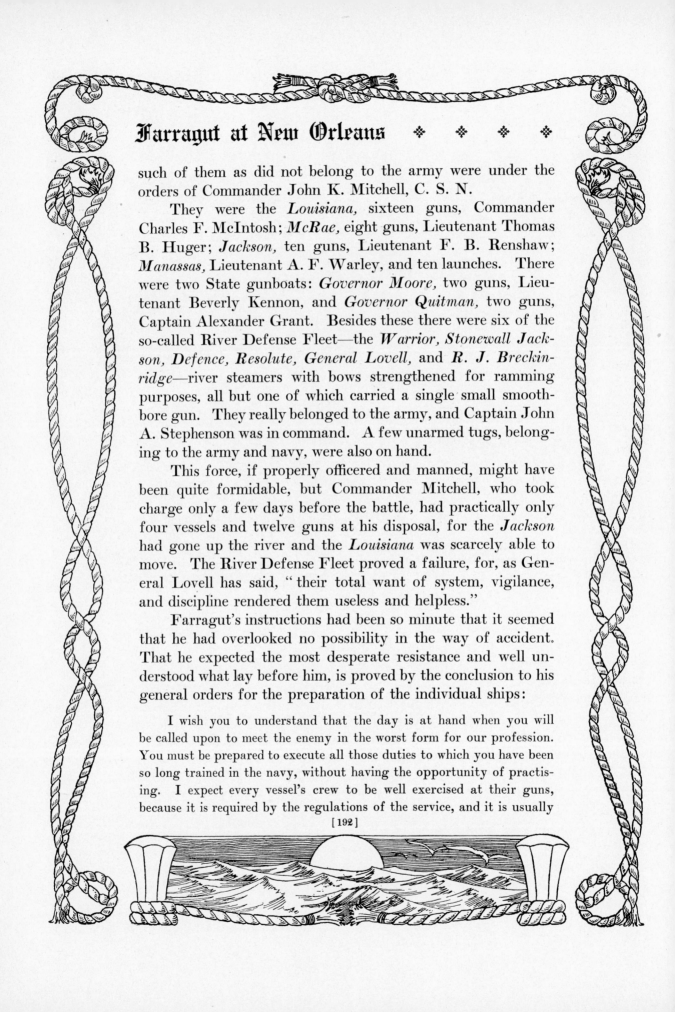

such of them as did not belong to the army were under the orders of Commander John K. Mitchell, C. S. N.

They were the *Louisiana,* sixteen guns, Commander Charles F. McIntosh; *McRae,* eight guns, Lieutenant Thomas B. Huger; *Jackson,* ten guns, Lieutenant F. B. Renshaw; *Manassas,* Lieutenant A. F. Warley, and ten launches. There were two State gunboats: *Governor Moore,* two guns, Lieutenant Beverly Kennon, and *Governor Quitman,* two guns, Captain Alexander Grant. Besides these there were six of the so-called River Defense Fleet—the *Warrior, Stonewall Jackson, Defence, Resolute, General Lovell,* and *R. J. Breckinridge*—river steamers with bows strengthened for ramming purposes, all but one of which carried a single small smooth-bore gun. They really belonged to the army, and Captain John A. Stephenson was in command. A few unarmed tugs, belonging to the army and navy, were also on hand.

This force, if properly officered and manned, might have been quite formidable, but Commander Mitchell, who took charge only a few days before the battle, had practically only four vessels and twelve guns at his disposal, for the *Jackson* had gone up the river and the *Louisiana* was scarcely able to move. The River Defense Fleet proved a failure, for, as General Lovell has said, "their total want of system, vigilance, and discipline rendered them useless and helpless."

Farragut's instructions had been so minute that it seemed that he had overlooked no possibility in the way of accident. That he expected the most desperate resistance and well understood what lay before him, is proved by the conclusion to his general orders for the preparation of the individual ships:

I wish you to understand that the day is at hand when you will be called upon to meet the enemy in the worst form for our profession. You must be prepared to execute all those duties to which you have been so long trained in the navy, without having the opportunity of practising. I expect every vessel's crew to be well exercised at their guns, because it is required by the regulations of the service, and it is usually

COPYRIGHT, 1911, REVIEW OF REVIEWS CO.

SAVED FROM AN UNTIMELY END—THE "SCIOTA"

This scene on the vessel's deck was photographed shortly after she had been raised after being sunk by a torpedo in Mobile Bay. Two days after the Federal flag was raised over the courthouse in Mobile, the "Sciota," while hurrying across the bay, ran into one of these hidden engines of destruction. A terrific explosion followed and the "Sciota" sank immediately in twelve feet of water. Four of her men were killed and six wounded and the vessel was badly damaged. This was on April 14, 1865. The navy never gives up one of its vessels as a total loss till everything has been done to prove that to be the case; by July 7th the "Sciota" had been raised, repaired, and sent around to Pensacola for her armament, with orders to proceed to New York and go into dry-dock. In the picture the man leaning against the bulwark, with one hand on his coat and the other in his trousers' pocket, is John S. Pearce, one of the engineers of the famous "Kearsarge." In Farragut's squadron below New Orleans the "Sciota," under Lieutenant Edward Donaldson, led the third division of vessels in charge of Commander Henry H. Bell. The "Sciota" did not get under fire of the forts till about 4 A.M. and passed them without much damage. Immediately behind her came the "Iroquois," which was attacked by the "McRae" and another Confederate vessel. The "McRae" was commanded by Lieutenant Thomas Huger, who had been serving on the "Iroquois" at the war's beginning. An 11-inch shell and a stand of cannister aimed from his old ship killed Huger and disabled the "McRae."

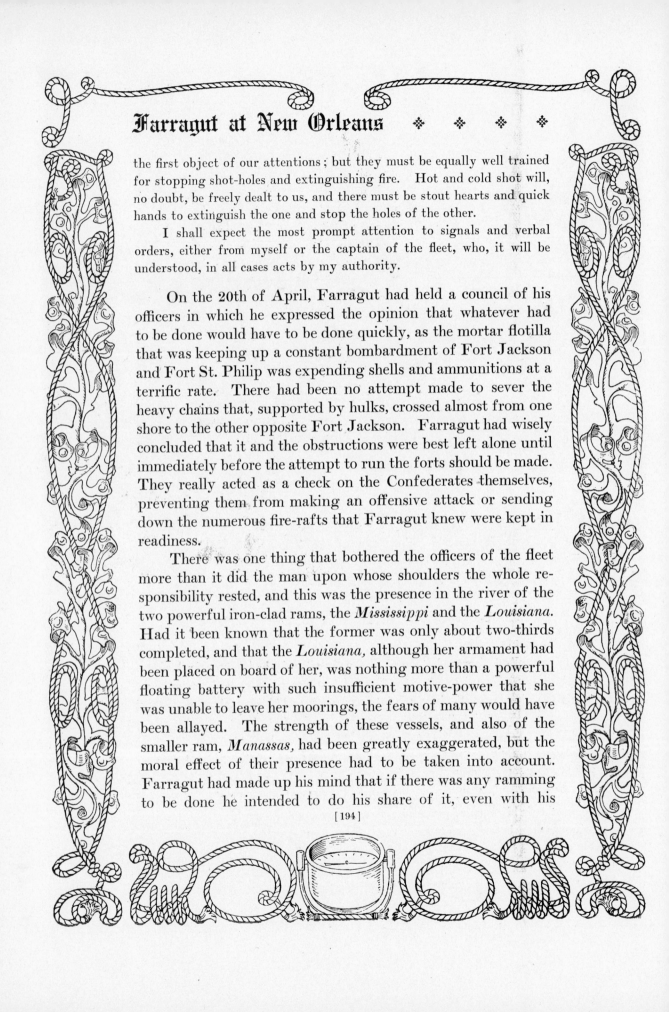

the first object of our attentions; but they must be equally well trained for stopping shot-holes and extinguishing fire. Hot and cold shot will, no doubt, be freely dealt to us, and there must be stout hearts and quick hands to extinguish the one and stop the holes of the other.

I shall expect the most prompt attention to signals and verbal orders, either from myself or the captain of the fleet, who, it will be understood, in all cases acts by my authority.

On the 20th of April, Farragut had held a council of his officers in which he expressed the opinion that whatever had to be done would have to be done quickly, as the mortar flotilla that was keeping up a constant bombardment of Fort Jackson and Fort St. Philip was expending shells and ammunitions at a terrific rate. There had been no attempt made to sever the heavy chains that, supported by hulks, crossed almost from one shore to the other opposite Fort Jackson. Farragut had wisely concluded that it and the obstructions were best left alone until immediately before the attempt to run the forts should be made. They really acted as a check on the Confederates themselves, preventing them from making an offensive attack or sending down the numerous fire-rafts that Farragut knew were kept in readiness.

There was one thing that bothered the officers of the fleet more than it did the man upon whose shoulders the whole responsibility rested, and this was the presence in the river of the two powerful iron-clad rams, the *Mississippi* and the *Louisiana.* Had it been known that the former was only about two-thirds completed, and that the *Louisiana,* although her armament had been placed on board of her, was nothing more than a powerful floating battery with such insufficient motive-power that she was unable to leave her moorings, the fears of many would have been allayed. The strength of these vessels, and also of the smaller ram, *Manassas,* had been greatly exaggerated, but the moral effect of their presence had to be taken into account. Farragut had made up his mind that if there was any ramming to be done he intended to do his share of it, even with his

COPYRIGHT, 1911, PATRIOT PUB. CO.

PORTER, WHOSE BOMB–VESSELS BACKED THE FLEET

Admiral David Dixon Porter was born in 1813 and died in 1891. The red blood of the sea-fighter had come down to him unto the third generation. He was the younger son of Commodore David Porter, who won fame in the "Constellation" and "Essex." His grandfather had served with distinction in the nondescript navy of the Colonies in the war for independence. Yet with such a lineage of the free and open sea, Porter, like Farragut, proved that he could adapt himself to the cramped arenas of bay and river. It was for his part in the fall of Vicksburg that he was made rear-admiral in 1863. It was he, too, that was chosen to command the North Atlantic squadron in 1864, when a courageous and steady hand was needed to guide the most important naval operations to a successful outcome. For his services at Fort Fisher he was made vice-admiral in 1866 and was retired with the rank of admiral in 1870.

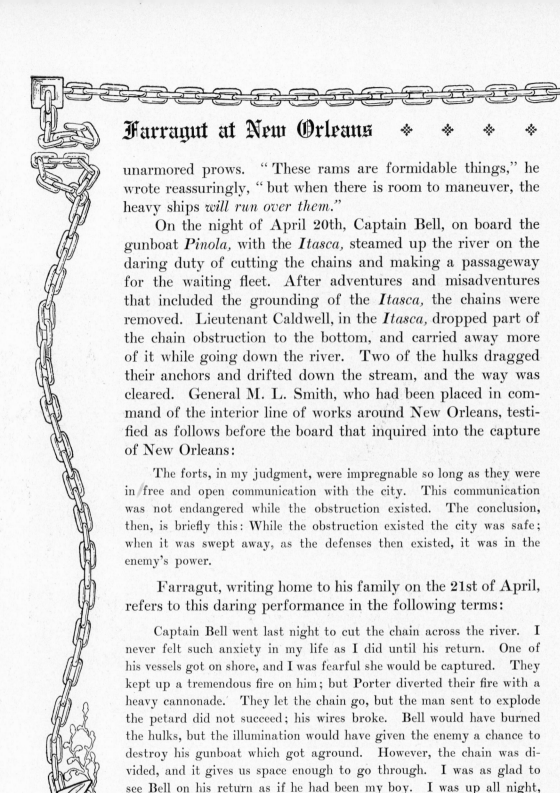

unarmored prows. "These rams are formidable things," he wrote reassuringly, "but when there is room to maneuver, the heavy ships *will run over them.*"

On the night of April 20th, Captain Bell, on board the gunboat *Pinola,* with the *Itasca,* steamed up the river on the daring duty of cutting the chains and making a passageway for the waiting fleet. After adventures and misadventures that included the grounding of the *Itasca,* the chains were removed. Lieutenant Caldwell, in the *Itasca,* dropped part of the chain obstruction to the bottom, and carried away more of it while going down the river. Two of the hulks dragged their anchors and drifted down the stream, and the way was cleared. General M. L. Smith, who had been placed in command of the interior line of works around New Orleans, testified as follows before the board that inquired into the capture of New Orleans:

The forts, in my judgment, were impregnable so long as they were in free and open communication with the city. This communication was not endangered while the obstruction existed. The conclusion, then, is briefly this: While the obstruction existed the city was safe; when it was swept away, as the defenses then existed, it was in the enemy's power.

Farragut, writing home to his family on the 21st of April, refers to this daring performance in the following terms:

Captain Bell went last night to cut the chain across the river. I never felt such anxiety in my life as I did until his return. One of his vessels got on shore, and I was fearful she would be captured. They kept up a tremendous fire on him; but Porter diverted their fire with a heavy cannonade. They let the chain go, but the man sent to explode the petard did not succeed; his wires broke. Bell would have burned the hulks, but the illumination would have given the enemy a chance to destroy his gunboat which got aground. However, the chain was divided, and it gives us space enough to go through. I was as glad to see Bell on his return as if he had been my boy. I was up all night, and could not sleep until he got back to the ship.

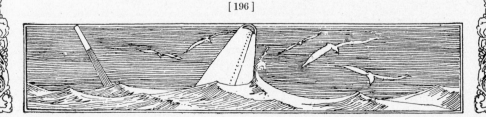

COPYRIGHT, 1911 REVIEW OF REVIEWS CO.

CLEARING THE WAY—DECK ON ONE OF PORTER'S MORTAR SCHOONERS

Twenty of these vessels accompanied Farragut's expedition. They were convoyed by six gunboats. Their huge mortars were capable of dropping shells of large caliber within the forts at a distance of 3,680 yards. The mortar schooners were divided into three divisions. Two were stationed behind a natural rampart formed by the west bank of the river, where they were screened from view by a thick growth of wood above which their mastheads rose, affording excellent lookouts. These were further concealed by branches of trees cleverly fastened upon them. Another division was stationed near the east bank, nearer to the forts and in plain view. A terrific bombardment was begun on the morning of April 16th, each mortar schooner firing at intervals of ten minutes throughout the day. Toward five o'clock flames were seen curling up in Fort Jackson. Commander Porter, who pulled up the river in a rowboat, ascertained that the fort itself was burning. It was indeed in a precarious position, as was learned afterward from Colonel Edward Higgins, the Confederate commander of the fort. Had the attempt to pass up the river been made next morning, it would probably have been much easier than on April 24th, when the fleet at last got under way. Throughout the succeeding days of waiting, the mortar flotilla kept up its vigorous bombardment, withdrawing, however, the division on the east bank, which had suffered in its exposed position during the first vigorous attack, and uniting it with the other vessels, which were protected by the screen on woods on the west bank.

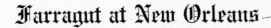

Farragut at New Orleans

Twice had Farragut been compelled to postpone the advance up the river, but on the night of the 23d everything was in readiness; Lieutenant Caldwell, in a ten-oared boat, made another daring reconnaissance on the evening of the 23d, and reported that the way through the obstructions was clear. Somehow, the Confederates must have known that the time had come, for as early as eleven o'clock they had lighted immense piles of wood along the shores and turned loose their burning rafts. It was five minutes to two on the morning of the 24th when two red lights appeared at the flagship's peak, the signal for getting under way. The first division of eight vessels under command of Captain Bailey passed through the opening in the obstructions and headed for Fort St. Philip. In less than ten minutes Bailey's vessels were replying to the concentrated fire that was poured in upon them. Commander Boggs, on the *Varuna,* accompanied by the *Oneida,* had kept in close to shore, and thus escaped a great deal of the fire of the heavy guns that had been elevated and pointed to cover the midchannel. But now Bailey's division found that there were more than land batteries to contend with—they had to meet the Confederate fleet. The *Varuna,* fired upon and rammed by the Louisiana State gunboat *Governor Moore* and River Defense ram *Stonewall Jackson,* was forced to run into shoal water where she promptly sunk to her topgallant forecastle. The Confederate vessels were so pierced by the *Varuna's* fire that they, too, were run ashore in flames. The *Oneida,* which had already disabled one of the Confederate gunboats, came up and received the surrender of the Confederate Commander Kennon and the crew of the burning *Governor Moore.*

As the *Brooklyn* came through the opening in the barrier, she ran afoul of the little *Kineo* and almost sank her. A few minutes later the ugly shape of the turtle-back ram *Manassas* appeared almost under the *Brooklyn's* bows. Had she not changed her course a little all would have been over, but the blow glanced from the chain armor slung along her sides. In

COPYRIGHT, 1911. REVIEW OF REVIEWS CO.

AFTER A SHOOTING–TRIP ASHORE—OFFICERS ON THE DECK OF THE "MIAMI"

From the time she ran the forts below New Orleans with Farragut, the "Miami" was ever on the go. During 1863–4, under the redoubtable Lieutenant-Commander C. W. Flusser, she was active in Carolina waters. In the Roanoke River, April 1, 1864, she met her most thrilling adventure when she and the "Southfield" were attacked by the powerful Confederate ram "Albemarle." The "Southfield" was sunk, but the "Miami" in a plucky running fight made her escape down the river and gave the alarm.

COPYRIGHT, 1911, REVIEW OF REVIEWS CO.

AN INDEFATIGABLE GUNBOAT—THE "MIAMI"

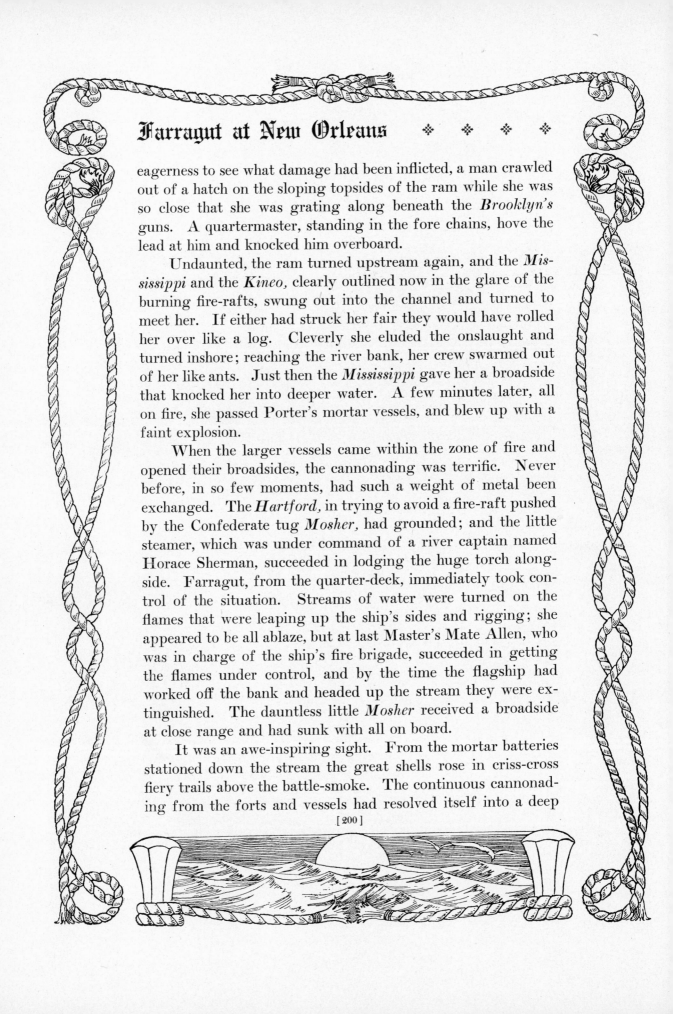

eagerness to see what damage had been inflicted, a man crawled out of a hatch on the sloping topsides of the ram while she was so close that she was grating along beneath the *Brooklyn's* guns. A quartermaster, standing in the fore chains, hove the lead at him and knocked him overboard.

Undaunted, the ram turned upstream again, and the *Mississippi* and the *Kineo,* clearly outlined now in the glare of the burning fire-rafts, swung out into the channel and turned to meet her. If either had struck her fair they would have rolled her over like a log. Cleverly she eluded the onslaught and turned inshore; reaching the river bank, her crew swarmed out of her like ants. Just then the *Mississippi* gave her a broadside that knocked her into deeper water. A few minutes later, all on fire, she passed Porter's mortar vessels, and blew up with a faint explosion.

When the larger vessels came within the zone of fire and opened their broadsides, the cannonading was terrific. Never before, in so few moments, had such a weight of metal been exchanged. The *Hartford,* in trying to avoid a fire-raft pushed by the Confederate tug *Mosher,* had grounded; and the little steamer, which was under command of a river captain named Horace Sherman, succeeded in lodging the huge torch alongside. Farragut, from the quarter-deck, immediately took control of the situation. Streams of water were turned on the flames that were leaping up the ship's sides and rigging; she appeared to be all ablaze, but at last Master's Mate Allen, who was in charge of the ship's fire brigade, succeeded in getting the flames under control, and by the time the flagship had worked off the bank and headed up the stream they were extinguished. The dauntless little *Mosher* received a broadside at close range and had sunk with all on board.

It was an awe-inspiring sight. From the mortar batteries stationed down the stream the great shells rose in criss-cross fiery trails above the battle-smoke. The continuous cannonading from the forts and vessels had resolved itself into a deep

COPYRIGHT, 1911, REVIEW OF REVIEWS CO.

THE "WINONA"—LAST IN THE LINE

This little vessel, mounting but two guns, brought up the rear of the third division in the passage of the New Orleans forts. Following the red stern-light of the "Itasca," she became entangled in the logs and driftwood of the Confederate obstructions on the smoke-clouded river. In backing out she fouled the "Itasca"; both vessels lost nearly half an hour in getting under way again. By this time most of the squadron had passed the forts and daylight was coming fast. Undaunted, Lieutenant Edward Tatnall Nichols of the "Winona" pressed on, a fair mark for the gunners of Fort Jackson. The first shot from the fort killed one man and wounded another; the third and fourth shots killed or wounded the entire gun-crew of her 30-pounder except one man. Still Lieutenant Nichols pressed on to Fort St. Philip. There his vessel and the "Itasca" became the center of such a terrific storm of shot that Commander David D. Porter, of the mortar-boat flotilla, signalled the two little vessels to retire. The "Itasca" had to be run ashore below the mortar-boats. The "Winona" had been "hulled several times, and the decks were wet fore and aft from the spray of the falling shot." She survived to run the batteries at Vicksburg with Farragut. She exchanged a few shells with Fort Morgan in Mobile Bay while on blockade duty there, August 30, 1862.

THE "HARTFORD" AFTER "PASSING THE FORTS" A SECOND TIME

The photographic chronicling of the "most daring deed" would remain incomplete without this presentment of the gallant "Hartford" as she paused at Baton Rouge on a second and peaceful visit in 1882. The rule against the inclusion of any but war-time scenes in this Photographic History has therefore been suspended in favor of this striking photograph—previously unpublished like the others. The people of New Orleans who remembered the "Hartford" in 1862 would hardly have recognized her when, twenty years afterward, she once more steamed up the river and dropped her anchor off the levee. Her appearance, it is seen, was greatly changed; her engines had been altered and she was a much faster vessel than before. When she had passed through the iron hail from the forts,

COPYRIGHT, 1911, REVIEW OF REVIEWS CO.

THE ALTERED APPEARANCE OF THE FAMOUS SHIP ON HER VOYAGE OF PEACE

she was not so trim as she is in this picture. Her top-gallant masts had been sent down and all but her lower yards were on deck; cables were slung along her sides and she was stripped for the fray. Lytle, the Confederate photographer, who had photographed the grand old flagship and her consorts in war-time, also took this photograph of her when she came as a peaceful visitor. The "Hartford" had been for a long time on the European station, and there was hardly a port at which she entered where her name and her fame had not preceded her. Her decks were constantly thronged with visitors, and among her crew were many of the men who had fought with Farragut. These prideful veterans could still point out some of her honorable scars as they told their adventures.

jarring note like the pedal-stop of some great organ; the air vibrated with the sound. Under the dropping arches of the shells the vessels of the second division became intermingled. The fire-rafts, pushed by the heroic little unarmored tugs, were among them. When the flames leaped up the *Hartford's* sides and some men of the broadside batteries drew back, Farragut, from the quarter-deck, called out in ringing tones:

"Don't flinch from that fire, boys! There's a hotter fire than that for those who don't do their duty."

An instant later, as the main-shrouds ignited and the scorched paint from the bulwarks licked about the ports, he raised his hands above his head, exclaiming, "My God! Is it to end this way?"

Among the other smaller vessels the battle became dispersed into single actions like that between the *Varuna* and the *Governor Moore,* the *Iroquois* and the *McRae,* when the latter was driven off and her commander killed, but before daylight every Federal ship but the *Itasca, Kennebec,* and *Winona,* which were forced to turn back, was above the forts, whose usefulness in protecting the city now was gone. In Farragut's fleet the casualties amounted to one hundred and eighty-four; the Confederate losses were never ascertained.

There were only two batteries now between the Federals and New Orleans. On the 25th of April, at one o'clock in the afternoon, the inhabitants of that city saw the fleet drop anchor off the levee. The two small batteries had only fired a shotted salute. On the 1st of May, General Butler arrived with transports, and the occupation was made complete. The forts had surrendered to Porter on the 28th of April. Baton Rouge and Natchez were given up by the civil authorities within a week or so. The opening of the Mississippi from the south had begun.

VIII

FIGHTING
ON
THE MISSISSIPPI

GUNBOAT "NUMBER 53"—AN OFFICER SPYING THE SHORE OPPOSITE BATON ROUGE

A POWERFUL REËNFORCEMENT TO THE RIVER FLEET

This huge vessel was one of the first attempts to develop the Eads type of gunboat. She, with the "Tuscumbia," the "Indianola," the "Lafayette," and the "Chillicothe," was added to the Mississippi squadron after Admiral Porter took command, and all received their baptism in the operations of the Vicksburg campaign, the "Indianola" being captured and destroyed by the Confederates. They were flat-bottomed vessels with side-wheels three-quarters of the way aft, each wheel acting independently of the other so as to give facility in turning in narrow channels, which rendered the broadside guns more effective. They were designed as light-drafts, requiring from five to seven feet of water. The "Choctaw" and her sister-vessel, the "Lafayette," required nine feet. The "Choctaw" mounted three 9-inch smooth-bores and a rifled

COPYRIGHT, 1911, REVIEW OF REVIEWS CO.

THE MONSTER IRONCLAD "CHOCTAW"

100-pounder in her forward casemate. She had a second casemate forward of the wheel where she mounted two 24-pounder howitzers, and a third casemate abaft the wheel containing two 30-pounder Parrott rifled guns. Under Lieutenant-Commander F. M. Ramsay, she was active in the flotilla co-operating with General W. T. Sherman against Haynes' Bluff and Drumgould's Bluff, Mississippi, to distract attention from Grant's famous movement to the south of Vicksburg. She accompanied the expedition that captured Yazoo City on May 21, 1863, and destroyed $2,000,000 worth of Confederate vessels, yards, mills, and other property. On June 7, 1863, she, with the little "Lexington," drove off the Confederate attack on Milliken's Bend, Louisiana. In 1864, she accompanied Admiral Porter on the Red River expedition.

THE "RATTLER"—LEADER OF THE "LAND CRUISE" IN 1863

This little "tinclad" Number 1, the "Rattler," was the flagship of Lieutenant-Commander Watson Smith. Admiral Porter sent him to enter the Yazoo River through Moon Lake, Cold Water, and the Tallahatchie River to attack Vicksburg from that side. This was the most daring and hazardous undertaking attempted by the river navy. The army engineers had cut the levee higher up the Mississippi, but after the water was let in it took some days for it to attain a sufficient level in the vast area flooded. Late in February, Smith and his squadron started out with transports carrying 6,000 troops. Struggling against overhanging trees and masses of driftwood, pausing to remove great trees which the Confederates had felled in their way, the gunboats managed to pick a channel, and approached Fort Pemberton on March 11, 1863. Many of the gunboats had suffered severely from this amphibious warfare. The "Romeo" had her stacks carried away, the "Petrel" had lost her wheel, and the "Chillicothe" had started a plank by running upon a submerged stump. The soldiers were grumbling at the constant labor of "digging the gunboats out of the woods." The channel was so obstructed and narrow that only one gunboat at a time could effectually engage Fort Pemberton. After a few days of ineffectual bombardment the expedition was abandoned and the gunboats returned to the Mississippi over the same long, difficult course.

A VIGILANT PATROLLER—THE "SILVER LAKE"

In the picture the "Silver Lake" is lying off Vicksburg after its fall. While Admiral Porter was busy attacking Vicksburg with the Mississippi squadron, Lieutenant-Commander Le Roy Fitch, with a few small gunboats, was actively patrolling the Tennessee and Cumberland Rivers. It was soon seen that the hold upon Tennessee and Kentucky gained by the Federals by the fall of Forts Henry and Donelson would be lost without adequate assistance from the navy, and Admiral Porter was authorized to purchase small light-draft river steamers and add them to Fitch's flotilla as rapidly as they could be converted into gunboats. One of the first to be completed was the "Silver Lake." The little stern-wheel steamer first distinguished herself on February 3, 1863, at Dover, Tennessee, where she (with Fitch's flotilla) assisted in routing 4,500 Confederates, who were attacking the Federals at that place. The little vessel continued to render yeoman's service with the other gunboats, ably assisted by General A. W. Ellet's marine brigade.

THE NAVY'S FRESH-WATER SAILORS

In this group the crew of the "Carondelet" is crowding to get within range of the camera. One of the earliest of the river ironclads, the "Carondelet" was frequently the flagship of Admiral Porter; and her crew, at first recruited from among men who had had little experience afloat, soon learned the art of warfare on inland waters.   Great difficulty was experienced at first in manning the river gunboats.   Men of the old navy could not be spared, and a large proportion of landsmen had to be enlisted to make up the required complement.   Crude as the early crews appeared to the officers of the navy who commanded them, they soon proved their worth; having gotten their sea-legs and sailorlike spirit in the fighting along the rivers, many of them saw service afterward in the blockading squadrons along the coast.

COPYRIGHT, 1911 REVIEW OF REVIEWS CO.

VETERANS IN THE MAKING—CREW OF THE "LAFAYETTE"

In this fine group on the Mississippi ironclad "Lafayette," the photographer has arranged the crew so that a better idea of the faces of the men can be gathered. Many of them are seen to be foreigners, while of the native Americans boys and youths as usual predominate. There is none of the unmistakable look that characterized the crews of the gunboats and ships in Eastern waters. In only a few instances is there any sign of that indescribable sea-faring appearance that marks the old salt. Yet these men could fight as bravely and endure hardship as uncomplainingly as their salt-water comrades. Most of them were recruited from the river towns and communities in the West.

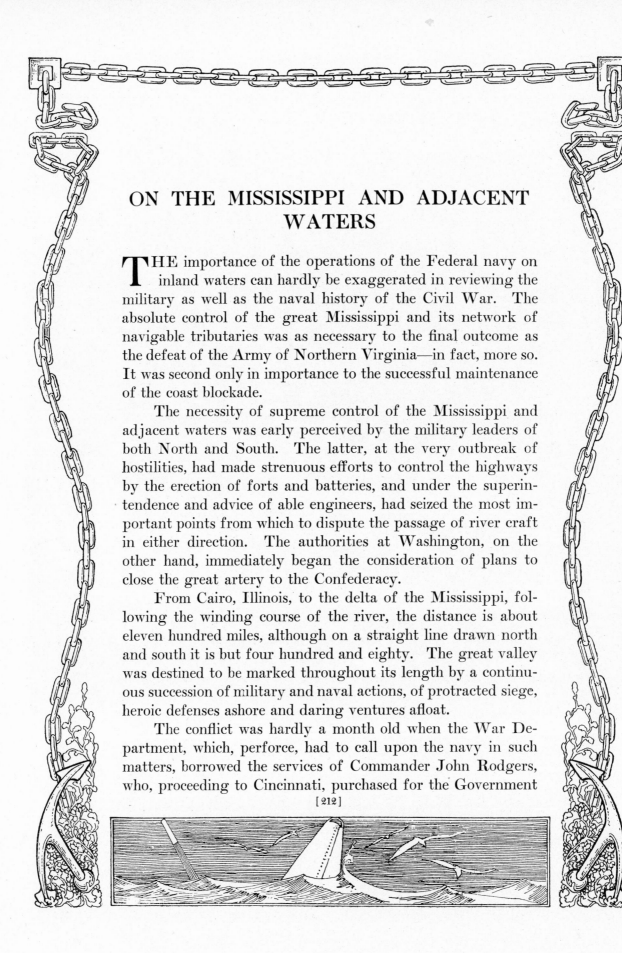

ON THE MISSISSIPPI AND ADJACENT WATERS

THE importance of the operations of the Federal navy on inland waters can hardly be exaggerated in reviewing the military as well as the naval history of the Civil War. The absolute control of the great Mississippi and its network of navigable tributaries was as necessary to the final outcome as the defeat of the Army of Northern Virginia—in fact, more so. It was second only in importance to the successful maintenance of the coast blockade.

The necessity of supreme control of the Mississippi and adjacent waters was early perceived by the military leaders of both North and South. The latter, at the very outbreak of hostilities, had made strenuous efforts to control the highways by the erection of forts and batteries, and under the superintendence and advice of able engineers, had seized the most important points from which to dispute the passage of river craft in either direction. The authorities at Washington, on the other hand, immediately began the consideration of plans to close the great artery to the Confederacy.

From Cairo, Illinois, to the delta of the Mississippi, following the winding course of the river, the distance is about eleven hundred miles, although on a straight line drawn north and south it is but four hundred and eighty. The great valley was destined to be marked throughout its length by a continuous succession of military and naval actions, of protracted siege, heroic defenses ashore and daring ventures afloat.

The conflict was hardly a month old when the War Department, which, perforce, had to call upon the navy in such matters, borrowed the services of Commander John Rodgers, who, proceeding to Cincinnati, purchased for the Government

COPYRIGHT. 1911. REVIEW OF REVIEWS CO.

THE WESTERN NAVAL BASE OF THE UNION—MOUND CITY IN 1862

After Captain Andrew H. Foote took command of the Mississippi flotilla on September 6, 1861, one of his first acts was to establish a depot for the repair of his vessels at Cairo. Since the Government owned no land at this point, the navy-yard was literally afloat in wharf-boats, old steamers, tugs, flat-boats, and rafts. Later, this depot was removed to Mound City, just above Cairo, where ten acres of land were secured. This was frequently under water from freshets, however, and the machine-shops, carpenter-shops, and the like were still maintained in steamers. Captain A. M. Pennock was placed in charge of this depot, and continued to render efficient service in that capacity, looking after the gunboats till the close of the war.

the nucleus of the subsequent river force in the three little wooden steamers, *Conestoga, Lexington,* and *Tyler.* About the time that these small craft had been converted into practicable gunboats, the department made a contract with James B. Eads, of St. Louis, for the construction of seven iron-clad steamers, and so, late in 1861 and early in 1862, there came into being the famous fighters, *Cairo, Carondelet, Cincinnati, Louisville, Mound City, Pittsburgh,* and *St. Louis.* To these were simultaneously added the powerful, converted snag-boats, *Benton* and *Essex,* almost twice the size of any of those built by Eads. The *Benton* proved, despite her slowness, to be the most formidable vessel on the river. She was armored with 3-inch plating, was about one thousand tons burden, and carried two 9-inch guns, seven rifled 42-pounders, and seven 32-pounders, a total of sixteen guns. Thirty-eight mortar-boats completed the Western Flotilla, as first organized.

It was soon evident that friction was bound to exist as long as naval officers were subject to the orders of innumerable military officials who happened to rank them. Nevertheless, it was not until October 1, 1862, that the Western Flotilla was transferred to the control of the Navy Department, and henceforth was called the Mississippi Squadron. During the year 1861 there had been little done by either the army or the navy along the Western border. But the early months of 1862 saw both gunboats and troops in active employment, and so they continued until practically the close of hostilities.

The separate actions that took place have already been covered in detail in previous volumes of this history. The first action of any moment was the capture of Fort Henry, on February 6th, where Flag-Officer Foote's flotilla consisted of the *Cincinnati* (flagship), *Carondelet, St. Louis,* and *Essex,* to which formidable force were added the three small wooden gunboats, *Lexington, Tyler,* and *Conestoga.* This was a joint army and navy movement, a combination of the two able minds of Ulysses S. Grant and Andrew H. Foote. General Lloyd

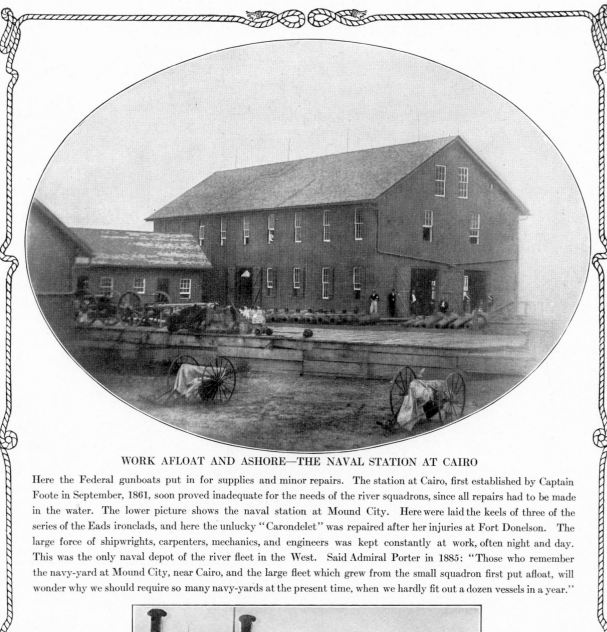

WORK AFLOAT AND ASHORE—THE NAVAL STATION AT CAIRO

Here the Federal gunboats put in for supplies and minor repairs. The station at Cairo, first established by Captain Foote in September, 1861, soon proved inadequate for the needs of the river squadrons, since all repairs had to be made in the water. The lower picture shows the naval station at Mound City. Here were laid the keels of three of the series of the Eads ironclads, and here the unlucky "Carondelet" was repaired after her injuries at Fort Donelson. The large force of shipwrights, carpenters, mechanics, and engineers was kept constantly at work, often night and day. This was the only naval depot of the river fleet in the West. Said Admiral Porter in 1885: "Those who remember the navy-yard at Mound City, near Cairo, and the large fleet which grew from the small squadron first put afloat, will wonder why we should require so many navy-yards at the present time, when we hardly fit out a dozen vessels in a year."

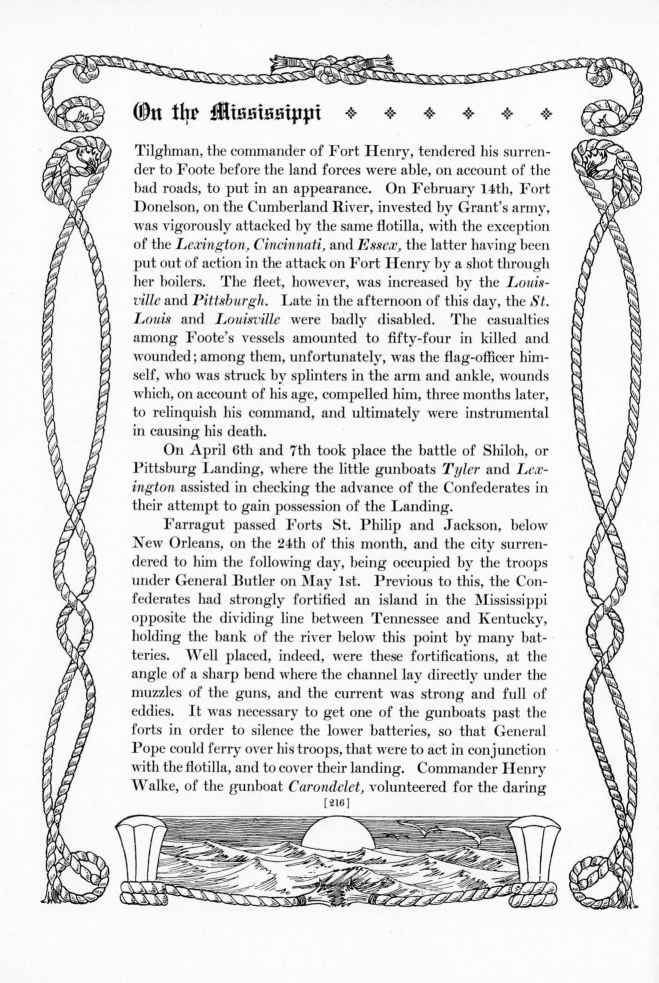

On the Mississippi ❖ ❖ ❖ ❖ ❖

Tilghman, the commander of Fort Henry, tendered his surrender to Foote before the land forces were able, on account of the bad roads, to put in an appearance. On February 14th, Fort Donelson, on the Cumberland River, invested by Grant's army, was vigorously attacked by the same flotilla, with the exception of the *Lexington, Cincinnati,* and *Essex,* the latter having been put out of action in the attack on Fort Henry by a shot through her boilers. The fleet, however, was increased by the *Louisville* and *Pittsburgh.* Late in the afternoon of this day, the *St. Louis* and *Louisville* were badly disabled. The casualties among Foote's vessels amounted to fifty-four in killed and wounded; among them, unfortunately, was the flag-officer himself, who was struck by splinters in the arm and ankle, wounds which, on account of his age, compelled him, three months later, to relinquish his command, and ultimately were instrumental in causing his death.

On April 6th and 7th took place the battle of Shiloh, or Pittsburg Landing, where the little gunboats *Tyler* and *Lexington* assisted in checking the advance of the Confederates in their attempt to gain possession of the Landing.

Farragut passed Forts St. Philip and Jackson, below New Orleans, on the 24th of this month, and the city surrendered to him the following day, being occupied by the troops under General Butler on May 1st. Previous to this, the Confederates had strongly fortified an island in the Mississippi opposite the dividing line between Tennessee and Kentucky, holding the bank of the river below this point by many batteries. Well placed, indeed, were these fortifications, at the angle of a sharp bend where the channel lay directly under the muzzles of the guns, and the current was strong and full of eddies. It was necessary to get one of the gunboats past the forts in order to silence the lower batteries, so that General Pope could ferry over his troops, that were to act in conjunction with the flotilla, and to cover their landing. Commander Henry Walke, of the gunboat *Carondelet,* volunteered for the daring

THE "ALBATROSS": WITH THE "HARTFORD," THE ONLY SHIP THAT
FOUGHT PAST PORT HUDSON

While Porter had been fighting on the upper Mississippi, Farragut had been busy attending to his large command in the Gulf, but on the 14th of March, 1863, he appeared below Port Hudson. General Banks was to make a simultaneous land-attack upon that post and Farragut was to run the river batteries and join his vessels to those of Porter in an effectual blockade of the Red River, from which the Confederacy drew its trans-Mississippi supplies. The Federal vessels, lashed two and two together, started on their dangerous attempt at eleven o'clock at night, but the Port Hudson garrison discovered them. Lighting bonfires, the Confederates opened with their heavy guns from the bluff a hundred feet above. Lashed to the gallant old flagship "Hartford" was the "Albatross," Lieutenant-Commander John E. Hart. Both vessels in the dense smoke that settled on the river were nearly carried ashore by the five-mile current. The "Hartford" actually did touch ground under the guns of one of the batteries, but with the assistance of the "Albatross" backed off and passed safely above the line of fire. Not so fortunate was the "Genesee," the fastest boat of the squadron. She was lashed to the "Richmond," the slowest boat, and just as they had reached the last battery a plunging shot penetrated to the engine-room of the "Richmond" and so damaged her safety-valves that her engines became useless. Not even with the aid of the "Genesee" could the "Richmond" longer stem the current, and the two had to proceed downstream again past the gauntlet of the Confederate batteries for the second time. Disaster overtook all the other vessels of the squadron, and the "Mississippi" grounded and blew up.

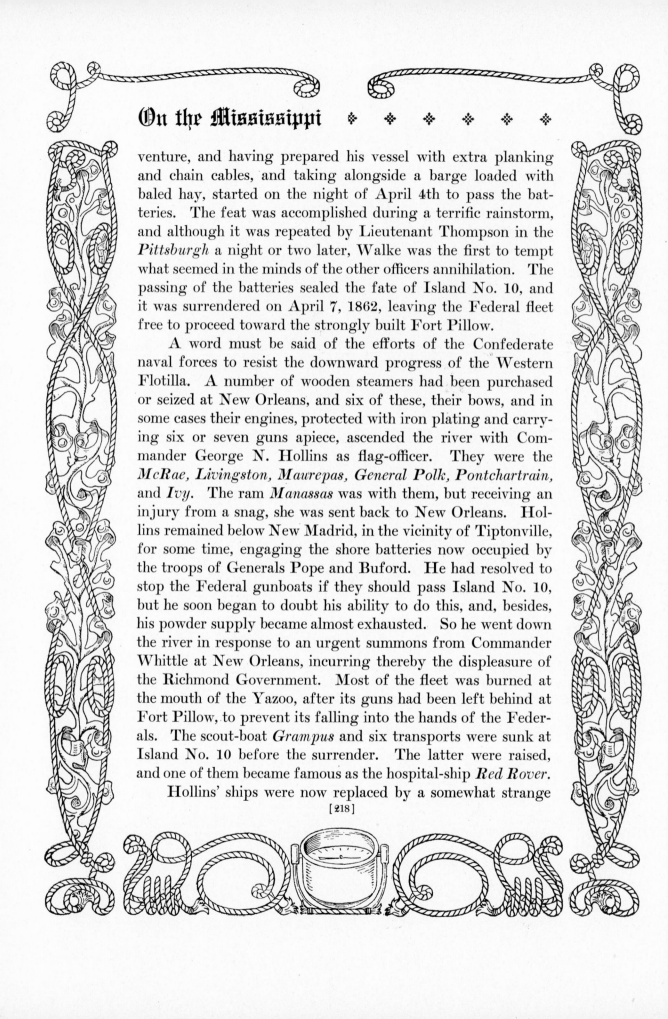

venture, and having prepared his vessel with extra planking and chain cables, and taking alongside a barge loaded with baled hay, started on the night of April 4th to pass the batteries. The feat was accomplished during a terrific rainstorm, and although it was repeated by Lieutenant Thompson in the *Pittsburgh* a night or two later, Walke was the first to tempt what seemed in the minds of the other officers annihilation. The passing of the batteries sealed the fate of Island No. 10, and it was surrendered on April 7, 1862, leaving the Federal fleet free to proceed toward the strongly built Fort Pillow.

A word must be said of the efforts of the Confederate naval forces to resist the downward progress of the Western Flotilla. A number of wooden steamers had been purchased or seized at New Orleans, and six of these, their bows, and in some cases their engines, protected with iron plating and carrying six or seven guns apiece, ascended the river with Commander George N. Hollins as flag-officer. They were the *McRae, Livingston, Maurepas, General Polk, Pontchartrain,* and *Ivy.* The ram *Manassas* was with them, but receiving an injury from a snag, she was sent back to New Orleans. Hollins remained below New Madrid, in the vicinity of Tiptonville, for some time, engaging the shore batteries now occupied by the troops of Generals Pope and Buford. He had resolved to stop the Federal gunboats if they should pass Island No. 10, but he soon began to doubt his ability to do this, and, besides, his powder supply became almost exhausted. So he went down the river in response to an urgent summons from Commander Whittle at New Orleans, incurring thereby the displeasure of the Richmond Government. Most of the fleet was burned at the mouth of the Yazoo, after its guns had been left behind at Fort Pillow, to prevent its falling into the hands of the Federals. The scout-boat *Grampus* and six transports were sunk at Island No. 10 before the surrender. The latter were raised, and one of them became famous as the hospital-ship *Red Rover.*

Hollins' ships were now replaced by a somewhat strange

"MY EXECUTIVE OFFICER, MR. DEWEY"

THE FUTURE ADMIRAL AS CIVIL WAR LIEUTENANT

In the fight with the batteries at Port Hudson, March 14, 1863, Farragut, in the "Hartford" lashed to the "Albatross," got by, but the fine old consort of the "Hartford," the "Mississippi," went down—her gunners fighting to the last. Farragut, in anguish, could see her enveloped in flames lighting up the river. She had grounded under the very guns of a battery, and not until actually driven off by the flames did her men leave her. When the "Mississippi" grounded, the shock threw her lieutenant-commander into the river, and in confusion he swam toward the shore; then, turning about, he swam back to his ship. Captain Smith thus writes in his report: "I consider that I should be neglecting a most important duty should I omit to mention the coolness of my executive officer, Mr. Dewey, and the steady, fearless, and gallant manner in which the officers and men of the 'Mississippi' defended her, and the orderly and quiet manner in which she was abandoned after being thirty-five minutes aground under the fire of the enemy's batteries. There was no confusion in embarking the crew, and the only noise was from the enemy's cannon." Lieutenant-Commander George Dewey, here mentioned at the age of 26, was to exemplify in Manila Bay on May 1, 1898, the lessons he was learning from Farragut.

lot of craft, under the control of the army, and known as the River Defense Fleet. They were river steamers, with bows enclosed in iron, and were designed for use as rams. Fourteen vessels in all were thus prepared, and eight were sent up the river in charge of Captain James E. Montgomery to try conclusions with Flag-Officer Foote's powerful ironclads. The opportunity was not long in coming.

Foote, suffering from the wound received at Fort Donelson, was relieved by Captain Charles H. Davis on May 9th. The new commander, who was soon to be promoted to flag-officer, selected the *Benton,* commanded by Lieutenant S. L. Phelps, as his flagship. On May 10th, the bombardment of Fort Pillow by the mortar-boats, which had been going on since the 14th of April, was unexpectedly interrupted by the advance of the River Defense Fleet, which came up bravely from its position under the guns of the fort and actually took the Federal vessels by surprise, the *Cincinnati* being called upon at first to bear the brunt of the onslaught alone. Both she and the *Mound City* had to be beached on account of the injuries they received. There is no doubt that Captain Montgomery, the Confederate commander, showed great bravery in making the attack, but he also proved his discretion by withdrawing upon the advance of the belated *Benton* and *St. Louis,* for with but slight loss and damage he retreated down the river, and had his vessels in good shape four weeks later at Memphis.

A new departure in river fighting began when Colonel Charles Ellet, Jr., came down with his nine rams, which consisted of old stern-wheelers and side-wheelers strengthened by bulkheads, their boilers protected by oak and iron and their bows reenforced with heavy metal sheathing. Colonel Ellet, who had long advocated this style of offensive vessel, had been given independent charge, his orders being simply to cooperate with Flag-Officer Davis and the flotilla. In fact, throughout the whole war, the Ellet rams were under the direction of the War Department. The vessels were unarmed until after the

COPYRIGHT, 1911, REVIEW OF REVIEWS CO.

A BESIEGING "TINCLAD"—THE "MARMORA"

This little "tinclad" Number 2, the "Marmora," under Acting Volunteer Lieutenant Robert Getty, played a lively part in the operations of Admiral Porter's squadron against Vicksburg. She and the "Signal" were the "tinclads" that reconnoitered up the torpedo-infested Yazoo, Dec. 11, 1862, and it was while protecting the "Marmora" from the Confederates along the bank that the luckless "Cairo" met her fate. The "Marmora" was with the fleet in Sherman's futile attack at Chickasaw Bayou. After the fall of Vicksburg, the squadron was divided into detachments to patrol the Mississippi and its tributaries, and the "Marmora" was assigned to the detachment of Lieutenant George M. Bache, the brave commander of the lost "Cincinnati." He, in the little veteran "Lexington," accompanied by the "Cricket" and "Marmora," went up the White River where the Confederates were massing. In the middle of August, 1863, the three little gunboats completely broke up the expedition that was being set afoot by the indefatigable General Price, whom it would have required an army of 20,000 to drive back. The pontoon-bridges in the river were destroyed, completely stopping the advance, and the "Cricket" captured the two vessels in his flotilla.

THE RAM "VINDICATOR" OFF VICKSBURG

battle of Memphis. On June 4th, Fort Pillow was evacuated, and the Federal gunboats and the Ellet rams steamed quietly down the river and anchored not far above the city of Memphis, under whose bluffs now lay the River Defense Fleet.

Long before this, however, Farragut had passed up the Mississippi as far as Vicksburg, the advance ships reaching that place on May 18th, but seeing that it was useless to attempt to reduce the batteries without the aid of troops, he steamed down again, and on May 29th was once more at New Orleans.

The 6th of June was memorable for the meeting at Memphis, in which no land forces lent aid or were concerned; where the ramming tactics used by both sides completely proved that this harking-back to an ancient form of naval warfare in confined waters was more destructive than well-aimed guns or heavy broadsides. Three ships were put out of action within fifteen minutes, the Federal *Queen of the West,* under command of Colonel Ellet, sinking the *General Lovell,* and in turn being rammed by the *General Beauregard* so hard that it was necessary to put her ashore. An accidental collision by the *General Beauregard* and the *General Price,* two Confederate vessels, put the latter out of commission. The Federal ram *Monarch's* charge upon the *Beauregard* took place just as the latter had received a deadly shot from the *Benton* through her boiler. Only one Confederate ram, the *General Van Dorn,* escaped destruction. Memphis was now at the mercy of the naval force, and the river was open to the south as far as Vicksburg.

A terrible disaster happened on June 17th to the gunboat *Mound City,* which, in company with the *St. Louis, Lexington,* and *Conestoga,* had been sent up the White River to convoy troops and transports and to assist in an attack on the Confederate batteries at St. Charles, Arkansas. A shot from a masked gun on the bank penetrated the casemate of the *Mound City* just above a gun-port, killed three men, and exploded the steam-drum. Nearly eighty men were scalded to death immediately, and forty-three others were drowned or shot by

COPYRIGHT, 1911, REVIEW OF REVIEWS CO.

In the picture above of gunboat "Number 54," the "Nymph," is seen—a typical example of the river steamers that were purchased by the Government and converted into the so-called "tinclads." This kind of vessel was acquired at the suggestion of Flag-Officer Davis, who saw the necessity of light-draft gunboats to operate in shallow waters against the Confederates constantly harassing the flotilla from along shore. These "tinclads" were mostly stern-wheel steamers drawing not more than three feet. They were covered from bow to stern with iron plate a half to three-quarters of an inch thick. When Admiral Porter succeeded Davis in the command of the Mississippi squadron, it had already been reënforced by a number of these extremely useful little vessels. One of Porter's first acts was to use the "tinclads" to prevent the erection of Confederate fortifications up the Yazoo. The "Queen City" ("tinclad" Number 26) was commanded in the Vicksburg campaign by Acting Volunteer Lieutenant J. Goudy, one of those to receive special mention in Admiral Porter's official report on the fall of the besieged town. In June, 1864, the "Queen City" was stationed on the White River, patrolling the stream between Clarendon and Duvall's Bluff, under command of Acting Volunteer Lieutenant G. W. Brown. On the 24th, she was surprised by a Confederate force under General Shelby, who attacked her with artillery about four in the morning. After a sharp struggle of twenty minutes the little "tinclad," with her thin armor riddled with shot, surrendered. After stripping her of the nine guns and her supplies, the Confederates scuttled and burned her. Such were the chances that the "tinclads" constantly took.

TWO WARSHIPS

OF THE

"MOSQUITO FLEET"

"NYMPH" (ABOVE)

AND THE

"QUEEN CITY"

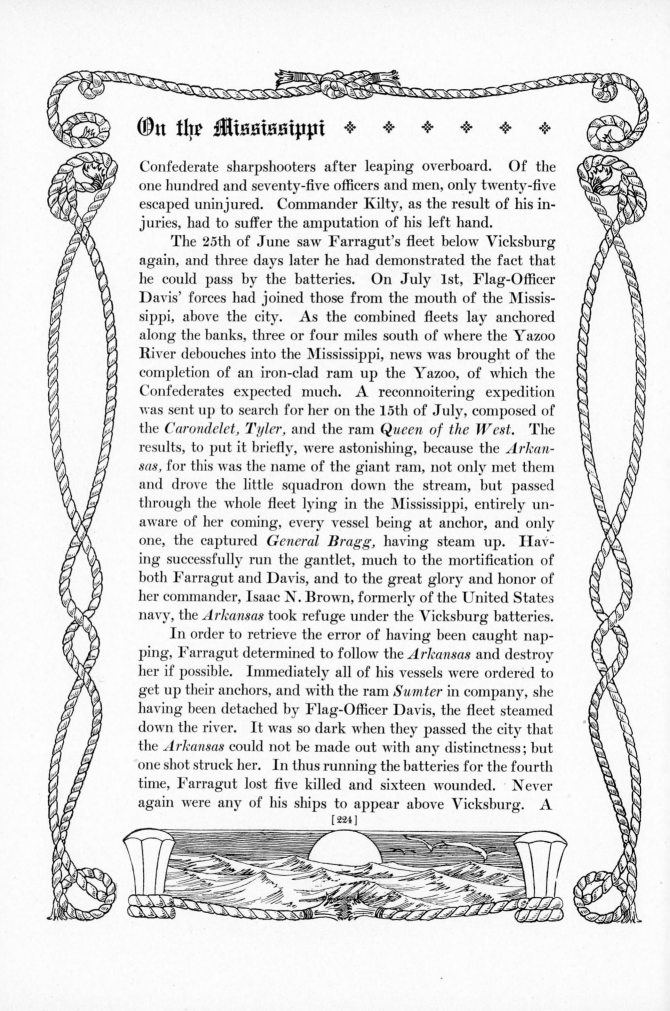

Confederate sharpshooters after leaping overboard. Of the one hundred and seventy-five officers and men, only twenty-five escaped uninjured. Commander Kilty, as the result of his injuries, had to suffer the amputation of his left hand.

The 25th of June saw Farragut's fleet below Vicksburg again, and three days later he had demonstrated the fact that he could pass by the batteries. On July 1st, Flag-Officer Davis' forces had joined those from the mouth of the Mississippi, above the city. As the combined fleets lay anchored along the banks, three or four miles south of where the Yazoo River debouches into the Mississippi, news was brought of the completion of an iron-clad ram up the Yazoo, of which the Confederates expected much. A reconnoitering expedition was sent up to search for her on the 15th of July, composed of the *Carondelet, Tyler,* and the ram *Queen of the West.* The results, to put it briefly, were astonishing, because the *Arkansas,* for this was the name of the giant ram, not only met them and drove the little squadron down the stream, but passed through the whole fleet lying in the Mississippi, entirely unaware of her coming, every vessel being at anchor, and only one, the captured *General Bragg,* having steam up. Having successfully run the gantlet, much to the mortification of both Farragut and Davis, and to the great glory and honor of her commander, Isaac N. Brown, formerly of the United States navy, the *Arkansas* took refuge under the Vicksburg batteries.

In order to retrieve the error of having been caught napping, Farragut determined to follow the *Arkansas* and destroy her if possible. Immediately all of his vessels were ordered to get up their anchors, and with the ram *Sumter* in company, she having been detached by Flag-Officer Davis, the fleet steamed down the river. It was so dark when they passed the city that the *Arkansas* could not be made out with any distinctness; but one shot struck her. In thus running the batteries for the fourth time, Farragut lost five killed and sixteen wounded. Never again were any of his ships to appear above Vicksburg. A

COPYRIGHT, 1911, REVIEW OF REVIEWS CO.

THE TRANSPORT "BLACK HAWK" AFTER HER FIERY TEST—MAY, 1864

The vessel shows the treatment accorded the thirty army transports which, convoyed by Porter's gunboats, went up the Red River in the futile expedition, the object of which was to reach Shreveport. The stacks and pilot-house of the "Black Hawk" have been riddled with Confederate bullets, and she shows the evidences of the continuous struggle through which the fleet passed in the retreat from Grand Ecore. For nearly a month the Federal vessels worked their way slowly down the river. The water was falling rapidly and the vessels, as they nosed their way through the shallow and unfamiliar channel, were constantly running aground. As the military forces had withdrawn to Alexandria, the Confederates, who lined both banks of the river, seized every opportunity to attack the discomfited vessels, and almost daily attempts were made to damage or capture them. The river was full of snags and the vessels had to be lightened; they were "jumped" over sand-bars and logs, fighting every inch of the difficult and laborious journey. Even Admiral Porter himself described the obstacles to be overcome as enough to appall the stoutest heart.

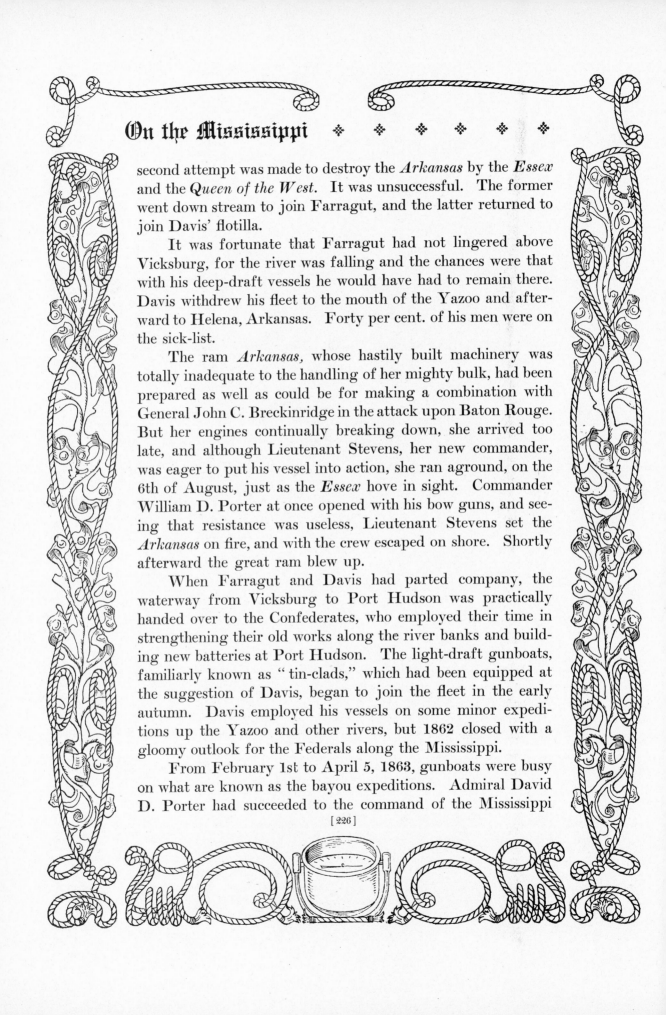

second attempt was made to destroy the *Arkansas* by the *Essex* and the *Queen of the West*. It was unsuccessful. The former went down stream to join Farragut, and the latter returned to join Davis' flotilla.

It was fortunate that Farragut had not lingered above Vicksburg, for the river was falling and the chances were that with his deep-draft vessels he would have had to remain there. Davis withdrew his fleet to the mouth of the Yazoo and afterward to Helena, Arkansas. Forty per cent. of his men were on the sick-list.

The ram *Arkansas,* whose hastily built machinery was totally inadequate to the handling of her mighty bulk, had been prepared as well as could be for making a combination with General John C. Breckinridge in the attack upon Baton Rouge. But her engines continually breaking down, she arrived too late, and although Lieutenant Stevens, her new commander, was eager to put his vessel into action, she ran aground, on the 6th of August, just as the *Essex* hove in sight. Commander William D. Porter at once opened with his bow guns, and seeing that resistance was useless, Lieutenant Stevens set the *Arkansas* on fire, and with the crew escaped on shore. Shortly afterward the great ram blew up.

When Farragut and Davis had parted company, the waterway from Vicksburg to Port Hudson was practically handed over to the Confederates, who employed their time in strengthening their old works along the river banks and building new batteries at Port Hudson. The light-draft gunboats, familiarly known as "tin-clads," which had been equipped at the suggestion of Davis, began to join the fleet in the early autumn. Davis employed his vessels on some minor expeditions up the Yazoo and other rivers, but 1862 closed with a gloomy outlook for the Federals along the Mississippi.

From February 1st to April 5, 1863, gunboats were busy on what are known as the bayou expeditions. Admiral David D. Porter had succeeded to the command of the Mississippi

COPYRIGHT, 1911, REVIEW OF REVIEWS CO.

A CRITICAL MOMENT IN THE RED RIVER EXPEDITION OF APRIL, 1864—FEDERAL TRANSPORTS BELOW THE FALLS

On the second Red River expedition, in 1864, Alexandria was garrisoned and made the base for the army and navy operating both above and below that point, in the effort that had for its ultimate object the recovery of Texas to the Union. The fleet under Admiral Porter started up the Red River from Vicksburg with the transports carrying A. J. Smith's column of 10,000 men. Fort De Russy was captured, and Alexandria and Natchitoches fell into Union hands as they advanced. Banks with his army arrived a week later. At Sabine Cross Roads the vanguard met the Confederates in force. Sufficient care had not been taken to keep the several Union bodies together, and the Confederates under General Taylor defeated Franklin April 8th, and drove him back with a loss of 3,000 out of 11,000 engaged. At Pleasant Hill, A. J. Smith made a stand on April 9th, but was unable to hold his own. An immediate retreat was made, without waiting to bury the dead, and the fleet came near being cut off by low water at Alexandria, but the ingenuity of Colonel Bailey in constructing a dam and water-way enabled it to escape. In the picture the level in front of the hotel is piled with ammunition and supplies—elaborate preparations all wasted.

ENTRAPPED ABOVE THE FALLS—GLOOMY DAYS OF WAITING AND NARROW ESCAPES

Here lies a part of the unlucky fleet that Admiral Porter came near losing in the fruitless expedition up the Red River, which imperilled some of the most valuable gunboats possessed by the Federal navy. First in line is the tow-boat "Brown"; next the steamer "Benefit," whose escape the month before was hair-breadth; then the tug "Dahlia," the tender to Porter's flagship, while the ironclads "Neosho" and "Chillicothe" bring up the rear. The expedition on the part of the navy was undertaken in the assurance that the Red River would, according to its custom, rise at this season of the year. For twenty years it had never failed to rise, but now, in 1864, it did exactly the opposite. Only the light-draft gunboats could be run above the falls by the end of March. Since it was rumored that the Confederates had some formidable ironclads up the Red River, the gunboat "Eastport" was at last hauled over the rocks of the rapids by main strength to lead the expedition. It proved to be her last; she grounded on the return from Grand Ecore, and after

COPYRIGHT, 1911, REVIEW OF REVIEWS CO.

THE FEDERAL FLOTILLA ABOVE ALEXANDRIA, HELD BY THE LOW WATER OF MAY, 1864

heroic efforts to get her off, during which the Confederates kept up constant fighting, she had to be destroyed and abandoned. It looked for a time as if the other vessels of Porter's fleet were to meet the same fate. General Banks had been ordered to give up the expedition and was chafing to get his troops in motion. Meanwhile the officers and men of the navy were working with characteristic courage and determination to save their vessels, now exposed to constant attacks from the Confederates, who grew more and more threatening. The little steamer "Benefit," seen in the picture, had a narrow escape at Grappe's Bluff, where she was attacked on the evening of April 10th, and in less than twenty minutes lost forty-five of her eighty men. Gloomy indeed were the days of waiting above the falls, for both officers and men. One difficulty and disaster followed another. It seemed almost certain that the fated expedition would cost the navy its heaviest and most humiliating loss during the war, but courage and determination won out

COPYRIGHT, 1911, REVIEW OF REVIEWS CO.

HELP AT HAND—THE GUNBOAT "SIGNAL" TOWING MATERIALS FOR THE DAM

On the 1st of May, 1864, thousands of men were set to work upon the famous dam by which Bailey raised the water sufficiently to enable the entrapped vessels to get below the falls. The "Signal" is busily at work towing materials to fill the cribs. Stones were gathered, deserted brick buildings were pulled down, and a large sugar-house a mile below the falls was wrecked and its woodwork, together with its machinery and kettles, were towed up to become a part of the dam. More dangerous work waited the "Signal," however, for on May 4th she and the "Covington," the best two gunboats below the falls, were despatched to convoy the transport "Warner," on which was Lieutenant Simpson of Banks' staff, bearing despatches to Grant, Sherman, and Rosecrans. Near David's Ferry the two gallant little gunboats fought for five hours, on May 5th, against tremendous odds. The Confederates had posted twenty pieces of artillery on the river bank, and against their fire the gunboats stood up bravely. The odds were too heavily against them, however, and the "Covington" was at last abandoned and destroyed, while the "Signal" fell a captive to the Confederates, who sunk her in the channel as an obstruction. Admiral Porter said: "Many of the actions heralded to the world during the late war were much less worthy of notice than this contest between two little gunboats only musket-proof and twenty pieces of artillery."

COPYRIGHT, 1911, REVIEW OF REVIEWS CO.

TRANSPORTS WAITING FOR THE UNION ARMY

COPYRIGHT, 1911, REVIEW OF REVIEWS CO.

THE ARMY SAVING THE NAVY IN MAY, 1864

Here the army is saving the navy by a brilliant piece of engineering that prevented the loss of a fleet worth $2,000,000. The Red River expedition was one of the most humiliating ever under-taken by the Federals. Porter's fleet, which had so boldly advanced above the falls at Alexandria, was ordered back, only to find that the river was so low as to imprison twelve vessels. Lieut.-Colonel Joseph Bailey, acting engineer of the Nineteenth Corps, obtained permission to build a dam in order to make possible the passage of the fleet. Begun on April 30, 1864, the work was finished on the 8th of May, almost entirely by the soldiers, working incessantly day and night, often up to their necks in water and under the broiling sun. Bailey succeeded in turning the whole current into one channel and the squadron passed below to safety. Not often have inland lumbermen been the means of saving a navy.

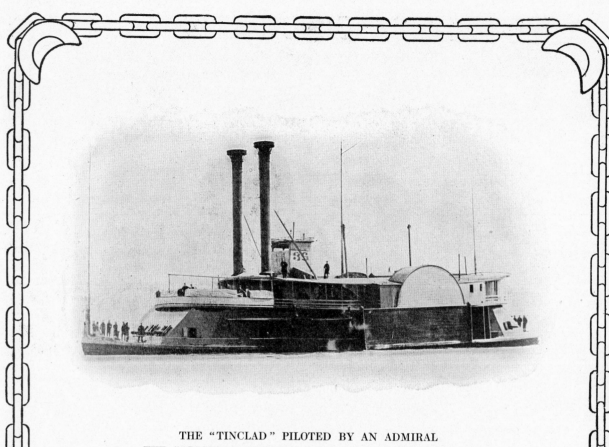

THE "TINCLAD" PILOTED BY AN ADMIRAL
THE "CRICKET"—PORTER'S FLAGSHIP ON THE RETURN

After capturing single-handed two Confederate steamers on the White River, this little fourth-rate vessel took an active part in the bombardment of Vicksburg under command of Acting Master A. R. Langthorne. On the Red River expedition came her great opportunity for distinction. She was chosen by Admiral Porter as his flagship for the return, as the falling water made it necessary to send the heavier vessels ahead with all speed. Porter with the "Cricket," "Fort Hindman," and "Juliet" remained behind to assist Lieutenant-Commander Phelps in his efforts to save the unlucky "Eastport." After getting the injured vessel about fifty miles down the river from Grand Écore, the tinclads were compelled to abandon her, since the river banks were now swarming with hostile forces bent on the capture of the entire squadron. About twenty miles below the wreck of the "Eastport," a Confederate battery had been planted and opened on the "tinclads." The other vessels retreated up-stream, but Porter on the "Cricket" forced his way through. It was all over in five minutes, but in that time the frail vessel was struck 38 times, and 19 shells pierced her. The pilot was wounded and Admiral Porter with great coolness and skill seized the wheel and saved the vessel. So furious was the fight while it lasted that out of the "Cricket's" crew of 50, twelve were killed and nineteen wounded.

COPYRIGHT, 1911, REVIEW OF REVIEWS CO.

FEDERAL GUNBOATS ON THE UPPER TENNESSEE

Federal success at Chattanooga made it important to patrol the upper Tennessee River, and a number of small gunboats were built for that purpose. They were actively engaged above Mussel Shoals in keeping open communications and convoying loaded transports. The "General Grant," under Acting Ensign J. Watson, with the other sturdy little vessels of the land-locked flotilla, aided in restoring order in the thinly settled districts along the river. She and the "General Burnside" engaged a battery which the Confederates had erected above Decatur, Ala., Dec. 12, 1864. On the 22d the "General Thomas" had a brush with some Confederate troops near the same place and they returned her fire with fury. Early in January of 1865 the "Grant," single-handed, silenced Confederate batteries at Guntersville and Beard's Bluff, Ala. Returning a few days later, she destroyed the entire town of Guntersville as punishment for hostile demonstrations against the gunboats. Thus these little vessels were kept busily at work till the close of the war. The "General Sherman" was commanded by Acting Master J. W. Morehead; her executive officer was G. L. McClung, by whose courtesy these fine pictures appear here. The vessels shown above, as they lay in the Tennessee near Bridgeport in March, 1865, are, from left to right, the "General Sherman," No. 60; the "General Thomas," No. 61; the "General Grant," No. 62; and the "General Burnside," No. 63; all named after the military leaders whose strategy had resulted in the recovery of Tennessee to the Union.

COPYRIGHT, 1911, REVIEW OF REVIEWS CO

GOVERNMENT STEAMBOAT USED ON THE UPPER TENNESSEE IN 1864–65

Squadron, as the Western Flotilla was now called, and had control of the river between Vicksburg and Port Hudson. Farragut once more entered the river and ran two vessels of his squadron past the works at Port Hudson on the 14th of March, 1863. In doing so, however, the old side-wheeler *Mississippi* grounded under the guns of the fort, where she was set on fire and abandoned. For weeks now the fleet was employed in assisting Grant's army that was slowly closing in upon Vicksburg, which stronghold was to fall on the 4th of July.

The expedition to Shreveport up the Red River, where the fleet under Porter cooperated with the troops under Banks, was a dire failure and came near resulting in a great loss to the squadron. The water in March, 1864, was exceedingly low, and many of the deep-draft vessels could not get above the rapids at Alexandria. However, with some thirty transports, fourteen of the gunboats were dragged up the stream, only to find themselves, when they wished to return at the end of April, helpless above the falls by the receding water. Their rescue, through the aid of the genius, resource, and indefatigable efforts of Lieutenant-Colonel Joseph Bailey, of the Fourth Wisconsin Volunteers, makes a thrilling story. He succeeded in damming the river, thus banking up the water, and by the 13th of May, amid the mighty cheers of the spectators and the lumbermen from Maine and Wisconsin who had built the helpful barrier, the twelve vessels which had been caught had passed down to safety. After Port Hudson fell, except for the Red River expedition, minor skirmishers, and the shelling of guerillas and batteries along the wooded shores, the operations of the navy on the Mississippi and its tributaries were practically over.

When the Federals occupied Chattanooga after the battle of Chickamauga, late in 1863, they needed gunboats on the upper Tennessee River, but none of Admiral Porter's fleet could cross the Mussel Shoals. So several light-draft vessels were built near Bridgeport. They were useful to the army, but saw little active service.

IX

THE ACTIONS WITH THE FORTS

A NAVY GUN ON LAND, 1863

THIS PIECE WAS PLACED ON MORRIS ISLAND IN THE ATTEMPT
TO REDUCE THE CHARLESTON FORTS

THE ACTIONS WITH THE FORTS

By Captain O. E. Hunt, U. S. A., and James Barnes

THE reduction and final capture of the Confederate strong-holds that guarded the important ports of entry of the Confederacy on the Atlantic coast and the Gulf were in every case a cooperation between the navy and the army, and to both belong the honor of the successful outcome, which, singly and alone, neither branch of the service could have accomplished.

The old brick and mortar fortress of Pulaski guarded the entrance to the Savannah River. Late in 1861, almost entirely through the use of the navy, the Federals had control of the Atlantic coast, and in the vicinity of Savannah their ships were patrolling the waters of Ossabaw and Wassaw sounds, and their gunboats had penetrated up the Edisto River in the direction of the city. But Pulaski's frowning guns afforded shelter for any blockade-runners that might succeed in eluding the blockading fleet. It was necessary to reduce this strong fortress before a stop could be put to the attempts of the venturesome runners. General Q. A. Gillmore directed the placing of batteries of rifled guns and mortars upon Big Tybee Island, and by the end of February, 1862, other batteries were erected in the rear of the fort, completely enfilading it.

On the 10th of April, 1862, thirty-six heavy rifled cannon and mortars began the bombardment, and after two days of uninterrupted firing, although the fort was gallantly defended, it was so badly battered that it was forced to surrender. But Fort McAllister, at the mouth of the Ogeechee, did not fall until W. T. Sherman had arrived at the end of his march from Atlanta and General Hazen's troops carried the battery by assault.

THE DEMOLISHED BARRIER—FORT PULASKI

These three pictures speak eloquently of the ruin wrought by the combined efforts of the army and navy to gain possession of Fort Pulaski. At the left an 8-inch smooth-bore points upward as the Confederates swung it for use as a mortar against the Federal batteries. Beside it lies one of the mortars, dismounted and rendered useless by the fire from the Federal batteries, while in the lower picture the huge breaches made in the walls of the fort are vividly apparent. It was no easy task to accomplish all this. Without the assistance of the navy it would have been impossible. The "web-footed" gunboats, as Lincoln called them, formed an essential part of the land expedition; floundering through mud, they protected the troops from Tattnall's flotilla while guns were dragged with difficulty over the marshy surface of Jones Island and placed in position. The doomed garrison refused to surrender on April 10, 1862, and for two days withstood a terrible bombardment from the thirty-six heavy-rifled cannon and mortars. Only when the battered fort became utterly untenable was it surrendered on April 12th to the besiegers that surrounded it, ready to open fire again.

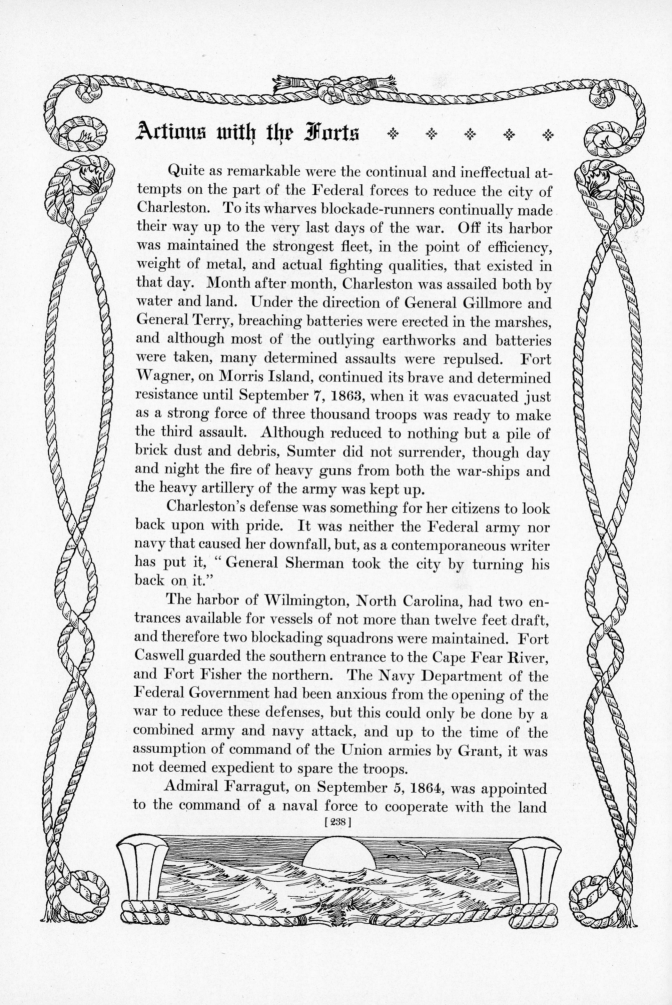

Actions with the Forts ❖ ❖ ❖ ❖ ❖

Quite as remarkable were the continual and ineffectual attempts on the part of the Federal forces to reduce the city of Charleston. To its wharves blockade-runners continually made their way up to the very last days of the war. Off its harbor was maintained the strongest fleet, in the point of efficiency, weight of metal, and actual fighting qualities, that existed in that day. Month after month, Charleston was assailed both by water and land. Under the direction of General Gillmore and General Terry, breaching batteries were erected in the marshes, and although most of the outlying earthworks and batteries were taken, many determined assaults were repulsed. Fort Wagner, on Morris Island, continued its brave and determined resistance until September 7, 1863, when it was evacuated just as a strong force of three thousand troops was ready to make the third assault. Although reduced to nothing but a pile of brick dust and debris, Sumter did not surrender, though day and night the fire of heavy guns from both the war-ships and the heavy artillery of the army was kept up.

Charleston's defense was something for her citizens to look back upon with pride. It was neither the Federal army nor navy that caused her downfall, but, as a contemporaneous writer has put it, "General Sherman took the city by turning his back on it."

The harbor of Wilmington, North Carolina, had two entrances available for vessels of not more than twelve feet draft, and therefore two blockading squadrons were maintained. Fort Caswell guarded the southern entrance to the Cape Fear River, and Fort Fisher the northern. The Navy Department of the Federal Government had been anxious from the opening of the war to reduce these defenses, but this could only be done by a combined army and navy attack, and up to the time of the assumption of command of the Union armies by Grant, it was not deemed expedient to spare the troops.

Admiral Farragut, on September 5, 1864, was appointed to the command of a naval force to cooperate with the land

HEROIC SACRIFICES AT CHARLESTON—THE FLOATING BATTERY AND THE "CHICORA"

It would have been almost sacrilege to retouch in any way the dim and faded photographs from which these pictures were made. Taken by a Confederate photographer at Charleston in the early part of the war, long lost to view, they preserve sights that inspired the men and women of the South with an intensity of purpose rarely exampled in history. In the upper picture is the famous floating battery built by subscription by the women of Charleston. Its guns were first fired in the attack on Fort Sumter that began the war. From that time forth every nerve was being strained by the Confederacy to put an ironclad flotilla in commission. South Carolina was conspicuous in its efforts to this end. Flag-Officer Duncan N. Ingraham superintended the navy-yard at Charleston and under his direction the "Palmetto State" and the "Chicora" were built. The keel of the latter was laid behind the Charleston post-office in March, 1862, and she was launched the following August. Five hundred tons of iron were required for her armor and the country was scoured by willing searchers for every scrap of metal that could be melted up. On January 31, 1863, the "Chicora" and the "Palmetto State" suddenly came down from Charleston and disabled both the "Mercedita" and the "Keystone State," receiving the former's surrender.

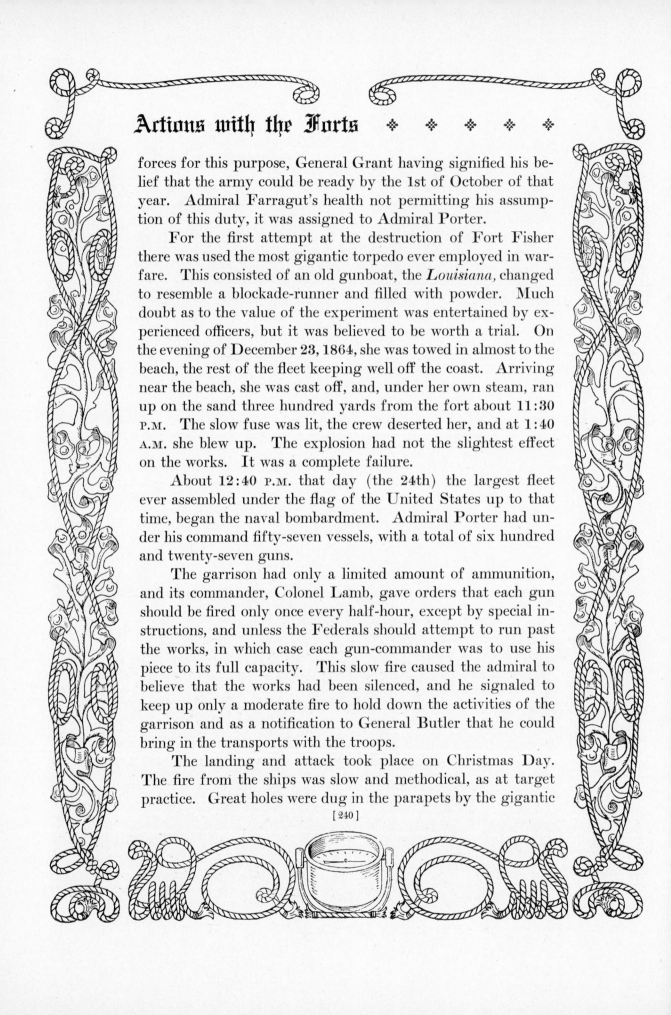

forces for this purpose, General Grant having signified his belief that the army could be ready by the 1st of October of that year. Admiral Farragut's health not permitting his assumption of this duty, it was assigned to Admiral Porter.

For the first attempt at the destruction of Fort Fisher there was used the most gigantic torpedo ever employed in warfare. This consisted of an old gunboat, the *Louisiana,* changed to resemble a blockade-runner and filled with powder. Much doubt as to the value of the experiment was entertained by experienced officers, but it was believed to be worth a trial. On the evening of December 23, 1864, she was towed in almost to the beach, the rest of the fleet keeping well off the coast. Arriving near the beach, she was cast off, and, under her own steam, ran up on the sand three hundred yards from the fort about 11:30 P.M. The slow fuse was lit, the crew deserted her, and at 1:40 A.M. she blew up. The explosion had not the slightest effect on the works. It was a complete failure.

About 12:40 P.M. that day (the 24th) the largest fleet ever assembled under the flag of the United States up to that time, began the naval bombardment. Admiral Porter had under his command fifty-seven vessels, with a total of six hundred and twenty-seven guns.

The garrison had only a limited amount of ammunition, and its commander, Colonel Lamb, gave orders that each gun should be fired only once every half-hour, except by special instructions, and unless the Federals should attempt to run past the works, in which case each gun-commander was to use his piece to its full capacity. This slow fire caused the admiral to believe that the works had been silenced, and he signaled to keep up only a moderate fire to hold down the activities of the garrison and as a notification to General Butler that he could bring in the transports with the troops.

The landing and attack took place on Christmas Day. The fire from the ships was slow and methodical, as at target practice. Great holes were dug in the parapets by the gigantic

COPYRIGHT, 1911, PATRIOT PUB. CO.

VIEW FROM FORT McALLISTER—UNION VESSELS IN THE ROADSTEAD

In this picture of December, 1864, the Federal vessels lie peaceful before the fort so impregnable to their attacks early the preceding year. The shore appearing below was lined with Georgia sharpshooters by Captain George W. Anderson, Jr., commander of the fort when the monitor "Montauk" and four gunboats advanced to the attack of Feb. 1, 1863. The "Montauk," under Commander John Lorimer Worden, hero of the original "Monitor," was the first Federal ironclad to arrive in Ossabaw Sound. Early on January 27th, it furiously attacked the fort. On this occasion the Federal vessels did not attempt to cross the line of piles and torpedoes. The Confederates were confident that in the second attack attempts would be made to land boat-parties to assault the works, and the sharpshooters were posted to prevent this. Commander Worden and his consorts, however, contented themselves with engaging the fort with their heavy guns and mortars. Although the Federals kept up a terrible fire, it failed to do more damage to the fort than could be repaired at night. The Confederate guns responded vigorously in kind, and the "Montauk" was struck forty-six times.

COPYRIGHT, 1911, PATRIOT PUB. CO.

IN FRONT OF THE PARAPET—FORT McALLISTER

COPYRIGHT, 1911, REVIEW OF REVIEWS CO

THE "HARTFORD" JUST AFTER THE BATTLE OF MOBILE BAY

QUARTERMASTER KNOWLES

This vivid photograph, taken in Mobile Bay by a war-time photographer from New Orleans, was presented by Captain Drayton of the "Hartford" to T. W. Eastman, U. S. N., whose family has courteously allowed its reproduction here. Never was exhibited a more superb morale than on the "Hartford" as she steamed in line to the attack of Fort Morgan at Mobile Bay on the morning of August 5, 1864. Every man was at his station thinking his own thoughts in the suspense of that moment. On the quarterdeck stood Captain Percival Drayton and his staff. Near them was the chief-quartermaster, John H. Knowles, ready to hoist the signals that would convey Farragut's orders to the fleet. The admiral himself was in the port main shrouds twenty-five feet above the deck. All was silence aboard till the "Hartford" was in easy range of the fort. Then the great broadsides of the old ship began to take their part in the awful cannonade. During the early part of the action Captain Drayton, fearing that some damage to the rigging might pitch Farragut overboard, sent Knowles on his famous mission. "I went up," said the old sailor, "with a piece of lead line and made it fast to one of the forward shrouds, and then took it around the admiral to the after shroud, making it fast there. The admiral said, 'Never mind, I'm all right,' but I went ahead and obeyed orders." Later Farragut, undoing the lashing with his own hands, climbed higher still.

COPYRIGHT, 1911, REVIEW OF REVIEWS CO.

FARRAGUT AT THE PINNACLE OF HIS FAME

Leaning on the cannon, Commander David Glasgow Farragut and Captain Percival Drayton, chief of staff, stand on the deck of the "Hartford," after the victory in Mobile Bay, of August, 1864. When Gustavus V. Fox, Assistant Secretary of the Navy, proposed the capture of New Orleans from the southward he was regarded as utterly foolhardy. All that was needed, however, to make Fox's plan successful was the man with spirit enough to undertake it and judgment sufficient to carry it out. Here on the deck of the fine new sloop-of-war that had been assigned to him as flagship, stands the man who had just accomplished a greater feat that made him a world figure as famous as Nelson. The Confederacy had found its great general among its own people, but the great admiral of the war, although of Southern birth, had refused to fight against the flag for which, as a boy in the War of 1812, he had seen men die. Full of the fighting spirit of the old navy, he was able to achieve the first great victory that gave new hope to the Federal cause. Percival Drayton was also a Southerner, a South Carolinian, whose brothers and uncles were fighting for the South.

WHERE THE CONFEDERATES FOUGHT FARRAGUT SHOT FOR SHOT

From these walls the gunners of Brigadier-General Richard L. Page, C. S. A., sighted their pieces and gave the Federal vessels shot for shot. It was a fight at close range, since the obstructions in the channel compelled the fleet to pass close under the guns of the fort. During the hour while the vessels were within range, the fort fired 491 shots, about eight a minute. When the fight was thickest the Confederate gunners fired even far more rapidly, enveloping the vessels, and especially the "Hartford" and the "Brooklyn," in a veritable hail of missiles. The fort was an old five-sided brick works mounting its guns in three tiers. It was built on the site of the little redoubt (Fort Bowyer) that had repelled the British fleet in 1814. Within the fort were mounted thirty-two smooth-bores and eight rifles.

COPYRIGHT, 1911, REVIEW OF REVIEWS CO.

INTERIOR OF FORT MORGAN, MOBILE BAY, IN 1864

The entire front wall was reënforced by enormous piles of sand-bags to enable its four feet eight inches of solid brick to withstand the broadsides of the fleet. Although the other fortifications at the entrance to Mobile Bay surrendered the day after the battle, it took more than Farragut's broadsides to reduce Fort Morgan. A siege-train had to be brought from New Orleans and a land attack made by the troops under General Gordon Granger, August, 22, 1864. Not till 3,000 missiles had been hurled into and around the fort by the combined guns of the army and navy did the brave garrison of Fort Morgan surrender after a gallant defense of twelve hours. In the picture some of the damaging effects of the terrific gunnery of the fleet are evident in the sea wall.

shells, until the whole face of the works began to take on the irregularity of the neighboring sand-dunes. The troops, about fifteen hundred men under command of General Weitzel, advanced their skirmish lines to within about seventy-five yards of the fort, capturing a small outwork and over two hundred men. By a personal reconnaissance, Weitzel ascertained that the two days' terrible bombardment by the fleet and the previous explosion of the powder-ship had done no practical injury to the parapets and interior. He therefore reported to Butler and to Admiral Porter that the works could not be taken by assault.

That evening, General Butler notified Admiral Porter that he was convinced that it was impossible to take the fort by assault as the naval fire had not damaged the works, and that he proposed to withdraw all his men and return to Fortress Monroe, which he did on the 27th. This ended the first combined attempt against Fort Fisher.

Admiral Porter was much disappointed at Butler's leaving him, and began to fear that the Confederates would abandon Fort Fisher and entrench themselves further up the river out of reach of his guns. So he attempted to deceive his foe. " I thought it best," he says, " under the circumstances, to let the enemy think we had abandoned the expedition entirely, and sent the fleet to a rendezvous off Beaufort, one or two at a time, to look as if they were crippled."

Evidently the Confederates did not anticipate the early return of the fleet. The supporting army was withdrawn to a point sixteen miles north of Wilmington. No lookout was kept up the coast, and, in consequence, the first tidings of the return were sent from Fort Fisher itself, when, on the evening of the 12th of January, 1865, its few defenders saw from the ramparts the Federal fleet returning.

At that time there were but eight hundred men in the garrison, and about one hundred of them were unfit for duty. The principal, and almost the only, organization represented was the Thirty-sixth North Carolina regiment. Sunrise revealed

COPYRIGHT 1911, REVIEW OF REVIEWS CO.

FORT MORGAN—A BOMBARDMENT BRAVELY ANSWERED

The battered walls of Fort Morgan, in 1864, tell of a terrific smashing by the Federal navy. But the gallant Confederates returned the blows with amazing courage and skill; the rapidity and accuracy of their fire was rarely equalled in the war. In the terrible conflict the "Hartford" was struck twenty times, the "Brooklyn" thirty, the "Octorora" seventeen, the "Metacomet" eleven, the "Lackawanna" five, the "Ossipee" four, the "Monongahela" five, the "Kennebec" two, and the "Galena" seven. Of the monitors the "Chickasaw" was struck three times, the "Manhattan" nine, and the "Winnebago" nineteen. The total loss in the Federal fleet was 52 killed and 170 wounded, while on the Confederate gunboats 12 were killed and 20 wounded. The night after the battle the "Metacomet" was turned into a hospital-ship and the wounded of both sides were taken to Pensacola. The pilot of the captured "Tennessee" guided the Federal ship through the torpedoes, and as she was leaving Pensacola on her return trip Midshipman Carter of the "Tennessee," who also was on the "Metacomet," called out from the wharf: "Don't attempt to fire No. 2 gun (of the "Tennessee"), as there is a shell jammed in the bore, and the gun will burst and kill some one." All felt there had been enough bloodshed.

COPYRIGHT 1911, REVIEW OF REVIEWS CO.

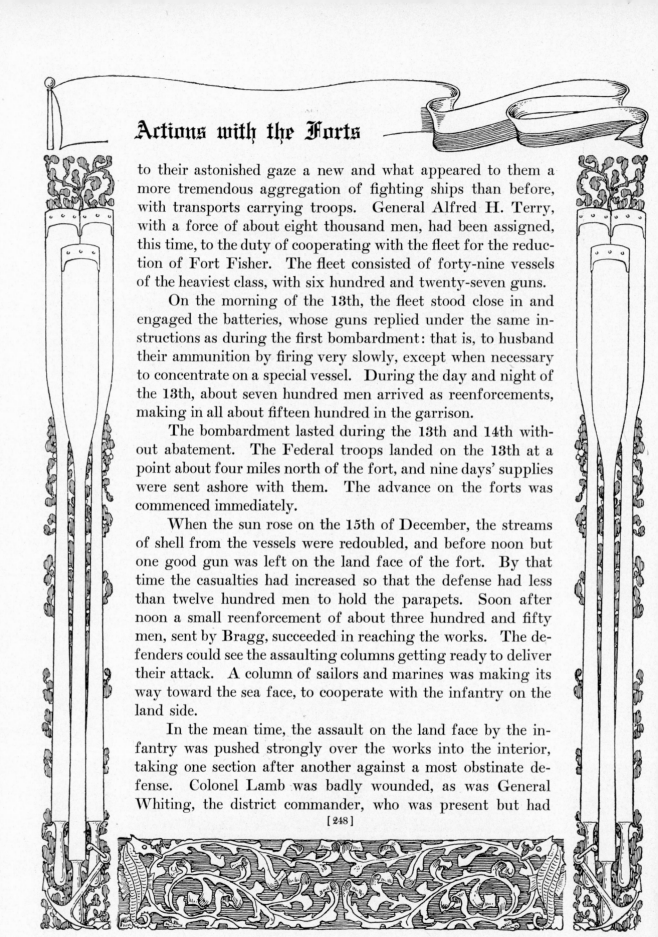

to their astonished gaze a new and what appeared to them a more tremendous aggregation of fighting ships than before, with transports carrying troops. General Alfred H. Terry, with a force of about eight thousand men, had been assigned, this time, to the duty of cooperating with the fleet for the reduction of Fort Fisher. The fleet consisted of forty-nine vessels of the heaviest class, with six hundred and twenty-seven guns.

On the morning of the 13th, the fleet stood close in and engaged the batteries, whose guns replied under the same instructions as during the first bombardment: that is, to husband their ammunition by firing very slowly, except when necessary to concentrate on a special vessel. During the day and night of the 13th, about seven hundred men arrived as reenforcements, making in all about fifteen hundred in the garrison.

The bombardment lasted during the 13th and 14th without abatement. The Federal troops landed on the 13th at a point about four miles north of the fort, and nine days' supplies were sent ashore with them. The advance on the forts was commenced immediately.

When the sun rose on the 15th of December, the streams of shell from the vessels were redoubled, and before noon but one good gun was left on the land face of the fort. By that time the casualties had increased so that the defense had less than twelve hundred men to hold the parapets. Soon after noon a small reenforcement of about three hundred and fifty men, sent by Bragg, succeeded in reaching the works. The defenders could see the assaulting columns getting ready to deliver their attack. A column of sailors and marines was making its way toward the sea face, to cooperate with the infantry on the land side.

In the mean time, the assault on the land face by the infantry was pushed strongly over the works into the interior, taking one section after another against a most obstinate defense. Colonel Lamb was badly wounded, as was General Whiting, the district commander, who was present but had

COPYRIGHT, 1911 REVIEW OF REVIEWS CO.

THE BRAVEST OF THE BRAVE—THE CONFEDERATE IRONCLAD RAM "TENNESSEE"

Mobile Bay, on the morning of August 5, 1864, was the arena of more conspicuous heroism than marked any naval battle-ground of the entire war. Among all the daring deeds of that day stands out superlatively the gallant manner in which Admiral Franklin Buchanan, C. S. N., fought his vessel, the "Tennessee." "You shall not have it to say when you leave this vessel that you were not near enough to the enemy, for I will meet them, and then you can fight them alongside of their own ships; and if I fall, lay me on one side and go on with the fight." Thus Buchanan addressed his men, and then, taking his station in the pilot-house, he took his vessel into action. The Federal fleet carried more power for destruction than the combined English, French, and Spanish fleets at Trafalgar, and yet Buchanan made good his boast that he would fight alongside. No sooner had Farragut crossed the torpedoes than Buchanan matched that deed, running through the entire line of Federal vessels, braving their broadsides, and coming to close quarters with most of them. Then the "Tennessee" ran under the guns of Fort Morgan for a breathing space. In half an hour she was steaming up the bay to fight the entire squadron single-handed. Such boldness was scarce believable, for Buchanan had now not alone wooden ships to contend with, as when in the "Merrimac" he had dismayed the Federals in Hampton Roads. Three powerful monitors were to oppose him at point-blank range. For nearly an hour the gunners in the "Tennessee" fought, breathing powder-smoke amid an atmosphere superheated to 120 degrees. Buchanan was serving a gun himself when he was wounded and carried to the surgeon's table below. Captain Johnston fought on for another twenty minutes, and then the "Tennessee," with her rudder and engines useless and unable to fire a gun, was surrendered, after a reluctant consent had been wrung from Buchanan, as he lay on the operating table.

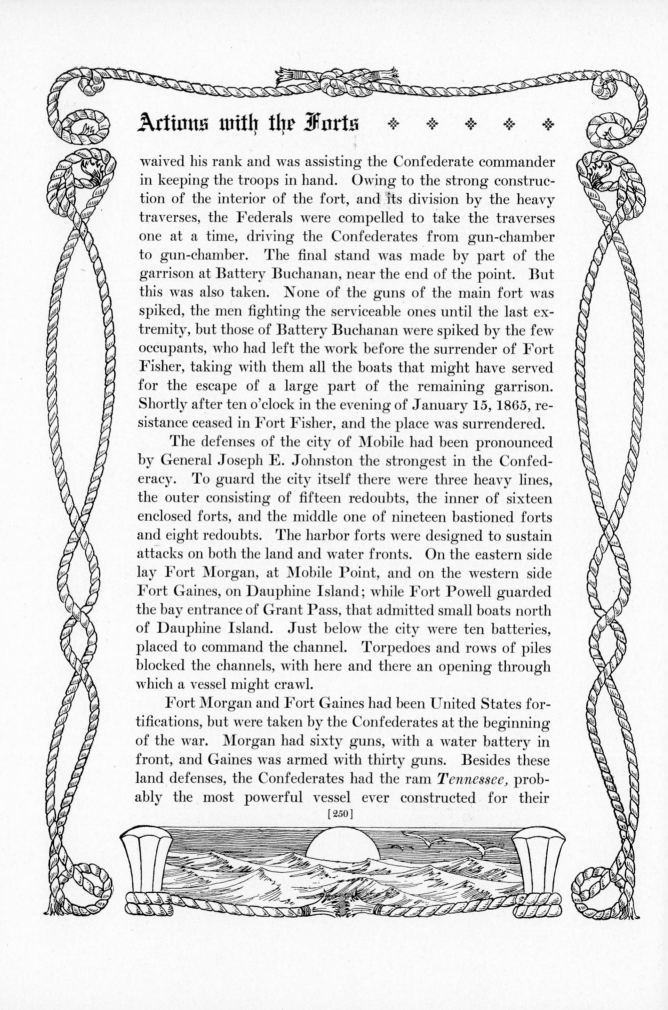

waived his rank and was assisting the Confederate commander in keeping the troops in hand. Owing to the strong construction of the interior of the fort, and its division by the heavy traverses, the Federals were compelled to take the traverses one at a time, driving the Confederates from gun-chamber to gun-chamber. The final stand was made by part of the garrison at Battery Buchanan, near the end of the point. But this was also taken. None of the guns of the main fort was spiked, the men fighting the serviceable ones until the last extremity, but those of Battery Buchanan were spiked by the few occupants, who had left the work before the surrender of Fort Fisher, taking with them all the boats that might have served for the escape of a large part of the remaining garrison. Shortly after ten o'clock in the evening of January 15, 1865, resistance ceased in Fort Fisher, and the place was surrendered.

The defenses of the city of Mobile had been pronounced by General Joseph E. Johnston the strongest in the Confederacy. To guard the city itself there were three heavy lines, the outer consisting of fifteen redoubts, the inner of sixteen enclosed forts, and the middle one of nineteen bastioned forts and eight redoubts. The harbor forts were designed to sustain attacks on both the land and water fronts. On the eastern side lay Fort Morgan, at Mobile Point, and on the western side Fort Gaines, on Dauphine Island; while Fort Powell guarded the bay entrance of Grant Pass, that admitted small boats north of Dauphine Island. Just below the city were ten batteries, placed to command the channel. Torpedoes and rows of piles blocked the channels, with here and there an opening through which a vessel might crawl.

Fort Morgan and Fort Gaines had been United States fortifications, but were taken by the Confederates at the beginning of the war. Morgan had sixty guns, with a water battery in front, and Gaines was armed with thirty guns. Besides these land defenses, the Confederates had the ram *Tennessee,* probably the most powerful vessel ever constructed for their

COPYRIGHT, 1911, REVIEW OF REVIEWS CO.

THE "MONONGAHELA"—A FEARLESS WOODEN SHIP

To this "heart of oak" belongs the distinction of being the first vessel to ram the huge Confederate ironclad "Tennessee." After Farragut, crying, "Damn the torpedoes!" had astounded both the Confederates and his own fleet by running the "Hartford" right through the line of submarine volcanoes, the "Tennessee" moved down with the intention of ramming the wooden ships in turn. She missed the "Hartford" and then the "Richmond," which escaped across the line of torpedoes like the flagship. In attempting to ram the "Lacka-wanna," the Confederate ironclad swung abeam of the channel, exposing her side full and fair to the "Mo-nongahela," which had been fitted with an artificial iron prow. Commander Strong endeavored to seize the opportunity to ram; but, owing to the fact that the "Kennebec" was lashed to her side, the "Mononga-hela" could not attain full speed, and only a glancing blow was struck. Later, when the "Tennessee" came up single-handed to attack the fleet above the forts, Farragut ordered the wooden vessels to try the effect of ramming the ironclad. Again the "Monongahela" was the first to advance to the attack and succeeded in striking the "Tennessee" fair amidships. So violent was the shock that many of the men on both vessels were knocked down. The blow, which would have sunk any vessel in the Federal fleet, did no more harm to the "Tennessee" than it did to the "Monongahela." Her iron prow was wrenched off and the butt-ends of her bow planks were shattered, while only a small leak was started in the "Tennessee."

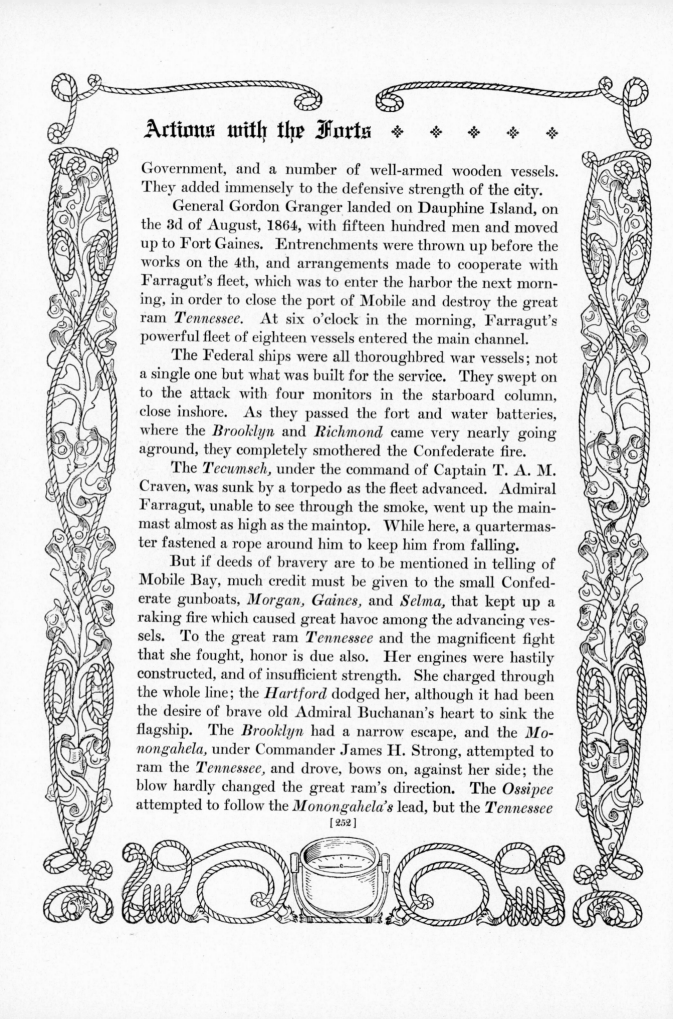

Actions with the Forts ✦ ✦ ✦ ✦

Government, and a number of well-armed wooden vessels. They added immensely to the defensive strength of the city.

General Gordon Granger landed on Dauphine Island, on the 3d of August, 1864, with fifteen hundred men and moved up to Fort Gaines. Entrenchments were thrown up before the works on the 4th, and arrangements made to cooperate with Farragut's fleet, which was to enter the harbor the next morning, in order to close the port of Mobile and destroy the great ram *Tennessee.* At six o'clock in the morning, Farragut's powerful fleet of eighteen vessels entered the main channel.

The Federal ships were all thoroughbred war vessels; not a single one but what was built for the service. They swept on to the attack with four monitors in the starboard column, close inshore. As they passed the fort and water batteries, where the *Brooklyn* and *Richmond* came very nearly going aground, they completely smothered the Confederate fire.

The *Tecumseh,* under the command of Captain T. A. M. Craven, was sunk by a torpedo as the fleet advanced. Admiral Farragut, unable to see through the smoke, went up the mainmast almost as high as the maintop. While here, a quartermaster fastened a rope around him to keep him from falling.

But if deeds of bravery are to be mentioned in telling of Mobile Bay, much credit must be given to the small Confederate gunboats, *Morgan, Gaines,* and *Selma,* that kept up a raking fire which caused great havoc among the advancing vessels. To the great ram *Tennessee* and the magnificent fight that she fought, honor is due also. Her engines were hastily constructed, and of insufficient strength. She charged through the whole line; the *Hartford* dodged her, although it had been the desire of brave old Admiral Buchanan's heart to sink the flagship. The *Brooklyn* had a narrow escape, and the *Monongahela,* under Commander James H. Strong, attempted to ram the *Tennessee,* and drove, bows on, against her side; the blow hardly changed the great ram's direction. The *Ossipee* attempted to follow the *Monongahela's* lead, but the *Tennessee*

COPYRIGHT, 1911 REVIEW OF REVIEWS CO.

LEADERS ON SEA AND LAND—FARRAGUT AND GRANGER AFTER THE BATTLE OF MOBILE BAY

This splendid picture shows the calm and finely-molded features of the great admiral just after the accomplishment of a feat which save in bravery o'er-topped his great achievement of the passage of the forts below New Orleans. There Farragut had done what was pronounced impossible, but at Mobile he had fought his way through dangers ten times more formidable. Here, with the modesty which ever characterized him, he sits within the captured Fort Gaines on Dauphin Island, discussing with General Gordon Granger plans for the combined attack by which Fort Morgan was taken on August 22, 1864. It was to Granger that Mobile finally surrendered·

passed between them, and made for the *Oneida,* which was not under steerageway.

It was at this exciting moment that the monitors drew up, and the *Winnebago,* forging ahead, took her position between the ram and her seemingly helpless prey. The Federal vessels had been hampered, in a measure, by being lashed side by side in couples, in the way that Farragut had run the batteries at Port Hudson, but now having passed the forts they began to cast off their lashings. Enabled, in the broader water, to maneuver and use their broadsides, they drove the little Confederate fleet before them, the *Selma* surrendering to the *Metacomet,* the *Gaines* being disabled and soon in flames. The *Morgan* sought the protection of Fort Morgan, and during the night steamed ahead to the inner harbor and anchored under the batteries protecting the city of Mobile. The Federal vessels, being now out of range of the forts, dropped anchor and their crews were sent to breakfast.

It was a meal that was never finished. Admiral Buchanan, who had passed through the whole Union line, stopped under the protecting guns of Fort Morgan and looked back up the bay. Turning to Commander Johnston, the brave old admiral, who had taught many of the commanders of the ships opposed to him their lessons in naval tactics, said, "Follow them up, Johnston; we can't let them off that way."

On came the *Tennessee,* one vessel against the entire Federal fleet! Signals flew from the flagship; the monitors were given orders to come into close action, and the *Monongahela, Lackawanna,* and *Ossipee,* which had false iron prows, were ordered to prepare to ram. The *Tennessee* was as unwieldy as a raft of logs; she made no attempt to dodge the blows of her more agile antagonists. The *Monongahela* struck her square amidships, with the only result that she carried away her own bow, and the *Lackawanna,* striking the *Tennessee* on the other side, suffered likewise. The Confederate ram was uninjured. The *Hartford* came bearing down upon her now; the ships met almost bows

THE FALLEN FORTRESS—TRAVERSES AT FORT FISHER IN 1865

COPYRIGHT, 1911, PATRIOT PUB. CO.

THE "MOUND"
AT
FORT FISHER

WHERE
BLOCKADE–RUNNERS
WERE SIGNALED

In the top picture appear six of the gun positions within Fort Fisher, from which the Confederates so long defied the blockading fleet covering the approach and departure of blockade-runners to and from Wilmington, N. C. Only after two powerful expeditions had been sent against it did the Federals finally gain possession of this well-constructed work. In the centre is seen a portion of the "Mound," an artificial eminence used as a lookout. It was on this that the light for the guidance of blockade-runners was established early in the war. The Confederates had destroyed all other aids to navigation along the coast, but it was of the utmost importance that vessels with cargoes for Wilmington should be able to make port and discharge their precious "ballast" in the form of munitions of war. In the view of the bomb-proof at the bottom of the page is evident the pains that have been taken to make the works impregnable. At the point where the brick chimney rises, the cooking for a section of the garrison was done in safety.

THE WELL-SHORED BOMB-PROOF

COPYRIGHT, 1911, PATRIOT PUB. CO.

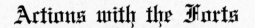

on, but the *Hartford's* anchor acted as a fender, and with their port sides touching, the two vessels scraped by each other. The solid 9-inch shot from the Federal flagship bounded off the *Tennessee's* sloping sides; she attempted to fire her broadside battery in turn, but her primers failed, and only one shot pierced the *Hartford's* side, exploding on the berth-deck, wounding an officer and killing several men.

In attempting to make a quick turn, with the object of again ramming, the *Hartford* came into collision with the *Lackawanna;* it was a narrow escape, for almost under the spot where Farragut was standing, the flagship was cut down within two feet of the water-line.

But now the monitors came up. From this minute on to the time that the *Tennessee* hauled down her flag, she never fired a shot and was literally hammered into submission. Even after the flag was lowered, the *Ossipee,* that had started another ramming charge and could not stop in time, struck her a slight blow. At the same moment the commanders of the two vessels recognized each other and passed a friendly hail. For over an hour the one-sided fight had been maintained. The *Tennessee* had lost two killed and nine wounded, and the Union fleet, in passing the forts and in the subsequent actions with the gunboats and the ram, had fifty-two killed and one hundred and seventy wounded. There were ninety-three lost by the sinking of the *Tecumseh.*

Fort Powell had been evacuated on the 5th, and Fort Gaines did not long survive the catastrophe to Buchanan's fleet. The siege was pressed, and the Confederates, appreciating that resistance was useless, asked for a truce to arrange terms of surrender. The arrangements were made on the 7th, and the surrender took place on the 8th.

The next day, General Granger moved his command, re-enforced by three new regiments, across the bay, landing at Navy Cove, four miles from Fort Morgan, on the bay side of Mobile Point. Each succeeding night slight advances were

COPYRIGHT, 1911, REVIEW OF REVIEWS CO.

PICKED MEN IN THE NAVY—PORTER AND HIS STAFF, DECEMBER, 1864

In this vivid portrait group of Admiral Porter and his staff, taken in December, 1864, appear the men selected by him to aid in accomplishing the fall of Fort Fisher and the conclusion of the navy's most important remaining tasks in the war. At the extreme left stands the young and indomitable Lieutenant W. B. Cushing, fresh from his famous exploit of blowing up the Confederate ram "Albemarle"; fifth from the left, with his arms folded, is Lieutenant-Commander K. R. Breese, another young officer scarcely less daring than Cushing and now Porter's fleet-captain. Lieutenant-Commander Henry A. Adams, Jr., stands on Porter's right. A number of volunteer officers are in the group. Porter was ever quick to recognize the bravery of the volunteers and their value to the service. From the decks of the "Malvern" (shown below) were directed the final operations at sea of the North Atlantic squadron in the war. Fort Fisher by 1864 had become the most formidable line of works in the Confederacy, and it was evident to the navy that this position at the mouth of the Cape Fear River, North Carolina, would have to be reduced if blockade-running into Wilmington was to be broken up. The first attack on Fort Fisher, December 24–25, 1864, was unsuccessful, owing to an unfortunate division in military authority in which General Benjamin F. Butler played an overweening part. After the second attack, January 13–15th, Admiral Porter, from the deck of the "Malvern," witnessed the gallant onslaught of General Terry's troops upon the land side of the fortifications, while 1,600 of his own sailors and 400 marines with pistol and cutlass tried to board the sea face. Amid the cheers of both army and navy, the news of the surrender of the garrison was received very soon afterward.

THE FLAGSHIP "MALVERN" AT NORFOLK

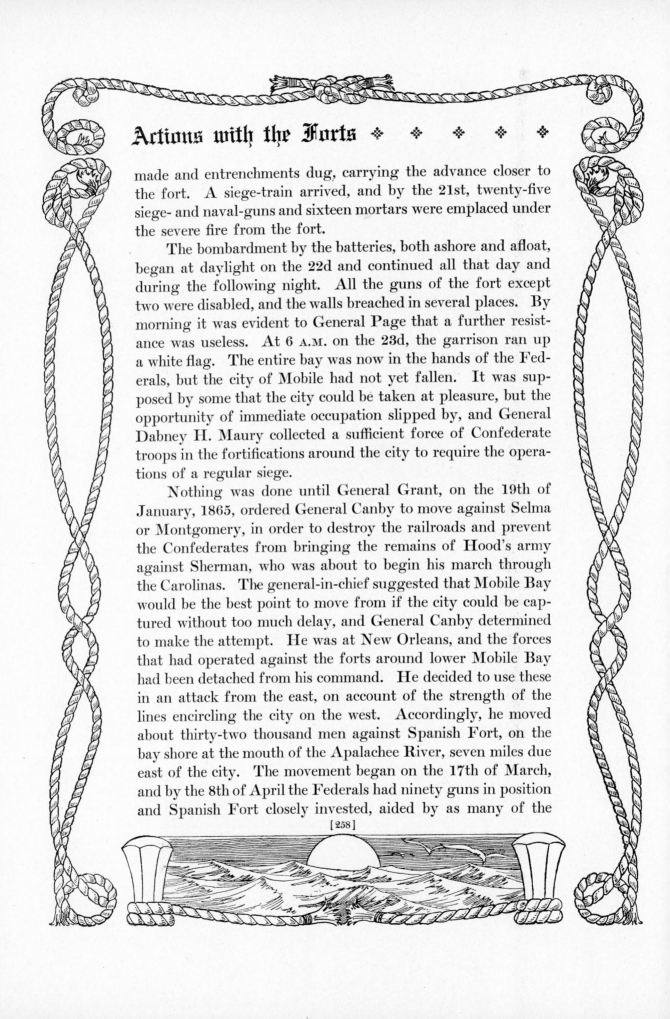

made and entrenchments dug, carrying the advance closer to the fort. A siege-train arrived, and by the 21st, twenty-five siege- and naval-guns and sixteen mortars were emplaced under the severe fire from the fort.

The bombardment by the batteries, both ashore and afloat, began at daylight on the 22d and continued all that day and during the following night. All the guns of the fort except two were disabled, and the walls breached in several places. By morning it was evident to General Page that a further resistance was useless. At 6 A.M. on the 23d, the garrison ran up a white flag. The entire bay was now in the hands of the Federals, but the city of Mobile had not yet fallen. It was supposed by some that the city could be taken at pleasure, but the opportunity of immediate occupation slipped by, and General Dabney H. Maury collected a sufficient force of Confederate troops in the fortifications around the city to require the operations of a regular siege.

Nothing was done until General Grant, on the 19th of January, 1865, ordered General Canby to move against Selma or Montgomery, in order to destroy the railroads and prevent the Confederates from bringing the remains of Hood's army against Sherman, who was about to begin his march through the Carolinas. The general-in-chief suggested that Mobile Bay would be the best point to move from if the city could be captured without too much delay, and General Canby determined to make the attempt. He was at New Orleans, and the forces that had operated against the forts around lower Mobile Bay had been detached from his command. He decided to use these in an attack from the east, on account of the strength of the lines encircling the city on the west. Accordingly, he moved about thirty-two thousand men against Spanish Fort, on the bay shore at the mouth of the Apalachee River, seven miles due east of the city. The movement began on the 17th of March, and by the 8th of April the Federals had ninety guns in position and Spanish Fort closely invested, aided by as many of the

COPYRIGHT, 1911, REVIEW OF REVIEWS CO.

ONE
THE NAVY LOST
LIEUTENANT SAM-
UEL W. PRESTON

This brave and promis-
ing young officer was an
ardent advocate of the
effectiveness of land de-
tachments of sailors and
marines against forts.
At Fort Fisher came the
coveted opportunity and
Preston paid for his be-
lief in it with his life.
The heavy loss on the
beach cast a gloom over
the navy despite the

success of the assaulting
column of soldiers under
General Terry. Ensign
(now Rear-Admiral) Rob-
ley D. Evans was one of
those severely wounded.
The 200-pounder Parrott
gun above was the for-
ward pivot-gun of the
"Wabash" and did as
much damage in the bom-
bardments of Fort Fisher
as any other single gun in
the fleet. The gun-crew
that served it was com-
posed of picked men
and every effective shot
aroused hearty cheers.

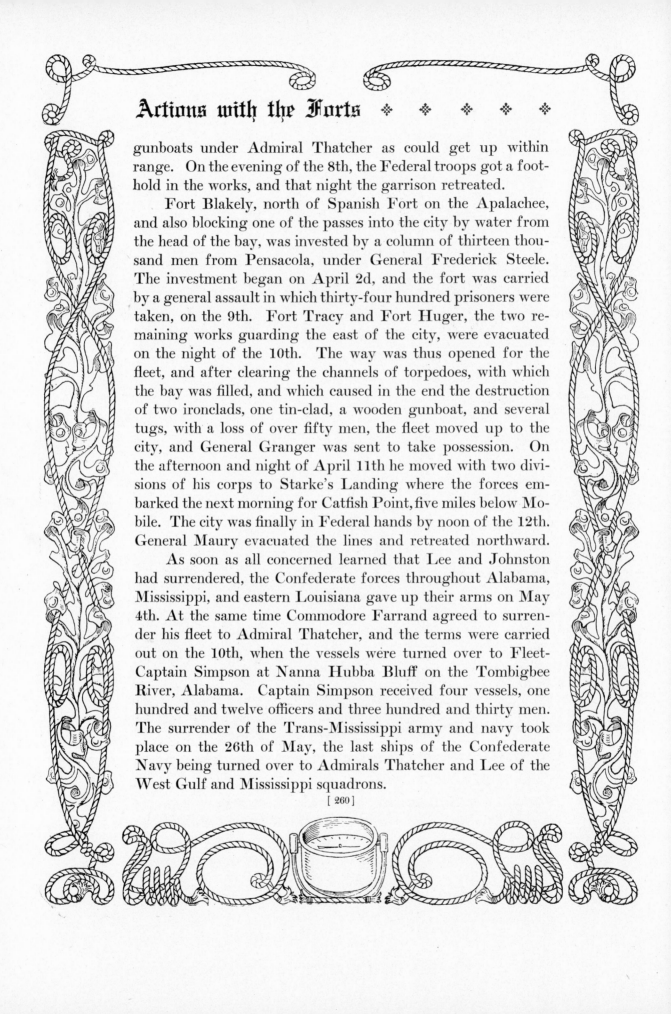

gunboats under Admiral Thatcher as could get up within range. On the evening of the 8th, the Federal troops got a foothold in the works, and that night the garrison retreated.

Fort Blakely, north of Spanish Fort on the Apalachee, and also blocking one of the passes into the city by water from the head of the bay, was invested by a column of thirteen thousand men from Pensacola, under General Frederick Steele. The investment began on April 2d, and the fort was carried by a general assault in which thirty-four hundred prisoners were taken, on the 9th. Fort Tracy and Fort Huger, the two remaining works guarding the east of the city, were evacuated on the night of the 10th. The way was thus opened for the fleet, and after clearing the channels of torpedoes, with which the bay was filled, and which caused in the end the destruction of two ironclads, one tin-clad, a wooden gunboat, and several tugs, with a loss of over fifty men, the fleet moved up to the city, and General Granger was sent to take possession. On the afternoon and night of April 11th he moved with two divisions of his corps to Starke's Landing where the forces embarked the next morning for Catfish Point, five miles below Mobile. The city was finally in Federal hands by noon of the 12th. General Maury evacuated the lines and retreated northward.

As soon as all concerned learned that Lee and Johnston had surrendered, the Confederate forces throughout Alabama, Mississippi, and eastern Louisiana gave up their arms on May 4th. At the same time Commodore Farrand agreed to surrender his fleet to Admiral Thatcher, and the terms were carried out on the 10th, when the vessels were turned over to Fleet-Captain Simpson at Nanna Hubba Bluff on the Tombigbee River, Alabama. Captain Simpson received four vessels, one hundred and twelve officers and three hundred and thirty men. The surrender of the Trans-Mississippi army and navy took place on the 26th of May, the last ships of the Confederate Navy being turned over to Admirals Thatcher and Lee of the West Gulf and Mississippi squadrons.

X

NAVAL ACTIONS
ALONG
THE SHORE

A BUSY SCENE ON THE JAMES, 1864

ARMY TUGS 4 AND 5 IN THE FOREGROUND; THE MONITOR "ONONDAGA" IN THE
OFFING—WITH GRANT AT CITY POINT, THE RIVER BECAME THE
ARTERY FOR ARMY AND NAVY COMMUNICATION

COPYRIGHT, 1911, REVIEW OF REVIEWS CO.

A FERRYBOAT READY FOR BATTLE

Take away the background of this picture of the "Commodore Perry," substitute for it the lonely shore of the Carolina sounds or the Virginia rivers lined with men in gray uniforms, and you have an exact reproduction of how this old converted ferryboat looked when going into action. Here the men have been called to quarters for gun-drill. The gun-captains are at their places and the crews with training lines in hand await the order from the officers above to aim and fire. Many times was this scene repeated aboard the "Commodore Perry" after she sailed with the motley fleet that Admiral Goldsborough led against Albemarle and Pamlico Sounds in January, 1862. In addition to her four 9-inch smooth-bores, the "Perry" carried a 12-pounder rifle and a 100-pounder rifle, it being the policy to equip the light-draft gunboats with the heaviest armament that they could possibly carry. Under command of the brave Lieutenant Charles W. Flusser, the guns of the "Perry" were kept hot as she skurried about the sounds and up the rivers, gaining a foothold for the Federal forces. Flusser, after a record of brilliant service in recovering inch by inch the waters of the Carolinas, lost his life in the "Miami" in the engagement with the "Albemarle."

COPYRIGHT, 1911, REVIEW OF REVIEWS CO.

AN EMERGENCY GUNBOAT FROM THE NEW YORK FERRY SERVICE

This craft, the "Commodore Perry," was an old New York ferryboat purchased and hastily pressed into service by the Federal navy to help solve the problem of patrolling the three thousand miles of coast, along which the blockade must be made effective. In order to penetrate the intricate inlets and rivers, light-draft fighting-vessels were required, and the most immediate means of securing these was to purchase every sort of merchant craft that could possibly be adapted to the purposes of war, either as a fighting-vessel or as a transport. The ferryboat in the picture has been provided with guns and her pilot-houses armored. A casemate of iron plates has been provided for the gunners. The Navy Department purchased and equipped in all one hundred and thirty-six vessels in 1861, and by the end of the year had increased the number of seamen in the service from 7,600 to over 22,000. Many of these new recruits saw their first active service aboard the converted ferryboats, tugboats, and other frail and unfamiliar vessels making up the nondescript fleet that undertook to cut off the commerce of the South. The experience thus gained under very unusual circumstances placed them of necessity among the bravest sailors of the navy.

The "Commodore Perry," under Lieutenant-Commander C. W. Flusser, was in the division of Commander Rowan, which distinguished itself at Roanoke Island. An old converted ferryboat, she was on the advance line of the action of February 10, 1862, when the signal for a dash at the Confederate gunboats was given. She pursued and captured the "Sea Bird," the flagship of Captain Lynch, C.S.N., upon that occasion, making prisoners of nearly all her officers and crew.

On July 9, 1862, she led two other frail gunboats up the Roanoke River on a reconnaissance. Commander Flusser's orders were to go to Hamilton; and despite the fact that the river banks were lined with sharpshooters, he braved their fire for ten hours, reached his destination, took possession of the Confederate steamer "Nelson," and returned with his prize. Flusser in the old "Perry" achieved a brilliant record on the shallow Carolina waters, where he finally lost his life.

A

PLUCKY

LIGHT–DRAFT

THE

"COMMODORE

PERRY"

THE NAVY ASHORE—CREW OF THE "FOSTER" WITH HOWITZERS

While the Federals with both army and navy closed in upon Richmond, heroic efforts were made by the Confederates to drive them back. Batteries were built along the river banks for the purpose of harassing the gunboats, and it was frequently necessary to land the crews of vessels—such as this detachment from the army gunboat "Foster," near Point of Rocks—in order effectually to drive off hostile detachments. In the lower picture the "Canonicus," one of the newer monitors, is seen coaling on the James. Under Commander E. G. Parrott, the "Canonicus" participated in the six-hour engagement with Battery Dantzler and the Confederate gunboats on June 21, 1864, and on August 16th and 18th, she, with other vessels, engaged the "Virginia" and the "Richmond" and Confederate troops under General R. E. Lee, to cover the

THE GUNBOAT "MASSASOIT"

advance of Federals under General Butler. The "Canonicus" participated in the Fort Fisher expedition, and to her belongs the honor of capturing the British blockade-runner "Deer" off Charleston, February 18, 1865. In the center appears the gunboat "Massasoit." In the last action that took place with the Confederate flotilla on the James, at Trent's Reach, January 24, 1865, it was the "Massasoit" that received the only damage from the guns of the hostile vessels and the battery at Howlett's house. In the two-hour action after the return of the "Onondaga" up-stream, five men on the "Massasoit" were wounded. She was one of the third-class double-ender armored vessels and mounted ten guns. During this action she was commanded by Lieutenant G. W. Sumner, who displayed the utmost coolness and bravery in handling his vessel.

THE MONITOR "CANONICUS"

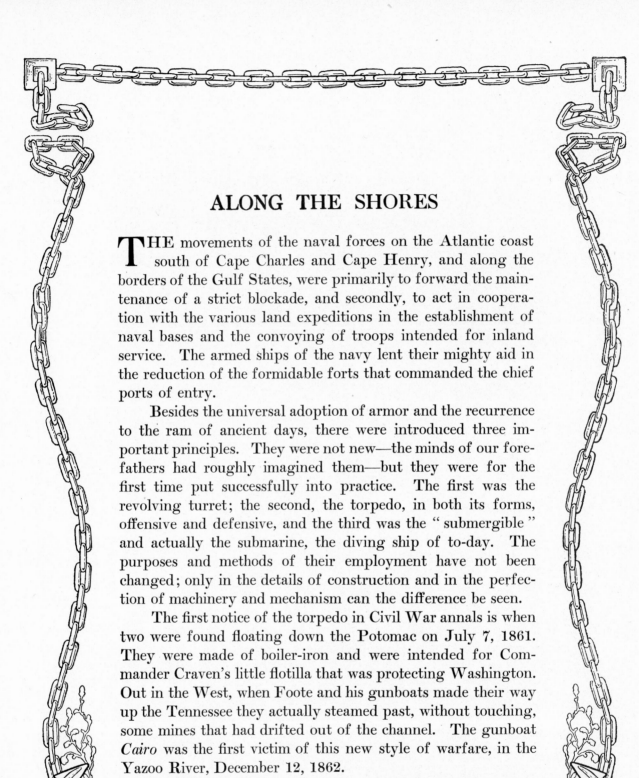

ALONG THE SHORES

THE movements of the naval forces on the Atlantic coast south of Cape Charles and Cape Henry, and along the borders of the Gulf States, were primarily to forward the maintenance of a strict blockade, and secondly, to act in cooperation with the various land expeditions in the establishment of naval bases and the convoying of troops intended for inland service. The armed ships of the navy lent their mighty aid in the reduction of the formidable forts that commanded the chief ports of entry.

Besides the universal adoption of armor and the recurrence to the ram of ancient days, there were introduced three important principles. They were not new—the minds of our forefathers had roughly imagined them—but they were for the first time put successfully into practice. The first was the revolving turret; the second, the torpedo, in both its forms, offensive and defensive, and the third was the " submergible " and actually the submarine, the diving ship of to-day. The purposes and methods of their employment have not been changed; only in the details of construction and in the perfection of machinery and mechanism can the difference be seen.

The first notice of the torpedo in Civil War annals is when two were found floating down the Potomac on July 7, 1861. They were made of boiler-iron and were intended for Commander Craven's little flotilla that was protecting Washington. Out in the West, when Foote and his gunboats made their way up the Tennessee they actually steamed past, without touching, some mines that had drifted out of the channel. The gunboat *Cairo* was the first victim of this new style of warfare, in the Yazoo River, December 12, 1862.

With the exception of the actions along the Potomac and in

[266]

THE BEGINNINGS OF SUBMARINE WARFARE

A CONFEDERATE PHOTOGRAPH OF '64—THE FIRST "DAVID," FIGURING IN AN HEROIC EXPLOIT

This peaceful scene, photographed by Cook, the Confederate photographer at Charleston, in 1864, preserves one of the most momentous inventions of the Confederate navy. Back of the group of happy children lies one of the "Davids" or torpedo-boats with which the Confederates made repeated attempts to destroy the Federal vessels in Charleston Harbor, and thus raise the blockade. The Confederates were the first to employ torpedoes in the war, at Aquia Creek, July 7, 1861. Captain F. D. Lee, C. S. N., was working on designs for a torpedo ram early in the war, and Captain M. M. Gray, C. S. N., in charge of the submarine defenses of Charleston, with a force of sixty officers and men under him, was particularly active in developing this mode of warfare. The "David" in the picture appears to be the first one built in the Confederacy; she was constructed at private expense by Theodore Stoney, of Charleston. She was driven by steam, and on the night of October 5, 1863, in command of Lieut. W. T. Glassell, with a crew of three volunteers from the Confederate gunboats, she succeeded in exploding a torpedo under the new "Ironsides," putting her out of commission for a time. The little "David" was almost swamped. Her crew took to the water to save themselves by swimming. Lieutenant Glassell and James Sullivan, fireman, were captured after being in the water nearly an hour. Engineer C. S. Tombs, seeing that the "David" was still afloat, swam back to her, where he found Pilot J. W. Cannon, who could not swim, clinging to her side. Tombs clambered aboard and pulled Cannon after him, and together they managed to build a fire under the boiler and bring the little vessel safely back to Charleston

Along the Shores ❖

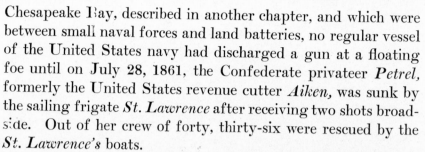

Chesapeake Bay, described in another chapter, and which were between small naval forces and land batteries, no regular vessel of the United States navy had discharged a gun at a floating foe until on July 28, 1861, the Confederate privateer *Petrel,* formerly the United States revenue cutter *Aiken,* was sunk by the sailing frigate *St. Lawrence* after receiving two shots broadside. Out of her crew of forty, thirty-six were rescued by the *St. Lawrence's* boats.

To the Federal navy belongs the honor of achieving the first signal success along the coast, in the bombardment and capture of Forts Hatteras and Clark at Hatteras Inlet, on the 28th and 29th of August, 1861. From Hatteras Inlet offensive operations could be carried on by means of light-draft vessels along the entire coast of North Carolina. The inlet was the key to Albemarle Sound, and was, besides, a good depot for outfitting and coaling, and a refuge, owing to its sheltered position, from the fierce winter storms that raged along the shore.

In the Gulf, there had been some skirmishing. The squadron under Captain John Pope that had been sent, after the escape of the *Sumter* to sea, to the mouth of the Mississippi, had a chance to bring on an action, in October, 1861, with several of the Confederate naval vessels. But Pope's ships got aground in the passes of the delta, and he and his captains exercising undue caution, refused offer of battle and made out into the Gulf. There were two brilliant bits of boat-work at Pensacola and Galveston. Lieutenant John H. Russell cut out and destroyed the unfinished Confederate privateer *Judah,* at the Pensacola Navy-Yard, on September 13, 1861, and Lieutenant James E. Jouett, of the frigate *Santee,* took and destroyed the privateer *Royal Yacht* in Galveston Harbor, in November.

Many were the gallant acts of the enlisted men and petty officers in the fighting along the shore. In the expedition under Flag-Officer Goldsborough against Roanoke Island, in February, 1862, there were two brave little fights between the

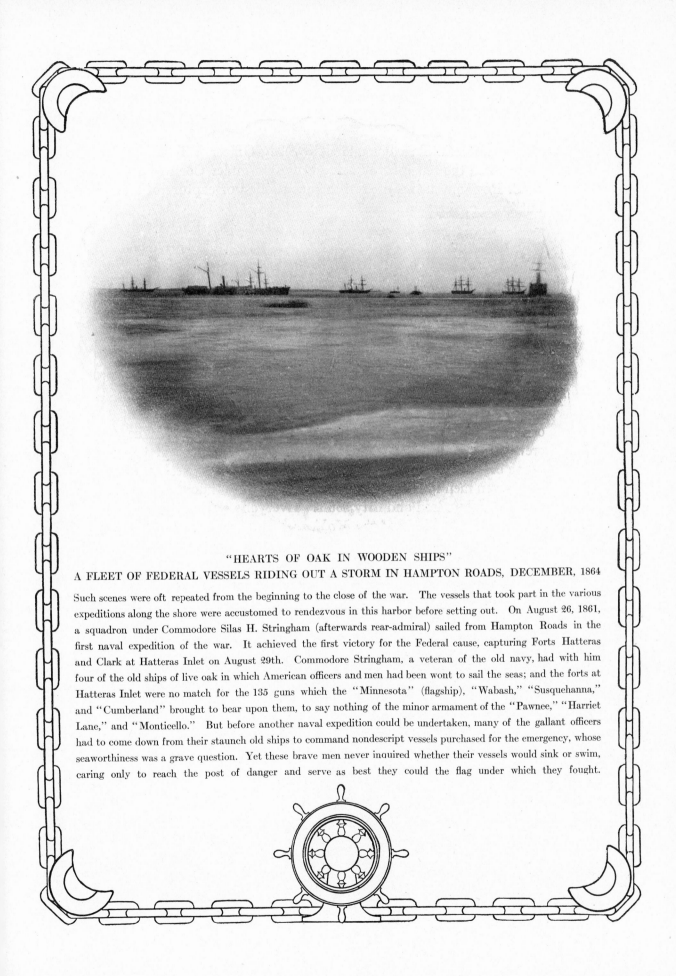

"HEARTS OF OAK IN WOODEN SHIPS"
A FLEET OF FEDERAL VESSELS RIDING OUT A STORM IN HAMPTON ROADS, DECEMBER, 1864

Such scenes were oft repeated from the beginning to the close of the war. The vessels that took part in the various expeditions along the shore were accustomed to rendezvous in this harbor before setting out. On August 26, 1861, a squadron under Commodore Silas H. Stringham (afterwards rear-admiral) sailed from Hampton Roads in the first naval expedition of the war. It achieved the first victory for the Federal cause, capturing Forts Hatteras and Clark at Hatteras Inlet on August 29th. Commodore Stringham, a veteran of the old navy, had with him four of the old ships of live oak in which American officers and men had been wont to sail the seas; and the forts at Hatteras Inlet were no match for the 135 guns which the "Minnesota" (flagship), "Wabash," "Susquehanna," and "Cumberland" brought to bear upon them, to say nothing of the minor armament of the "Pawnee," "Harriet Lane," and "Monticello." But before another naval expedition could be undertaken, many of the gallant officers had to come down from their staunch old ships to command nondescript vessels purchased for the emergency, whose seaworthiness was a grave question. Yet these brave men never inquired whether their vessels would sink or swim, caring only to reach the post of danger and serve as best they could the flag under which they fought.

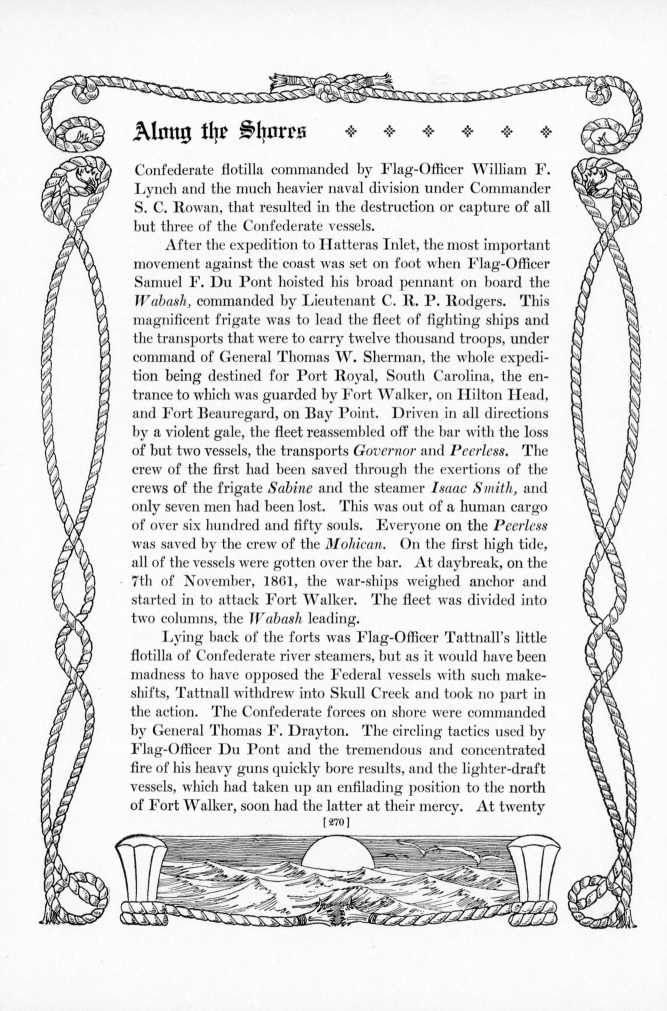

Confederate flotilla commanded by Flag-Officer William F. Lynch and the much heavier naval division under Commander S. C. Rowan, that resulted in the destruction or capture of all but three of the Confederate vessels.

After the expedition to Hatteras Inlet, the most important movement against the coast was set on foot when Flag-Officer Samuel F. Du Pont hoisted his broad pennant on board the *Wabash,* commanded by Lieutenant C. R. P. Rodgers. This magnificent frigate was to lead the fleet of fighting ships and the transports that were to carry twelve thousand troops, under command of General Thomas W. Sherman, the whole expedition being destined for Port Royal, South Carolina, the entrance to which was guarded by Fort Walker, on Hilton Head, and Fort Beauregard, on Bay Point. Driven in all directions by a violent gale, the fleet reassembled off the bar with the loss of but two vessels, the transports *Governor* and *Peerless.* The crew of the first had been saved through the exertions of the crews of the frigate *Sabine* and the steamer *Isaac Smith,* and only seven men had been lost. This was out of a human cargo of over six hundred and fifty souls. Everyone on the *Peerless* was saved by the crew of the *Mohican.* On the first high tide, all of the vessels were gotten over the bar. At daybreak, on the 7th of November, 1861, the war-ships weighed anchor and started in to attack Fort Walker. The fleet was divided into two columns, the *Wabash* leading.

Lying back of the forts was Flag-Officer Tattnall's little flotilla of Confederate river steamers, but as it would have been madness to have opposed the Federal vessels with such makeshifts, Tattnall withdrew into Skull Creek and took no part in the action. The Confederate forces on shore were commanded by General Thomas F. Drayton. The circling tactics used by Flag-Officer Du Pont and the tremendous and concentrated fire of his heavy guns quickly bore results, and the lighter-draft vessels, which had taken up an enfilading position to the north of Fort Walker, soon had the latter at their mercy. At twenty

COPYRIGHT, 1911, REVIEW OF REVIEWS CO.

MEN OF THE "UNADILLA," AFTER PLAYING THEIR PART IN THE NAVY'S CRUCIAL TEST

Under Lieutenant-Commander N. Collins, the "Unadilla" took part in the expedition that succeeded in capturing Port Royal, November 9, 1861. The "Unadilla" was but one of the fifty vessels that had assembled in Hampton Roads by October 27th to join the largest fleet ever commanded by an officer of the American navy up to that time. In contrast to the number of the vessels was the nondescript character of most of them. The "Unadilla" is described officially as a steam gunboat, but she was typical of the sort of hastily converted vessels that made up the fleet—river steamers, ferryboats, tugs, almost anything that would turn a wheel or propeller. These frail craft, loaded down with heavy guns, set forth in the face of foul weather to engage in battle for the first time with two of the strongest fortifications of the Confederacy. It was a momentous trial of wooden ships against most formidable earthworks. But Flag-Officer Du Pont, who possessed in an eminent degree all the qualities of a great commander, succeeded in demonstrating to Europe that even with a fleet of so uncertain a character the American navy could win by a masterly plan of battle, originated by him.

THE "UNADILLA"

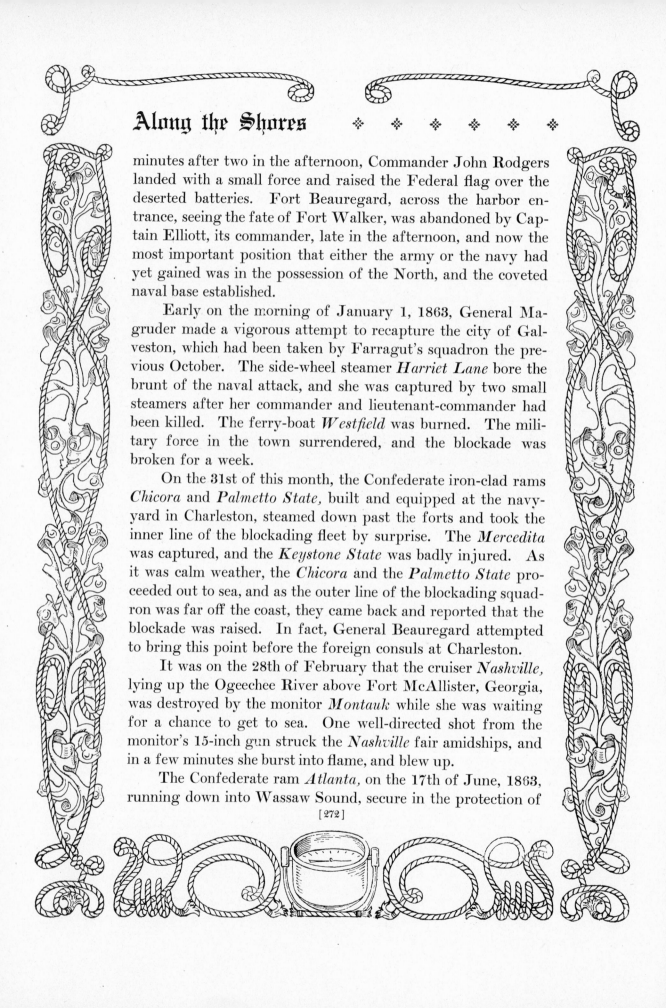

minutes after two in the afternoon, Commander John Rodgers landed with a small force and raised the Federal flag over the deserted batteries. Fort Beauregard, across the harbor entrance, seeing the fate of Fort Walker, was abandoned by Captain Elliott, its commander, late in the afternoon, and now the most important position that either the army or the navy had yet gained was in the possession of the North, and the coveted naval base established.

Early on the morning of January 1, 1863, General Magruder made a vigorous attempt to recapture the city of Galveston, which had been taken by Farragut's squadron the previous October. The side-wheel steamer *Harriet Lane* bore the brunt of the naval attack, and she was captured by two small steamers after her commander and lieutenant-commander had been killed. The ferry-boat *Westfield* was burned. The military force in the town surrendered, and the blockade was broken for a week.

On the 31st of this month, the Confederate iron-clad rams *Chicora* and *Palmetto State,* built and equipped at the navy-yard in Charleston, steamed down past the forts and took the inner line of the blockading fleet by surprise. The *Mercedita* was captured, and the *Keystone State* was badly injured. As it was calm weather, the *Chicora* and the *Palmetto State* proceeded out to sea, and as the outer line of the blockading squadron was far off the coast, they came back and reported that the blockade was raised. In fact, General Beauregard attempted to bring this point before the foreign consuls at Charleston.

It was on the 28th of February that the cruiser *Nashville,* lying up the Ogeechee River above Fort McAllister, Georgia, was destroyed by the monitor *Montauk* while she was waiting for a chance to get to sea. One well-directed shot from the monitor's 15-inch gun struck the *Nashville* fair amidships, and in a few minutes she burst into flame, and blew up.

The Confederate ram *Atlanta,* on the 17th of June, 1863, running down into Wassaw Sound, secure in the protection of

COPYRIGHT, 1911, PATRIOT PUB. CO.

A FEARLESS BLOCKADER—U. S. S. "KANSAS"

This little screw steamer, under Lieutenant-Commander P. G. Watmough, with four other vessels no more formidable than she, stood her ground when the great ironclad ram "Raleigh" came down from Wilmington on May 7, 1864, and attempted to raise the blockade at the mouth of the Cape Fear River. The "Raleigh" trained her ten guns on the little vessels for nine hours. But they replied with vigor, and finally Flag-Officer W. F. Lynch, C. S. N., under whose direction the "Raleigh" had been built, judged it best to retire, since she was hardly in a state of completion to warrant coming to close quarters. To the "Kansas" belongs the honor of capturing the famous blockade-runner "Tristram Shandy," May 15, 1864. The "Tristram Shandy" afterward became despatch vessel to Porter's fleet.

her heavy armor and big guns, was pounded into submission by the monitors *Weehawken* and *Nahant,* and surrendered after a stubborn defense.

The many attempts to gain possession of Charleston Harbor, that were animated as much by sentimental reasons as they were dictated by military necessity, were crowned by at least one success. Part of Morris Island was evacuated by the Confederates on September 7th. The enfilading and breaching batteries in the swamps, together with the combined efforts of the ironclads and other vessels, had not succeeded in the reduction of Fort Sumter. Every kind of invention was tried by the inhabitants of Charleston to raise the blockade. Floating mines were sent out on the receding tides by the score; many were anchored at night in places where the day before the Federal vessels had occupied vantage spots in the bombardment.

On September 6th it was that the *New Ironsides,* directly off Fort Wagner, lay over a huge mine whose two thousand pounds of powder would have been sufficient to have torn her in two. On shore, the engineering officer who had placed the mine and laid the wires, surrounded by a large body of officers, was making every effort to produce the contact that would destroy the hostile ironclad. It was all in vain. By the most miraculous circumstances the wagons that had been driven along the beach to gather sand for the reenforcement of the parapet had rubbed off the insulation of the wires, and they would not work.

It was now that the invention of the torpedo-boat and the submergible came to be enforced on the attention of the public. In all the history of any war there will be found no such record of continuous daring and almost certain death as is to be found in the story of the *H. L. Hunley,* the first submarine boat. This vessel, a cylindrical, cigar-shaped craft only thirty-five feet in length, could actually dive and be propelled under water and rise to the surface. The motive power was furnished by the crew, who, sitting *vis-à-vis* on benches, turned a crank

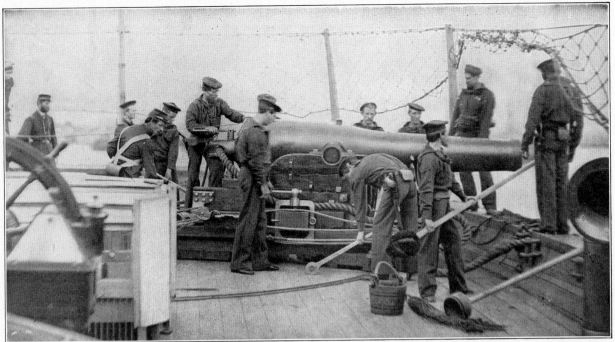

COPYRIGHT, 1911, REVIEW OF REVIEWS CO.

From the time General Grant established his headquarters at City Point, there was no rest for the gunboats in the James River. There was an active and determined foe to contend with, and alertness was the watchword for every officer and man in the Federal flotilla. Underneath, one of the huge 100-pounder Parrott guns is being brought into position on the gunboat "Mendota" in July,

1864, ready to be trained upon the Confederates whenever they attempted to plant batteries along the shores. The work of the "Mendota's" gunners on July 28th at Four Mile Creek spoke eloquently of their coolness and accuracy of aim. With equal smartness, and scarcely more excitement than is apparent in the picture above, they served their guns under fire of shot and shell.

CONSTANT

PREPAREDNESS

ON THE

"MENDOTA"

1864

LOOKING ALONG

THE

100-LB

PARROTT

GUN

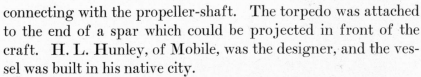

Along the Shores ❖

connecting with the propeller-shaft. The torpedo was attached
to the end of a spar which could be projected in front of the
craft. H. L. Hunley, of Mobile, was the designer, and the vessel was built in his native city.

After several unsuccessful and fatal attempts at Mobile
and Charleston, Hunley went to the latter city to take command
of his invention in person. Volunteers seemed easy to find, for
he picked six men, and starting out in the harbor made several
spectacular dives. She was gone overlong on one of these. It
was a week before she was brought to the surface. Her inventor and all of his crew were huddled together under one of
the manholes. Nothing daunted, Lieutenant George E. Dixon,
a friend of the boat's inventor, got together another crew, and
on the 17th of February, 1864, silently they moved out to where
the fine sloop-of-war *Housatonic* was lying at anchor. The
torpedo plunged against her side and exploded, blew her almost
out of the water and she sank immediately. But the little
Hunley never returned. She found a resting-place on the
ocean bed beside her gigantic victim.

On the 27th of October, 1864, the indomitable Lieutenant
W. B. Cushing, who had been constantly proposing wonderful
and almost impossible things, succeeded in getting eight miles
up the Roanoke River in North Carolina and sinking, in an
open launch, with a torpedo, the Confederate ram *Albemarle*.

The gunboat *Otsego* ran afoul of a torpedo in the Roanoke
River on December 9th and went to the bottom, and after the
fall of the last fort, Fort Fisher, the *Patapsco* was sunk in
Charleston Harbor, January 15, 1865, and officers and crew
were lost to the number of sixty. Still later in the war, in April,
the monitors *Milwaukee* and *Osage* suffered a like fate. They
were in Admiral Thatcher's fleet that was assisting Generals
Canby and Steele in the capture of Mobile. After the forts had
been taken by the army, the war-ship advanced up the torpedo-
filled channel. A tin-clad, a wooden gunboat, and several tugs
were also blown up before the ships anchored off the city.

[276]

XI

THE SEA LIFE
OF '61

A "POWDER-MONKEY" ON A DEEP-SEA CRAFT

This smart little "monkey" is a sailor, every inch.   In the old navy, the powder, before the days of "fixed ammunitions," was brought up in canvas bags or powder buckets, and during an action these brave little fellows were constantly on the run from their divisions to the magazine.   Under the break of the poop-deck behind the little lad are to be seen the cutlasses that every sailor wore in the old days and that have now disappeared from the service.

THE MEN OF THE "MENDOTA"

Gathered here on the after-deck are the crew of the gunboat "Mendota," some busy at banjo-playing, checkers, and other diversions more idle. More than one nationality is represented. Although there are many men who probably have followed no other calling than that of the seaman, there are doubtless men from inland towns and farms who, flocking to the seaports, had chosen to enlist in the service. But there is another reason for the foreign-looking faces; the higher pay of the United States navy and the chance for adventure and prize money had caused a good many foreign ships to find it difficult to procure merchant-sailors. Englishmen,

COPYRIGHT, 1911, REVIEW OF REVIEWS CO.

AN IDLE HOUR ON THE AFTER-DECK

Swedes and Norwegians, Danes, Russians, Germans, Frenchmen, Spaniards, and Portugese were to be found on almost every United States ship. To a certain extent sea-language, so far as the terms and orders are concerned, are the same the world over. There was no educational qualification required. Some of the seamen could scarcely speak English. In the foreground is a marine and an able seaman playing the jack-tar's favorite game of checkers, while a bright-faced little "powder-monkey," leaning picturesquely against the capstan, has looked up to pose for the camera man who has preserved this typical scene of the sailors' idle hour.

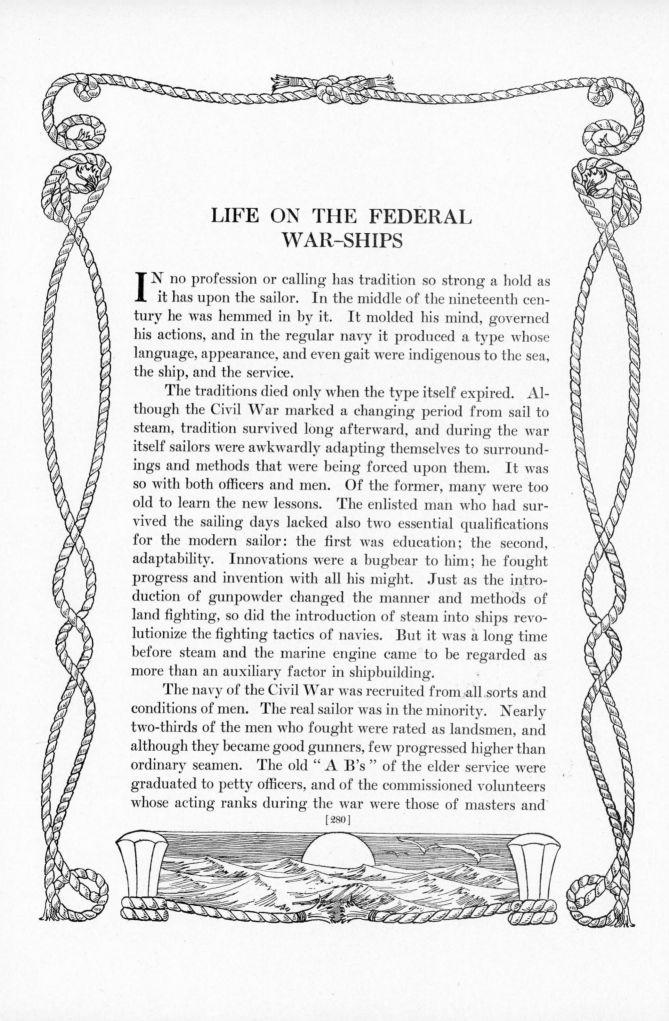

LIFE ON THE FEDERAL
WAR-SHIPS

IN no profession or calling has tradition so strong a hold as it has upon the sailor. In the middle of the nineteenth century he was hemmed in by it. It molded his mind, governed his actions, and in the regular navy it produced a type whose language, appearance, and even gait were indigenous to the sea, the ship, and the service.

The traditions died only when the type itself expired. Although the Civil War marked a changing period from sail to steam, tradition survived long afterward, and during the war itself sailors were awkwardly adapting themselves to surroundings and methods that were being forced upon them. It was so with both officers and men. Of the former, many were too old to learn the new lessons. The enlisted man who had survived the sailing days lacked also two essential qualifications for the modern sailor: the first was education; the second, adaptability. Innovations were a bugbear to him; he fought progress and invention with all his might. Just as the introduction of gunpowder changed the manner and methods of land fighting, so did the introduction of steam into ships revolutionize the fighting tactics of navies. But it was a long time before steam and the marine engine came to be regarded as more than an auxiliary factor in shipbuilding.

The navy of the Civil War was recruited from all sorts and conditions of men. The real sailor was in the minority. Nearly two-thirds of the men who fought were rated as landsmen, and although they became good gunners, few progressed higher than ordinary seamen. The old " A B's " of the elder service were graduated to petty officers, and of the commissioned volunteers whose acting ranks during the war were those of masters and

COPYRIGHT, 1911, REVIEW OF REVIEWS CO.

AMUSEMENT DURING THE BLOCKADE

MINSTRELS ON THE FLAGSHIP "WABASH"

A ship's company is a little world by itself. As one of the principal objects of the inhabitants of the earth is to amuse themselves, so it is with the crew of a vessel at sea. The man who can sing, dance, play the banjo or the fiddle is always sure of an appreciative audience in the hours off duty. On many of the larger craft there were formed orchestras, amateur theatrical companies, and minstrel troupes who used to get together to rehearse, and gave entertainments to which very often the officers of all the ships of the fleet were glad to be invited. Time grew heavy and the hours lagged in each other's laps during the tedious blockade. The flagship "Wabash" became renowned throughout the fleet for her minstrels, whose good music and amusing songs helped to pass many a long evening. On more than one occasion regular balls were given that, although not attended by the fair sex, did not lack in gaiety. "A busy ship is a happy one," is an old adage with sea-faring men, but the wise captain was he who remembered also an old saying well known and equally true both afloat and ashore: "All work and no play makes Jack a dull boy."

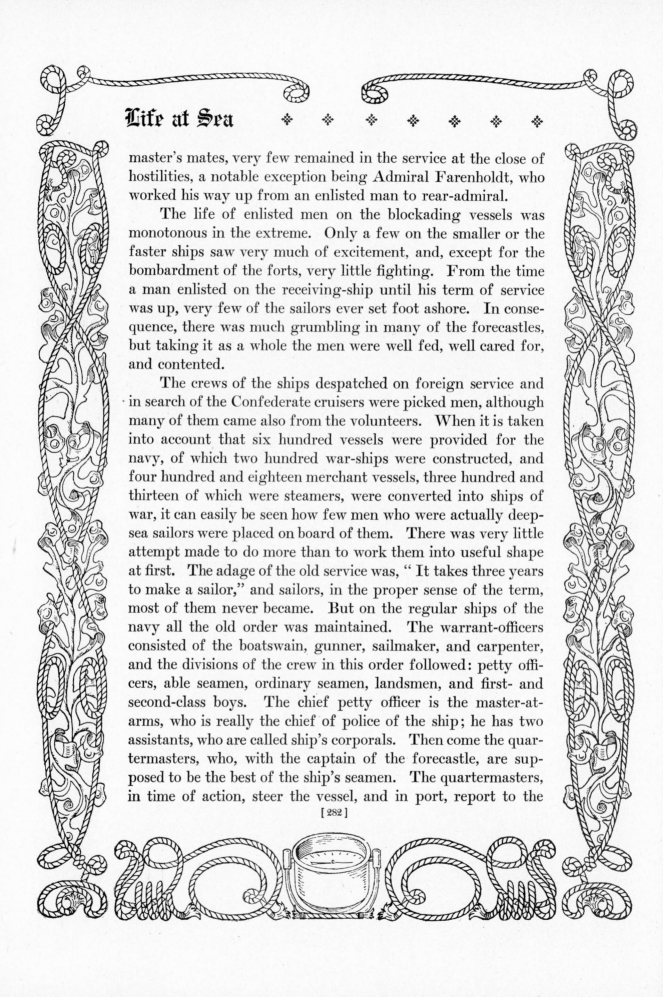

master's mates, very few remained in the service at the close of hostilities, a notable exception being Admiral Farenholdt, who worked his way up from an enlisted man to rear-admiral.

The life of enlisted men on the blockading vessels was monotonous in the extreme. Only a few on the smaller or the faster ships saw very much of excitement, and, except for the bombardment of the forts, very little fighting. From the time a man enlisted on the receiving-ship until his term of service was up, very few of the sailors ever set foot ashore. In consequence, there was much grumbling in many of the forecastles, but taking it as a whole the men were well fed, well cared for, and contented.

The crews of the ships despatched on foreign service and in search of the Confederate cruisers were picked men, although many of them came also from the volunteers. When it is taken into account that six hundred vessels were provided for the navy, of which two hundred war-ships were constructed, and four hundred and eighteen merchant vessels, three hundred and thirteen of which were steamers, were converted into ships of war, it can easily be seen how few men who were actually deep-sea sailors were placed on board of them. There was very little attempt made to do more than to work them into useful shape at first. The adage of the old service was, " It takes three years to make a sailor," and sailors, in the proper sense of the term, most of them never became. But on the regular ships of the navy all the old order was maintained. The warrant-officers consisted of the boatswain, gunner, sailmaker, and carpenter, and the divisions of the crew in this order followed: petty officers, able seamen, ordinary seamen, landsmen, and first- and second-class boys. The chief petty officer is the master-at-arms, who is really the chief of police of the ship; he has two assistants, who are called ship's corporals. Then come the quartermasters, who, with the captain of the forecastle, are supposed to be the best of the ship's seamen. The quartermasters, in time of action, steer the vessel, and in port, report to the

COPYRIGHT, 1911, PATRIOT PUB. CO.

"AL FRESCO" COOKING ON THE FAMOUS "MONITOR"

This is the deck of the original "Monitor," with part of the crew that had participated in the fight in Hampton Roads. The savory smoke is blowing away from the fire, where the ship's cook is preparing the mid-day meal. The crew are awaiting the mess-call, and in the foreground are seated two of the fire-room force. There was one thing that the men on the monitors had a right to complain of: it was the intense heat generated between decks after a day's exposure to the sun. It was difficult to obtain proper ventilation in this class of vessel at the best. The wooden ships, with their high top sides, their hanging "wind sails" or canvas ventilators, and their ranges of open ports, admitted the free passage of the air; but in the iron-decked mon-

itors, whose metal plating often got so hot that it was almost scorching to the feet, the fire-rooms, the galley, and the men's sleeping-quarters became almost unbearable. In still water, while on blockading duty, it became customary for the ship's cook to prepare the men's messes up on deck, and for this purpose stoves were erected that could be easily taken below in time of action, and the men took their meals *al fresco* in the open air. The crew of the "Monitor" were picked men, in a sense, for they were all old sailors who had volunteered for the unknown work that lay before them. Their devotion to the officers who had brought them so successfully through the famous engagement was little short of worship; it is sad to think that most of these men went down with their vessel when she foundered in the storm off Hatteras a few weeks after this picture was taken.

officer of the deck, taking care of signals and other movements in the harbor. Boatswains' mates are assistants to the boatswain, and the medium through which the officers' orders are communicated to the crew. The gunners' mates and quarter-gunners have the guns and all their paraphernalia under their especial charge; to each gun-deck there is a gunner's mate, and a quarter-gunner to each division. The crew proper is divided primarily into two watches, starboard and port watch; and secondarily into subdivisions which in the old days were entitled forecastlemen, foretopmen, maintopmen, mizzentopmen, afterguard, and waisters.

The ship's guns were divided into divisions, each generally under command of a lieutenant, assisted by a midshipman, and to each gun was assigned a crew that, in the muzzle-loading days, was made up of (for the heavier guns) one captain, one second captain, two loaders, two rammers and spongers, four side-tacklemen, five train-tacklemen, and a powder-boy—sixteen in all. Their names indicate distinctly their positions at the gun in action.

On board the faster vessels which acted as scouts on the outer line of the blockading squadrons, things often reached a pitch of great excitement. The appearance of low-lying, black lines of smoke against the horizon late in the afternoon was a sure precursor of the dash of a runner, either to make port or to reach shoal water along the beach—anyhow, to get through if possible. Rich as were the hauls, however, when the vessel was captured, they did not begin to compare in value with those taken from outward-bound blockade-runners loaded with cotton. Some of the blockading vessels had once been in the very business themselves, and there are instances of chases lasting fifty-six hours before the runner either escaped or was brought to, with most of her cargo jettisoned. In 1863, one noted blockade-runner loaded to the gunwales with cotton, brought as prize-money to the captain of the vessel that captured her twenty thousand dollars, and even the cabin-boys

WILLIAM YOUNG
GUNNER'S MATE
OF THE
"ESSEX"

Below appear four picked men from the crew of the "Essex." Seated on the right in the front row is "Bill Young," the medal of honor man whose portrait appears above. W. L. Park, to his left, was a quarter gunner, as were Thomas T. Drew, standing to the right, and Gordon F. Terry beside him. All four are typical faces of the best that service in the inland navy could produce. The firm features of these men tell of a simple heroism that so often rose to great heights in the battles of the gunboats. These men fought under "Bill" (Com. W. D.) Porter, elder brother of the admiral, in a ship named after the famous flagship of their father, Commodore David Porter, in the War of 1812. In that old namesake Farragut had his first training as a fighter and about the newer "Essex" there hung much of the spirit of the navy of former days. Aboard of her too there was abundant opportunity to exemplify that spirit as nobly as was ever done by sailors anywhere. From Fort Henry till

the fall of Port Hudson the "Essex" was always in the thick of the fight. One of the "Essex's" most important services came in the action of July 15, 1862. On Aug. 7 the "Arkansas" and two gunboats were lying above Baton Rouge ready to coöperate with the Confederate troops in a combined attack on that place. The troops with the aid of the Federal gunboats were defeated. Then Commander W. D. Porter started up-stream with the "Essex." As he approached the "Arkansas," a few well-directed shots disabled her so that she became unmanageable. Porter, seeing his advantage, loaded with incendiary shells, but at the first discharge the "Arkansas" was seen to be already ablaze. Porter and his men redoubled their efforts. The "Arkansas" managed to get near enough in-shore to make fast but her cable burnt away, and drifting again into the current she blew up. The "Essex" had accomplished the destruction of the last Confederate ram operating on the Mississippi River.

FOUR PICKED MEN
GUNNERS' CREW
OF THE "ESSEX"

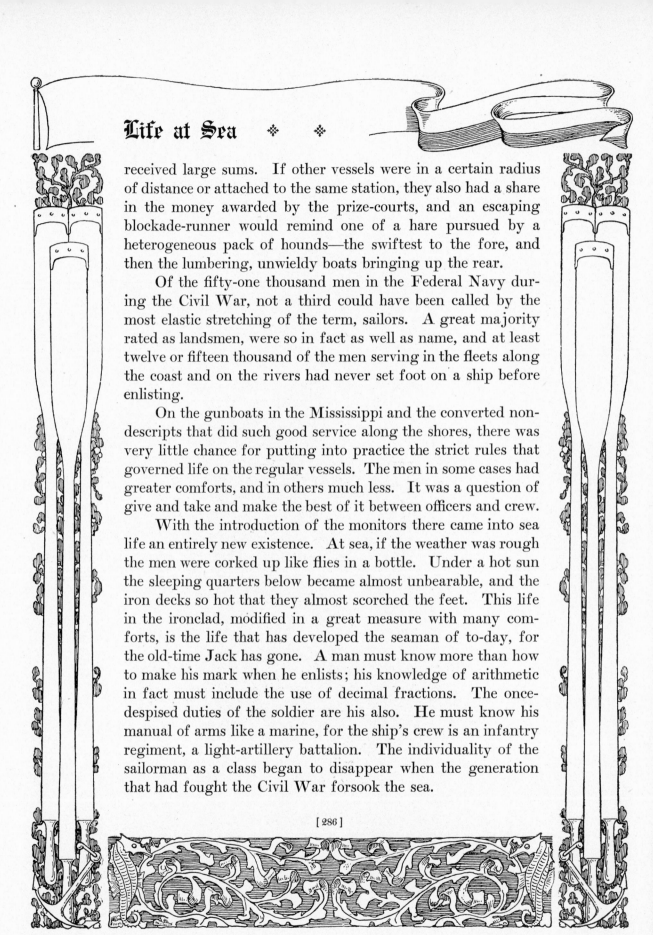

received large sums. If other vessels were in a certain radius of distance or attached to the same station, they also had a share in the money awarded by the prize-courts, and an escaping blockade-runner would remind one of a hare pursued by a heterogeneous pack of hounds—the swiftest to the fore, and then the lumbering, unwieldy boats bringing up the rear.

Of the fifty-one thousand men in the Federal Navy during the Civil War, not a third could have been called by the most elastic stretching of the term, sailors. A great majority rated as landsmen, were so in fact as well as name, and at least twelve or fifteen thousand of the men serving in the fleets along the coast and on the rivers had never set foot on a ship before enlisting.

On the gunboats in the Mississippi and the converted nondescripts that did such good service along the shores, there was very little chance for putting into practice the strict rules that governed life on the regular vessels. The men in some cases had greater comforts, and in others much less. It was a question of give and take and make the best of it between officers and crew.

With the introduction of the monitors there came into sea life an entirely new existence. At sea, if the weather was rough the men were corked up like flies in a bottle. Under a hot sun the sleeping quarters below became almost unbearable, and the iron decks so hot that they almost scorched the feet. This life in the ironclad, modified in a great measure with many comforts, is the life that has developed the seaman of to-day, for the old-time Jack has gone. A man must know more than how to make his mark when he enlists; his knowledge of arithmetic in fact must include the use of decimal fractions. The once-despised duties of the soldier are his also. He must know his manual of arms like a marine, for the ship's crew is an infantry regiment, a light-artillery battalion. The individuality of the sailorman as a class began to disappear when the generation that had fought the Civil War forsook the sea.

XII

THE CONFEDERATE CRUISERS
AND
THE "ALABAMA"

AFTER THE SINKING OF THE "ALABAMA"—
ADMIRAL SEMMES (ABOVE) AND COMMAND-
ER KELL WITH THEIR ENGLISH HOSTESSES

REAR-ADMIRAL RAPHAEL SEMMES

A PHOTOGRAPH IMMEDIATELY AFTER THE ALABAMA'S FIGHT WITH THE KEARSARGE

Very few officers in the Civil War had the opportunity of serving in both the army and navy: Admiral Semmes of the Confederate service was one of the small number. This fine likeness represents him at Southampton, England, whither he was taken by the *Deerhound* when the unlucky *Alabama* sank to her watery grave. Upon his return to America he was appointed rear-admiral and put in charge of the James River Squadron. This was February 10, 1865. On April 2d came the order from Secretary Mallory to destroy the ships, for Richmond was to be evacuated. His occupation gone, Semmes did not stand idly by and witness the ruin of his Government, but with a commission of brigadier-general undauntedly led a marine brigade in the last efforts of the expiring Confederacy.

COMMANDER JOHN McINTOSH KELL

THE RIGHT-HAND MAN OF CAPTAIN SEMMES

As first-lieutenant, Kell was Captain Semmes' executive officer on the *Alabama*. The captain gave him "great credit for the fine condition in which the ship went into action" and further stated that he rendered him "great assistance by his coolness and judgment as the fight proceeded." Kell, like his superior, was rescued by the *Deerhound* and taken to Southampton, where this photograph was made. On his return to the Confederate States, he was appointed commander and given the ironclad *Richmond*, in the James River Squadron. The fine features and resolute bearing of these naval officers go far to explain the daring and effective handling of the famous *Alabama*. With such sailors, an extensive Confederate Navy would have added even more dramatic chapters to history.

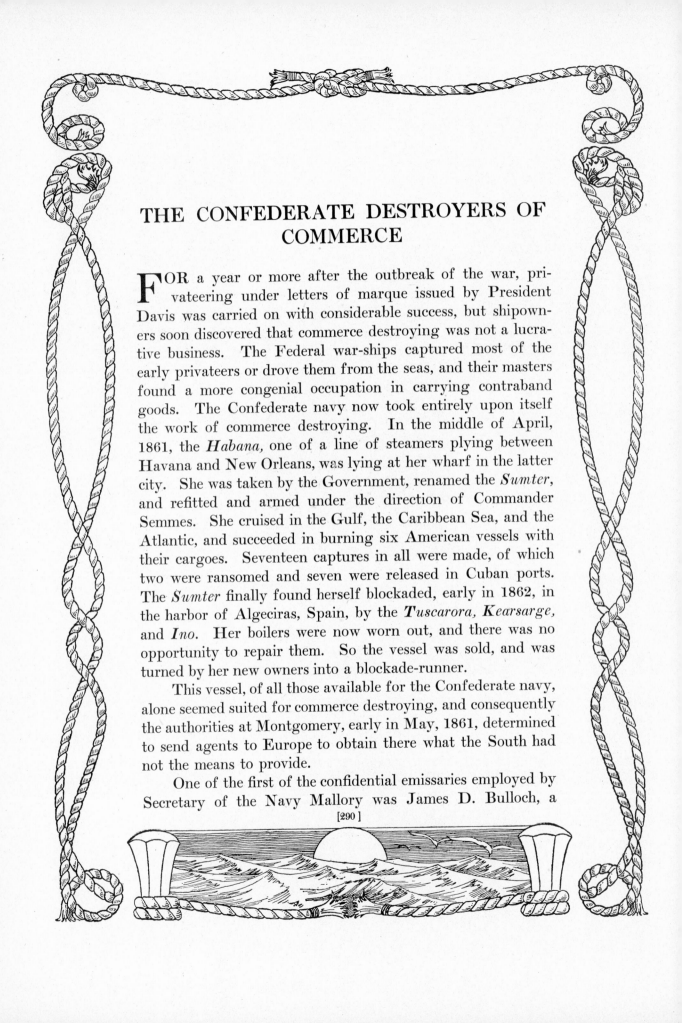

THE CONFEDERATE DESTROYERS OF COMMERCE

FOR a year or more after the outbreak of the war, privateering under letters of marque issued by President Davis was carried on with considerable success, but shipowners soon discovered that commerce destroying was not a lucrative business. The Federal war-ships captured most of the early privateers or drove them from the seas, and their masters found a more congenial occupation in carrying contraband goods. The Confederate navy now took entirely upon itself the work of commerce destroying. In the middle of April, 1861, the *Habana,* one of a line of steamers plying between Havana and New Orleans, was lying at her wharf in the latter city. She was taken by the Government, renamed the *Sumter,* and refitted and armed under the direction of Commander Semmes. She cruised in the Gulf, the Caribbean Sea, and the Atlantic, and succeeded in burning six American vessels with their cargoes. Seventeen captures in all were made, of which two were ransomed and seven were released in Cuban ports. The *Sumter* finally found herself blockaded, early in 1862, in the harbor of Algeciras, Spain, by the *Tuscarora, Kearsarge,* and *Ino.* Her boilers were now worn out, and there was no opportunity to repair them. So the vessel was sold, and was turned by her new owners into a blockade-runner.

This vessel, of all those available for the Confederate navy, alone seemed suited for commerce destroying, and consequently the authorities at Montgomery, early in May, 1861, determined to send agents to Europe to obtain there what the South had not the means to provide.

One of the first of the confidential emissaries employed by Secretary of the Navy Mallory was James D. Bulloch, a

A. P. MASON

JOHN SLIDELL

JOHN BIGELOW

CAPT. JAMES N. MAFFIT,
C. S. N,

The names of Mason and Slidell were linked throughout the war with the diplomatic efforts made in behalf of the Confederacy at the courts of England and France. The most concrete evidence of these efforts were the vessels that were built in English and French shipyards and, eluding the "vigilance" of the two Governments, passed into the hands of the Confederates to strike telling blows at American commerce, then next to the largest on the seas. Actively opposed to Mason and Slidell was John Bigelow, consul at Paris for the Federal Government during the war. His efforts to circumvent the construction of Confederate cruisers were untiring and in great measure successful in keeping in check the foreign tendency to encourage the division of the United States. At the very outset of this diplomatic struggle the Federal Government narrowly escaped becoming involved in war with England when Captain Charles Wilkes, in the "San Jacinto," seized Mason and Slidell aboard the British steamer "Trent," Nov. 8, 1861. Had not the captain of the "Trent" forgotten to throw his vessel on the hands of Captain Wilkes as a prize, hostilities could scarcely have been prevented. While Mason and Slidell were paving the way with diplomacy, a commission of Confederate naval officers, with headquarters in London, were striving energetically to arrange for the purchase

and building of vessels to be used as blockade-runners or privateers. Particularly active among these officers was Captain James Newland Maffit, C. S. N., and he was given command of the first cruiser built with Confederate funds that safely put to sea. In the "Oreto," Captain Maffit proceeded to Nassau; after she had been released by the British authorities there, her armament was again put aboard her and she began her career as the "Florida." She had been out but five days when yellow fever broke out on board. It reduced the working force to one fireman and four deckhands. Maffit, himself stricken, ran into Cardenas, but was soon ordered by the Cuban authorities to bring his ship to Havana. Maffit determined to escape. On Sept. 4, 1862, he took the "Florida" boldly through the blockading squadron into Mobile Bay. The vessel was refitted, and on the night of Jan. 15, 1863, Captain Maffit ran out with her and got safely to sea. He continued to command the cruiser on her adventurous voyages until the latter part of 1864, when his health was so broken that he was relieved. In January, 1865, he took the blockade-runner "Owl" out from Wilmington and over the bar near Fort Caswell, the very night that the forts surrendered to the Federal fleet. Maffit arrived at Bermuda in time to stop the sailing of five blockade-runners.

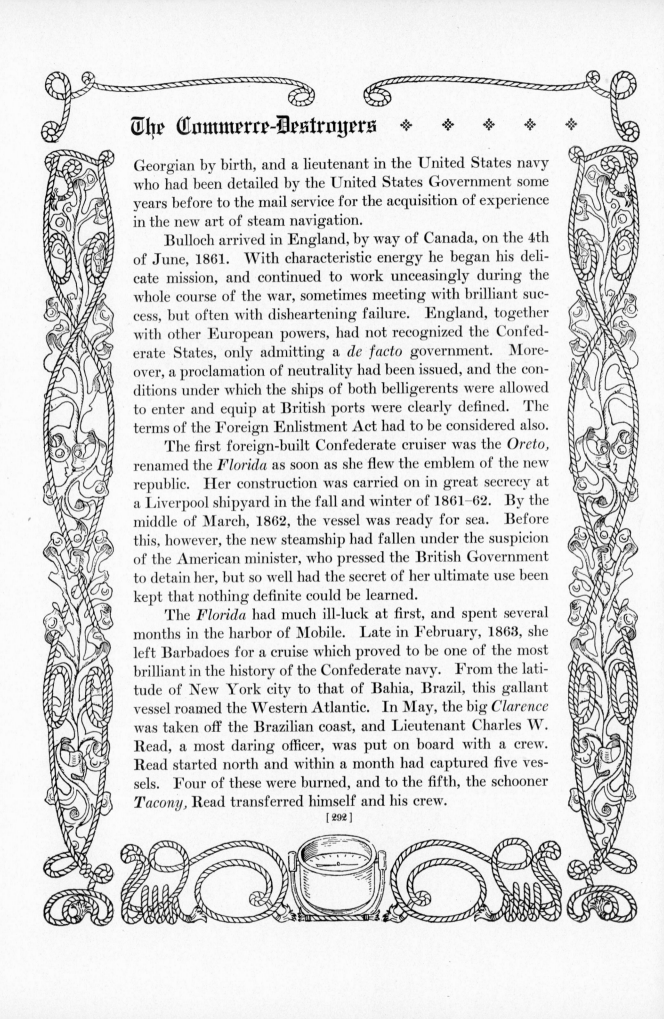

Georgian by birth, and a lieutenant in the United States navy who had been detailed by the United States Government some years before to the mail service for the acquisition of experience in the new art of steam navigation.

Bulloch arrived in England, by way of Canada, on the 4th of June, 1861. With characteristic energy he began his delicate mission, and continued to work unceasingly during the whole course of the war, sometimes meeting with brilliant success, but often with disheartening failure. England, together with other European powers, had not recognized the Confederate States, only admitting a *de facto* government. Moreover, a proclamation of neutrality had been issued, and the conditions under which the ships of both belligerents were allowed to enter and equip at British ports were clearly defined. The terms of the Foreign Enlistment Act had to be considered also.

The first foreign-built Confederate cruiser was the *Oreto,* renamed the *Florida* as soon as she flew the emblem of the new republic. Her construction was carried on in great secrecy at a Liverpool shipyard in the fall and winter of 1861–62. By the middle of March, 1862, the vessel was ready for sea. Before this, however, the new steamship had fallen under the suspicion of the American minister, who pressed the British Government to detain her, but so well had the secret of her ultimate use been kept that nothing definite could be learned.

The *Florida* had much ill-luck at first, and spent several months in the harbor of Mobile. Late in February, 1863, she left Barbadoes for a cruise which proved to be one of the most brilliant in the history of the Confederate navy. From the latitude of New York city to that of Bahia, Brazil, this gallant vessel roamed the Western Atlantic. In May, the big *Clarence* was taken off the Brazilian coast, and Lieutenant Charles W. Read, a most daring officer, was put on board with a crew. Read started north and within a month had captured five vessels. Four of these were burned, and to the fifth, the schooner *Tacony,* Read transferred himself and his crew.

COPYRIGHT, 1911, REVIEW OF REVIEWS CO.

THE "TUSCARORA" NEAR GIBRALTAR, IN CHASE OF THE CONFEDERATE CRUISERS

The U. S. S. "Tuscarora" with other vessels during the latter half of 1861 was scouring the seas in search of the "Sumter"—the first of the Confederate cruisers to get to sea, eluding the blockading squadron at the mouth of the Mississippi, June 30, 1861. She was a 500-ton passenger steamer with a speed of but ten knots and had been declared unfit for naval service by a board of Confederate officers. Captain Raphael Semmes, upon seeing the report, said: "Give me that ship; I think I can make her answer the purpose." Within a week after she got away, the "Sumter" had made eight prizes. On Nov. 23d Semmes cleverly eluded the "Iroquois," then lying outside the harbor of St. Pierre, Martinique, and cruised to Gibraltar. There the "Sumter" was blockaded by the

"Tuscarora," the "Kearsarge," and the "Ino." Semmes, seeing that escape was impossible, sold his vessel and disbanded her crew. Her prizes totalled fifteen, and Semmes was soon making another record for himself in the "Alabama." The "Florida" was the first cruiser built for the Confederacy abroad. She was allowed to clear from Liverpool on March 22, 1862, under the name "Oreto." On August 7th she began her career under Captain John Newland Maffit, with a crew of but twenty-two men. She had an adventurous career till she ran into the harbor of Bahia, Oct. 5, 1864, where she encountered a vessel of Wilke's flying squadron, the "Wachusett." Commander Napoleon Collins, in violation of the neutrality laws, suddenly attacked the "Florida" and received her surrender.

The Commerce-Destroyers ❖ ❖ ❖ ❖

The *Clarence* was burned. Within two weeks the *Tacony* had ten prizes, and the coast between Chesapeake and Casco bays was in a state of terror. The dauntless schooner shared the fate of the *Clarence* when the better-suited *Archer* fell into her clutches. But the latter's career was short. Dashing into the harbor of Portland, Maine, Read cut out the revenue cutter *Caleb Cushing*. The next day he was attacked, captured, and sent as a prisoner to Fort Warren, in Boston Harbor.

The *Florida* had no less than fourteen prizes to her credit, when, late in August, 1863, she entered the harbor of Brest, France, greatly in need of repairs. Here she remained until February, 1864, and became in the mean time almost a new ship. Back and forth across the Atlantic she went, preying on the merchant vessels of the United States until, on the 5th of October, Lieutenant Morris brought her into the harbor of Bahia.

Commander N. Collins, of the United States war-ship *Wachusett,* then in that port, on October 7, 1864, broke the laws of neutrality and ran into and captured the *Florida*, which got him a court martial (and in course of time, promotion). The *Florida* was brought up to Chesapeake Bay, and after much international confabulation her prisoners were released, and she was ordered to be turned over to the Brazilian Government. But a blundering ferryboat ran her down, and Brazil received only an apology, for this time the *Florida* went to the bottom.

While the *Florida* was building, Captain Bulloch visited the shipyard of John Laird, at Birkenhead, and arranged to build a wooden screw despatch-vessel. This ship, when it finally went into commission on the 24th of August, 1862, was the famous *Alabama,* and she was under the charge of Commander Semmes of the dismantled *Florida*. In a month's cruise in the North Atlantic twenty American vessels were destroyed. Then she went south, swept the Gulf, and among her captures was the Federal war vessel *Hatteras*. The

COPYRIGHT, 1911, REVIEW OF REVIEWS CO.

AT ANTWERP—U. S. S. "NIAGARA" AND THE FIGHT THAT WAS NOT FOUGHT

No sooner did it become known that the "Stonewall" was abroad than the Federal vessels in foreign waters began an active search for her. At the very beginning of her cruise she was found to have sprung a leak, however, and put into Ferrol, Spain, for repairs. There, during the first week in February, 1865, the frigate "Niagara" and the sloop-of-war "Sacramento" found her and attempted to blockade her. On March 24th the "Stonewall" steamed out of Ferrol and cleared for action. Commander T. T. Craven, of the "Niagara," had already notified his Government that in a smooth sea the "Stonewall" would be a match for three such ships as the "Niagara." Twice when the sea was rough he had stood out and offered battle to the Confederate ram, but Captain Page refused the offer, choosing his own time on a day when the water was as smooth as glass and no slight advantage could accrue to the Federals. Commander Craven was equally determined not to give his antagonist an inexpensive victory and carefully avoided the encounter. The "Stonewall" after flaunting her flag in his face, sailed jauntily off to Lisbon with the intention of crossing the Atlantic and striking a blow at Port Royal and at the cities of the North, hoping thus to revive the waning cause of the Confederacy. Arriving at Havana early in May, Captain Page learned that the war was over, and surrendered his vessel to the captain-general of Cuba.

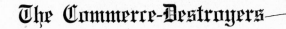

successful cruiser now visited Jamaica, landed her prisoners, and made necessary repairs. Semmes then cruised off the coast of Brazil, making ten prizes, and in company with one of them, taken into the Confederate service and renamed the *Tuscaloosa,* proceeded to the Cape of Good Hope. The vessel next spent six months in Eastern waters, even crossing the China Sea. On this cruise seven vessels were destroyed. In March, 1864, she was back at the Cape, and before the end of the month sailed for Europe. On June 11th, the *Alabama* entered the harbor of Cherbourg, France, in order to coal and to refit. What happened to her now will be told at the end of this chapter.

Among other Confederate cruisers was the *Georgia,* bought in March, 1863, by one of the Confederate agents, Commander Matthew F. Maury, the distinguished hydrographer. The *Georgia* started from England, but her sail power was found to be so small that she was constantly compelled to enter port to take on coal. This circumstance made her useless for long cruises, and she was taken to Liverpool and sold, after a year's activity in the Middle and South Atlantic. The *Victor,* an old despatch-boat of the British navy, was also bought by Commander Maury and, as the *Rappahannock,* was long detained in the harbor of Calais.

With neither of these vessels was it possible to duplicate the *Alabama,* and, as yet, the whaling industry in the Pacific had been quite free from the unwelcome attentions of the Confederate cruisers. The *Sea King* was purchased by the Southern agents in Europe in the summer of 1864. She was refitted and armed, and, as the *Shenandoah,* was sent to the Pacific under command of Lieutenant Waddell. In these far seas he destroyed a large number of whalers, keeping the work up until the end of June, 1865, in ignorance of the termination of the war. Lieutenant Waddell then returned to Liverpool and surrendered the *Shenandoah* to the British Government.

A ship of many names began her adventures as the blockade-runner *Atlanta,* in the summer of 1864. She made two

COPYRIGHT, 1911 PATRIOT PUB. CO.

THE "STONEWALL," A DREAD CONFEDERATE DESTROYER

In this picture, taken after the "Stonewall" was voluntarily delivered by Spain to the United States in July, 1865, is seen the tremendous power for harm possessed by the vessel. Commodore Craven, at his own request, was tried in a court of inquiry for his failure to engage the Confederate ram with the "Niagara" and "Sacramento" and was exonerated of all blame. By taking the less popular course he undoubtedly saved the Federal navy a grave disaster. His were wooden ships, while the "Stonewall" was heavily armored, and her great ram could easily have sunk both her antagonists even if her gunnery should have proved inaccurate. Although the "Niagara" was rated as one of the most powerful vessels of the old navy and perhaps the fastest sailing-ship afloat, under steam she was scarcely a match for the

COMMODORE
THOMAS T. CRAVEN

"Stonewall" in that particular. The condition of her boilers at the time was still further disadvantageous. The "Niagara" could not turn around in less than fifteen minutes, while the "Stonewall" could turn on her center while going either forward or backward in a minute and a half. The battery of the "Niagara" had been condemned as unserviceable by a board of survey. Her target-practice reports showed that the shot from her guns would "tumble." The "Niagara" carried twelve 9-inch smooth-bores and the "Sacramento" ten guns, but unless both ships could bring their broadsides to bear on their antagonist it was bound to be a one-sided battle, for the "Stonewall's" powerful and modern Armstrong rifles were mounted in two turrets and could be brought quickly to bear over a wide range.

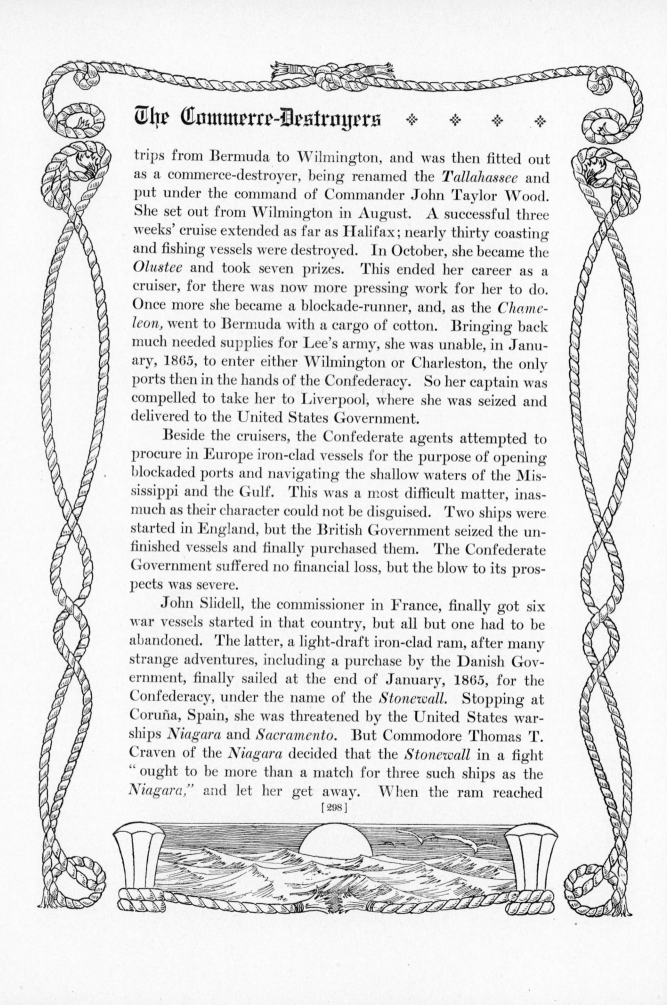

trips from Bermuda to Wilmington, and was then fitted out as a commerce-destroyer, being renamed the *Tallahassee* and put under the command of Commander John Taylor Wood. She set out from Wilmington in August. A successful three weeks' cruise extended as far as Halifax; nearly thirty coasting and fishing vessels were destroyed. In October, she became the *Olustee* and took seven prizes. This ended her career as a cruiser, for there was now more pressing work for her to do. Once more she became a blockade-runner, and, as the *Chameleon,* went to Bermuda with a cargo of cotton. Bringing back much needed supplies for Lee's army, she was unable, in January, 1865, to enter either Wilmington or Charleston, the only ports then in the hands of the Confederacy. So her captain was compelled to take her to Liverpool, where she was seized and delivered to the United States Government.

Beside the cruisers, the Confederate agents attempted to procure in Europe iron-clad vessels for the purpose of opening blockaded ports and navigating the shallow waters of the Mississippi and the Gulf. This was a most difficult matter, inasmuch as their character could not be disguised. Two ships were started in England, but the British Government seized the unfinished vessels and finally purchased them. The Confederate Government suffered no financial loss, but the blow to its prospects was severe.

John Slidell, the commissioner in France, finally got six war vessels started in that country, but all but one had to be abandoned. The latter, a light-draft iron-clad ram, after many strange adventures, including a purchase by the Danish Government, finally sailed at the end of January, 1865, for the Confederacy, under the name of the *Stonewall.* Stopping at Coruña, Spain, she was threatened by the United States warships *Niagara* and *Sacramento.* But Commodore Thomas T. Craven of the *Niagara* decided that the *Stonewall* in a fight "ought to be more than a match for three such ships as the *Niagara*," and let her get away. When the ram reached

THE CONFEDERATE RAM "STONEWALL"

Here are two striking views in the Port Royal dry-dock of the Confederate ram "Stonewall." When this powerful fighting-ship sailed from Copenhagen, Jan. 6, 1865, under command of Capt. T. J. Page, C.S.N., the Federal navy became confronted by its most formidable antagonist during the war. In March, 1863, the Confederacy had negotiated a loan of £3,000,000, and being thus at last in possession of the necessary funds, Captain Bulloch and Mr. Slidell arranged with M. Arman, who was a member of the *Corps-Legislatif* and proprietor of a large shipyard at Bordeaux, for the construction of ironclad ships of war. Mr. Slidell had already received assurances from persons in the confidence of Napoleon III that the building of the ships in the French yards would not be interfered with, and that getting them to sea would be connived at by the Government. Owing to the indubitable proof laid before the Emperor by the Federal diplomats at Paris, he was compelled to revoke the guarantee that had been given to Slidell and Bulloch. A plan was arranged, however, by which M. Arman should sell the vessels to various European powers; and he disposed of the ironclad ram "Sphinx" to the Danish Government, then at war with Prussia. Delivery of the ship at Copenhagen was not made, however, till after the war had ceased, and no trouble was experienced by the Confederates in arranging for the purchase of the vessel. On January 24, 1865, she rendezvoused off Quiberon, on the French coast; the remainder of her officers, crew, and supplies were put aboard of her;

the Confederate flag was hoisted over her, and she was christened the "Stonewall." Already the vessel was discovered to have sprung a leak, and Captain Page ran into Ferrol, Spain. Here dock-yard facilities were at first granted, but were withdrawn at the protest of the American Minister. While Captain Page was repairing his vessel as best he could, the "Niagara" and the "Sacramento" appeared, and after some weeks the "Stonewall" offered battle in vain.

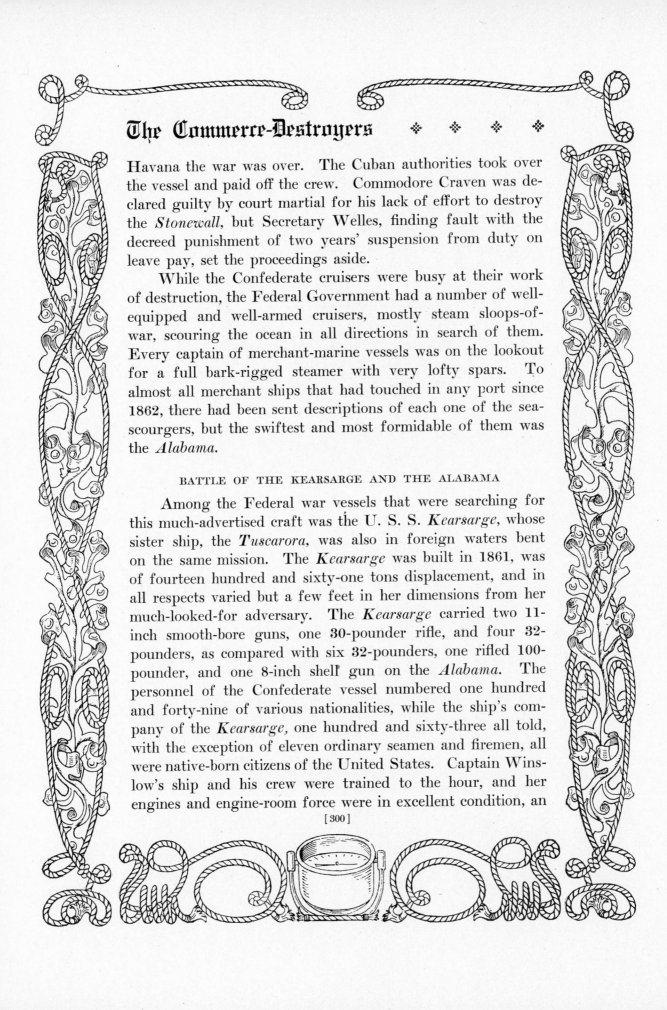

The Commerce-Destroyers ❖ ❖ ❖ ❖

Havana the war was over. The Cuban authorities took over the vessel and paid off the crew. Commodore Craven was declared guilty by court martial for his lack of effort to destroy the *Stonewall*, but Secretary Welles, finding fault with the decreed punishment of two years' suspension from duty on leave pay, set the proceedings aside.

While the Confederate cruisers were busy at their work of destruction, the Federal Government had a number of well-equipped and well-armed cruisers, mostly steam sloops-of-war, scouring the ocean in all directions in search of them. Every captain of merchant-marine vessels was on the lookout for a full bark-rigged steamer with very lofty spars. To almost all merchant ships that had touched in any port since 1862, there had been sent descriptions of each one of the sea-scourgers, but the swiftest and most formidable of them was the *Alabama*.

BATTLE OF THE KEARSARGE AND THE ALABAMA

Among the Federal war vessels that were searching for this much-advertised craft was the U. S. S. *Kearsarge*, whose sister ship, the *Tuscarora*, was also in foreign waters bent on the same mission. The *Kearsarge* was built in 1861, was of fourteen hundred and sixty-one tons displacement, and in all respects varied but a few feet in her dimensions from her much-looked-for adversary. The *Kearsarge* carried two 11-inch smooth-bore guns, one 30-pounder rifle, and four 32-pounders, as compared with six 32-pounders, one rifled 100-pounder, and one 8-inch shell gun on the *Alabama*. The personnel of the Confederate vessel numbered one hundred and forty-nine of various nationalities, while the ship's company of the *Kearsarge,* one hundred and sixty-three all told, with the exception of eleven ordinary seamen and firemen, all were native-born citizens of the United States. Captain Winslow's ship and his crew were trained to the hour, and her engines and engine-room force were in excellent condition, an

COPYRIGHT, 1911, REVIEW OF REVIEWS CO.

OFFICERS OF THE "ALABAMA" IN 1862

From left to right: First Lieut. John M. Kell; Surgeon David H. Llewellyn; Capt. Raphael Semmes; Third Lieut. Joseph D. Wilson; Lieut. P. Schroeder; Master J. P. Bullock; Lieut. Arthur Sinclair; Chief Engineer Miles D. Freeman; Lieut. Richard F. Armstrong; Capt.'s Clerk W. B. Smith; Surgeon Francis L. Galt; Asst. Engineer William P. Brooke; Midshipman Eugene Maffitt; Midshipman E. M. Anderson; Master's Mate George T. Fullman; Lieut. of Marines Becker K. Howell; Carpenter William Robinson; Paymaster Clarence R. Yonge; Fifth Lieut. John Lowe; Asst. Engineer S. W. Cummings. The portraits here grouped were taken in London in 1862 before the departure on August 13th in the steamer "Bahama" to join "Ship No. 290," built at the Lairds' shipyard, which received her guns and crew on the high seas off the Azores.

advantage that was proved completely in the action between the two well-matched vessels when at last they met.

June 19, 1864, was the momentous day of the meeting. The *Kearsarge* had located the *Alabama* in the harbor of Cherbourg, France, and on the 14th of the month had steamed in and passed out again without anchoring. This was both a challenge and a defiance, and Captain Semmes decided that he could "hardly do less than go out and meet her." So he wrote the *Alabama's* agent at Cherbourg, expressing the hope that the *Kearsarge* would not depart at once, as he intended to fight just as soon as the *Alabama* could be gotten ready. Through this channel, Winslow was informed of Semmes' intention by the United States consul. It was a bright Sunday morning when the *Alabama* steamed through the opening of the harbor, accompanied by the French man-of-war *Couronne,* and steered straight for her waiting adversary. Let us quote from a Confederate chronicle:

The late foul weather had given way to a gentle breeze, and the subsiding swell of the Atlantic wave under a clear sky made the day eminently favorable for the work in hand. All Cherbourg was on the heights above the town and along the bastions and the mole. Never did knightly tournament boast a more eager multitude of spectators. It chanced, fortunately, that an English steam-yacht, the *Deerhound,* with its owner, Mr. John Lancaster, and his family on board, was in harbor at the time. The *Deerhound* followed the *Alabama* at a respectful distance and was the closest witness of the fight. Some French pilot-boats hung as near as they considered prudent. At the limit of neutral waters the *Alabama* parted company with her escort, and the *Couronne* returned to within a league of the shore.

In three-quarters of an hour, at the distance of about a mile, the *Alabama* opened fire. It was some time before the *Kearsarge* replied. Captain Winslow soon perceived that, despite the supposed superiority of the *Alabama* in engine-power, he had the faster vessel, and the circling tactics which the two ships observed during the fight were made necessary

COPYRIGHT, 1911, REVIEW OF REVIEWS CO.

THE GUN THAT SUNK THE "ALABAMA"—ON BOARD U. S. S. "KEARSARGE"

On the main deck, showing one of the two 11-inch pivot-guns that were handled with superb skill in the famous fight with the "Alabama." The engagement was in reality a contest in skill between American and British gunners, since the crew of the "Alabama" was composed almost entirely of British sailors. Word was passed to the men in the "Kearsarge" to let every shot tell, and there followed an exhibition of that magnificent American gunnery that had characterized the War of 1812. The "Kearsarge" fired only 173 missiles, almost all of which took effect. The "Alabama" fired 370 missiles, of which but 28 struck her antagonist. An 11-inch shell from the pivot-gun of the "Kearsarge" entered the "Alabama's" 8-inch gun-port, mowing down most of the gun crew. It was quickly followed by another shell from the same gun, and then by another, all three striking in the same place. Although the gunnery aboard the "Alabama" was inferior, one of her 68-pound shells lodged in the sternpost of the "Kearsarge" but failed to explode. Had it done so, in all likelihood it would have been the "Kearsarge" and not the "Alabama" that went to the bottom of the English Channel. Although the "Kearsarge" was wrecked on Roncador Reef in 1894, her sternpost with the shell still imbedded in it was recovered and became a historic relic.

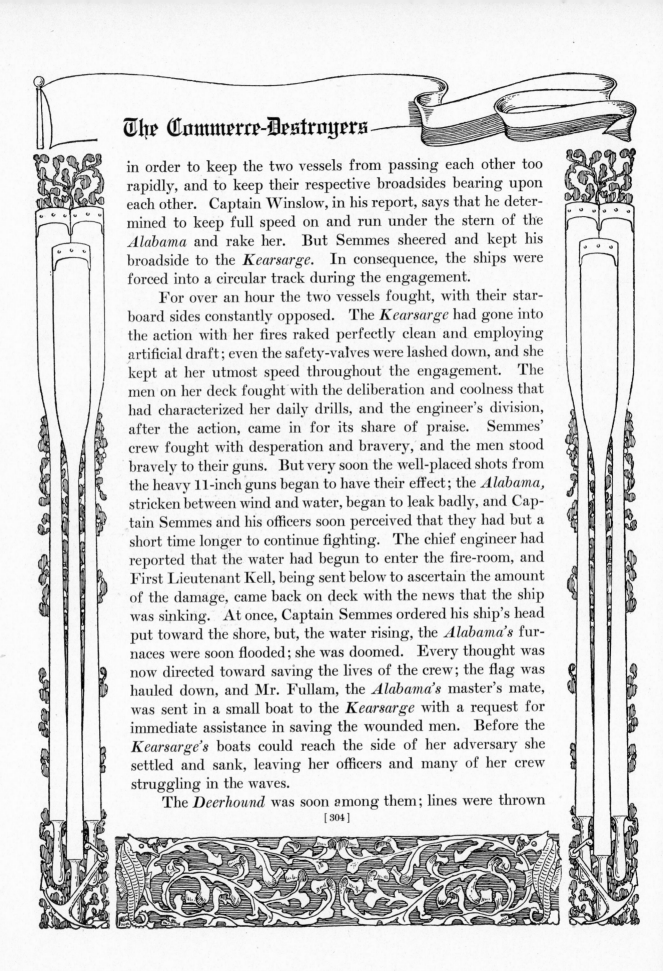

in order to keep the two vessels from passing each other too rapidly, and to keep their respective broadsides bearing upon each other. Captain Winslow, in his report, says that he determined to keep full speed on and run under the stern of the *Alabama* and rake her. But Semmes sheered and kept his broadside to the *Kearsarge*. In consequence, the ships were forced into a circular track during the engagement.

For over an hour the two vessels fought, with their starboard sides constantly opposed. The *Kearsarge* had gone into the action with her fires raked perfectly clean and employing artificial draft; even the safety-valves were lashed down, and she kept at her utmost speed throughout the engagement. The men on her deck fought with the deliberation and coolness that had characterized her daily drills, and the engineer's division, after the action, came in for its share of praise. Semmes' crew fought with desperation and bravery, and the men stood bravely to their guns. But very soon the well-placed shots from the heavy 11-inch guns began to have their effect; the *Alabama*, stricken between wind and water, began to leak badly, and Captain Semmes and his officers soon perceived that they had but a short time longer to continue fighting. The chief engineer had reported that the water had begun to enter the fire-room, and First Lieutenant Kell, being sent below to ascertain the amount of the damage, came back on deck with the news that the ship was sinking. At once, Captain Semmes ordered his ship's head put toward the shore, but, the water rising, the *Alabama's* furnaces were soon flooded; she was doomed. Every thought was now directed toward saving the lives of the crew; the flag was hauled down, and Mr. Fullam, the *Alabama's* master's mate, was sent in a small boat to the *Kearsarge* with a request for immediate assistance in saving the wounded men. Before the *Kearsarge's* boats could reach the side of her adversary she settled and sank, leaving her officers and many of her crew struggling in the waves.

The *Deerhound* was soon among them; lines were thrown

COPYRIGHT, 1911, REVIEW OF REVIEWS CO.

AFTER THE MOST FAMOUS SEA-FIGHT OF THE WAR
CAPTAIN WINSLOW AND HIS OFFICERS ON THE "KEARSARGE"

Here on the deck of the "Kearsarge" stand Captain John A. Winslow (third from left) and his officers after their return from the victorious battle with the "Alabama." On Sunday morning, June 19, 1864, Captain Winslow, who had been lying off the harbor of Cherbourg waiting for the Confederate cruiser to come out, was conducting divine service. Suddenly a cry—"She's coming, and heading straight for us"—rang out on the deck. Laying down his prayer-book and seizing his speaking-trumpet, Winslow ordered his ship cleared for action. He stood out to sea to make sure that the fight would occur beyond the neutrality limit. Meanwhile, people were crowding to every vantage-point along the coast with spy-glasses and camp-chairs, eager to witness the only great fight on the high seas between a Federal and a Confederate cruiser. The two ships were almost precisely matched in tonnage, number of men, and shot-weight of the guns brought into action on each side. The battle was begun by the "Alabama" at a range of 1,200 yards. The "Kearsarge," however, soon closed in to 900 yards, training her guns for more than an hour upon the "Alabama" with telling effect. Precisely an hour and thirteen minutes after the "Alabama" fired her first broadside, her colors were hauled down from her masthead; the 11-inch shells of the pivot-guns of the "Kearsarge" had pierced her again and again below the water-line; twenty-six of her men were killed and drowned and twenty-one wounded, while aboard the "Kearsarge" only three men were injured. Twenty minutes after the surrender the "Alabama" settled by the stern and sank. Some survivors escaped on the British steam-yacht "Deerhound."

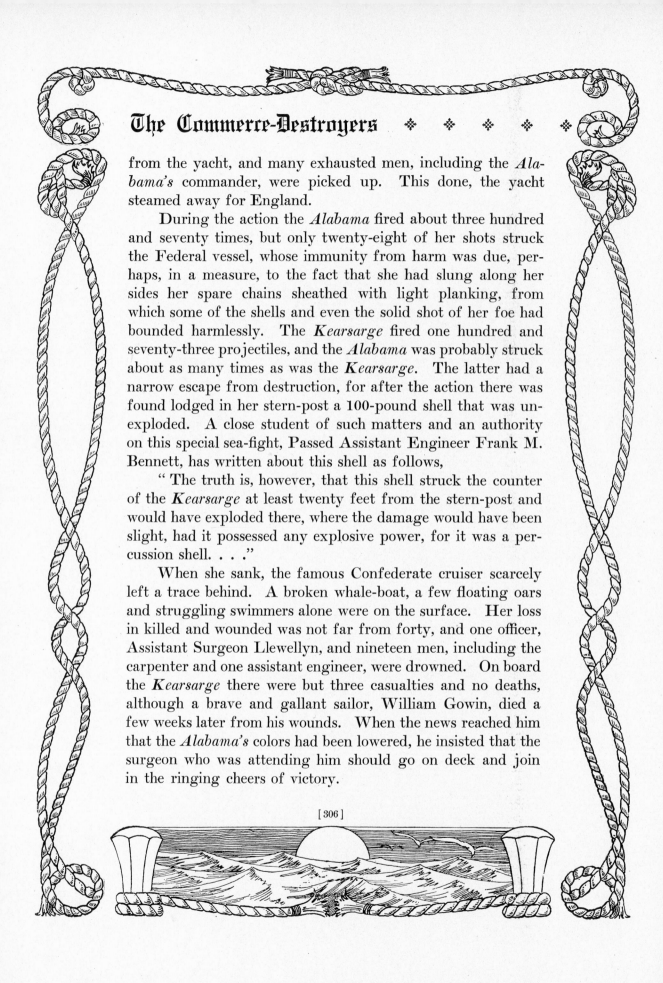

from the yacht, and many exhausted men, including the *Alabama's* commander, were picked up. This done, the yacht steamed away for England.

During the action the *Alabama* fired about three hundred and seventy times, but only twenty-eight of her shots struck the Federal vessel, whose immunity from harm was due, perhaps, in a measure, to the fact that she had slung along her sides her spare chains sheathed with light planking, from which some of the shells and even the solid shot of her foe had bounded harmlessly. The *Kearsarge* fired one hundred and seventy-three projectiles, and the *Alabama* was probably struck about as many times as was the *Kearsarge*. The latter had a narrow escape from destruction, for after the action there was found lodged in her stern-post a 100-pound shell that was unexploded. A close student of such matters and an authority on this special sea-fight, Passed Assistant Engineer Frank M. Bennett, has written about this shell as follows,

" The truth is, however, that this shell struck the counter of the *Kearsarge* at least twenty feet from the stern-post and would have exploded there, where the damage would have been slight, had it possessed any explosive power, for it was a percussion shell. . . ."

When she sank, the famous Confederate cruiser scarcely left a trace behind. A broken whale-boat, a few floating oars and struggling swimmers alone were on the surface. Her loss in killed and wounded was not far from forty, and one officer, Assistant Surgeon Llewellyn, and nineteen men, including the carpenter and one assistant engineer, were drowned. On board the *Kearsarge* there were but three casualties and no deaths, although a brave and gallant sailor, William Gowin, died a few weeks later from his wounds. When the news reached him that the *Alabama's* colors had been lowered, he insisted that the surgeon who was attending him should go on deck and join in the ringing cheers of victory.

CHAPTER XIII

NAVAL CHRONOLOGY

1861—1865

IMPORTANT NAVAL ENGAGEMENTS

OF THE CIVIL WAR

MARCH, 1861—JUNE, 1865

CHRONOLOGICAL summary of important actions in which the Federal and Confederate navies were engaged, based on official records. Minor engagements are omitted; also joint operations where the army played the principal part.

MARCH, 1861.

20.—Sloop *Isabella*, with provisions, for the Federal Navy-Yard at Pensacola, seized at Mobile by request of Gen. Bragg.

APRIL, 1861.

17.—Seizure of the U. S. transport *Star of the West*, at Indianola, by Texas troops under Col. Van Dorn.

19.—Ports of South Carolina, Georgia, Alabama, Florida, Mississippi, Louisiana, and Texas ordered blockaded by President Lincoln.

20 and 21.—Gosport Navy-Yard, Norfolk, Va., abandoned by Union officers in charge, and seized by Virginia State troops.

27.—Ports of Virginia and North Carolina included in the blockade.

MAY, 1861.

4.—S. S. *Star of the West* made the receiving ship of the Confed. navy, New Orleans, La.

9.—U. S. ships *Quaker City*, *Harriet Lane*, *Young America*, *Cumberland*, *Monticello*, and *Yankee* enforcing the blockade off Fort Monroe.

—Steamers *Philadelphia*, *Baltimore*, *Powhatan*, and *Mount Vernon* armed by U. S. Government, and cruising on the Potomac.

13.—Proclamation of neutrality issued by Queen Victoria, in which the subjects of Great Britain were forbidden to endeavor to break a blockade "lawfully and effectually established."

18 and 19.—Shots exchanged between U. S. S. *Freeborn* and *Monticello* and the Confed. battery at Sewell's Point, Va.

—U. S. S. *Harriet Lane* arrives off Charleston.

26.—U. S. S. *Brooklyn* commenced the blockade of the Mississippi River.

—Blockade of Mobile, Ala., commenced by U. S. S. *Powhatan*.

28.—U. S. S. *Minnesota* begins real blockade of Charleston.

—Blockade of Savannah initiated by U. S. gunboat *Union*.

31.—U. S. S. *Freeborn*, *Anacostia*, *Pawnee*, and *Resolute* attacked Confed. batteries at Aquia Creek, Va.

JUNE, 1861.

27.—Engagement between U. S. gunboats *Freeborn* and *Reliance* and Confed. batteries at Mathias Point, Va., Commander Ward of the *Freeborn* killed.

JULY, 1861.

2.—U. S. S. *South Carolina* begins blockade of Galveston.

4 to 7.—U. S. S. *South Carolina* captures or destroys 10 vessels off Galveston.

7.—"Infernal" machines detected floating in the Potomac.

19.—Captain-General of Cuba liberated all the vessels brought into Cuban ports as prizes by Confed. cruiser *Sumter*.

24.—Naval expedition from Fort Monroe to Back River, Va., by Lieut. Crosby and 300 men. Nine sloops and schooners of the Confederates burnt, and one schooner with bacon and corn captured.

COPYRIGHT, 1911, REVIEW OF REVIEWS CO.

COMMODORE VANDERBILT'S PRESENT TO THE GOVERNMENT

This side-wheel steamer was presented to the Government by Commodore Cornelius Vanderbilt in 1861, when the navy was sorely in need of ships, and she was christened after the donor. In Hampton Roads she led one of the two columns of fighting-vessels of all sorts that had been assembled to meet the "Merrimac," in case she made another attack upon the fleet after her encounter with the "Monitor." The "Vanderbilt" mounted fifteen guns and showed great speed. She was employed largely as a cruiser. Her first prize was the British blockade-runner "Peterhoff," captured off St. Thomas, February 25, 1863. On April 16th she caught the "Gertrude" in the Bahamas, and on October 30th the "Saxon," off the coast of Africa. Under command of Captain C. W. Pickering, she participated in both of the joint-expeditions against Fort Fisher.

28.—Confederate privateer *Petrel,* formerly U. S. revenue cutter *Aiken,* sunk by U. S. frigate *St. Lawrence* near Charleston.

AUGUST, 1861.

22.—The steamer *Samuel Orr* was seized at Paducah, Ky., by Confederates, and taken up the Tennessee River.

26.—Naval and military expedition to North Carolina coast sailed from Hampton Roads, Va., under command of Flag-Officer Stringham and Maj.-Gen. Butler.

28 and 29.—Bombardment and capture of Forts Hatteras and Clark, at Hatteras Inlet, N. C., 30 pieces of cannon, 1000 stand of arms, 3 vessels with valuable cargoes, and 750 prisoners were taken.

30.—Capt. Foote ordered to the command of U. S. naval forces on the Western waters.

SEPTEMBER, 1861.

4.—Engagement on the Mississippi River near Hickman, Ky., between U. S. gunboats *Tyler* and *Lexington* and the Confed. gunboat *Yankee* and shore batteries.

14.—An expedition from the U. S. frigate *Colorado,* under Lieut. J. H. Russell, destroyed the privateer *Judah,* under the Confed. guns at Pensacola.

16.—A naval expedition from Hatteras Inlet, under command of Lieut. J. Y. Maxwell, destroyed Fort Ocracoke, on Beacon Island, N. C.

17.—Ship Island, near the mouth of the Mississippi River, occupied by Federal forces from the steamer *Massachusetts.*

OCTOBER, 1861.

1.—U. S. steamer *Fanny,* with 35 men of the 9th N. Y. Volunteers, captured by the Confederates on the north shore of Hatteras Inlet.

4.—Commander Alden, U. S. S. *South Carolina,* captured two schooners off the S. W. Pass of the Mississippi, with four to five thousand stands of arms.

5.—Two boats from U. S. S. *Louisiana,* Lieut. A. Murray, destroyed a Confed. schooner, being fitted out for a privateer, at Chincoteague Inlet, Va.

12.—Five Confed. gunboats, the ram *Manassas,* and a fleet of fireships attacked the U. S. fleet at the passes of the Mississippi and were repulsed after considerable injury had been done to the U. S. fleet.

26.—Confed. steamer *Nashville,* commanded by Lieut. R. B. Pegram, escaped from Charleston, S. C.

28.—Three Confed. vessels were surprised and burnt at Chincoteague Inlet, Va., by a portion of the crew of U. S. gunboat *Louisiana,* under Lieut. A. Hopkins.

29.—Federal expedition sailed from Fort Monroe, under the command of Flag-Officer Samuel F. Du Pont, comprising 77 vessels of all classes. The land forces, numbering 20,000 men, were commanded by Brig.-Gen. Thos. W. Sherman.

NOVEMBER, 1861.

1.—A violent storm overtook the naval expedition off the N. C. coast. 3 vessels were disabled and returned, 2 were driven ashore, and 2 foundered. 7 lives lost.

7.—Federal fleet under Du Pont captured Forts Walker and Beauregard at Port Royal entrance, and took the town of, Beaufort, S. C.

7 and 8.—Two launches and 40 men, commanded by Lieut. Jas. E. Jouett, from the U. S. frigate *Santee,* off Galveston, Texas, surprised and cut out the Confed. privateer *Royal Yacht.*

8.—Capt. Chas. Wilkes, commanding U. S. screw sloop *San Jacinto,* removed by force Confed. Commissioners Jas. M. Mason and John Slidell from British mail steamer *Trent.*

18.—U. S. gunboat *Conestoga* engaged Confed. batteries on the Tennessee River, and silenced them.

19.—The ship *Harvey Birch* was captured and burnt in the English Channel by the Confed. steamer *Nashville.*

—First flotilla of the "Stone Fleet" sailed for the South, from Conn. and Mass.

24.—Tybee Island, in Savannah Harbor, was occupied by U. S. forces under Flag-Officer Du Pont.

COPYRIGHT, 1911, REVIEW OF REVIEWS CO

A SIGHT FOR THE OLD-TIME SAILOR—A GUN-CREW ON THE DECK OF THE FLAGSHIP "WABASH"

Here is a sight that will please every old-time sailor—a gun-crew on the old "Wabash" under the eyes of Admiral Du Pont himself, who stands with his hand on the sail. No finer sweep of deck or better-lined broadside guns were ever seen than those of the U. S. "Wabash," the finest type of any vessel of her class afloat at the outbreak of the Civil War. Everything about her marked the pride which her officers must take in having everything "ship-shape and Bristol fashion." She was at all times fit for inspection by a visiting monarch. The "Wabash" threw the heaviest broadside of any vessel in the Federal fleet. Her crew were practically picked men, almost all old sailors who had been graduated from the navy of sailing days. The engines of this magnificent frigate were merely auxiliary; she yet depended upon her towering canvas when on a cruise. Her armament was almost identically that of the "Minnesota," although her tonnage was somewhat less. She mounted two 10-inch smooth-bores, twenty-eight 9-inch guns on her gun-deck, fourteen 8-inch on her spar deck, and two 12-pounders. At the time this picture was taken she was flagship of the South Atlantic squadron, flying the broad pennant of Admiral Samuel F. Du Pont.

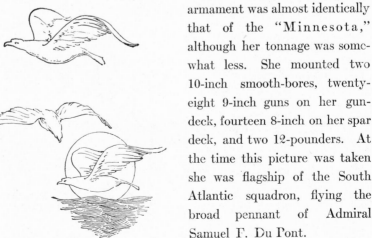

Important Naval Engagements of the Civil War

DECEMBER, 1861.

4.—Proclamation of Gen. Phelps, attached to Gen. Butler's expedition, on occupation of Ship Island, Mississippi Sound.

17.—Entrance to the harbor at Savannah, Ga., blocked by sinking 7 vessels laden with stone.

20.—The main ship-channel at Charleston Harbor was obstructed by sinking 16 vessels of the " Stone Fleet."

31.—Two boats under Acting-Masters A. Allen and H. L. Sturges, from the U. S. S. *Mount Vernon,* destroyed a light-ship off Wilmington, N. C., which the Confederates had fitted up for a gunboat.

—Capture of the town of Biloxi, Miss., by U. S. gunboats *Lewis, Water Witch,* and *New London,* with Federal forces from Ship Island.

JANUARY, 1862.

1.—Confed. Commissioners Mason and Slidell left Boston for England via Provincetown, Mass., where the British war steamer *Rinaldo* received them.

12.—Expedition sailed from Fort Monroe under command of Flag-Officer Goldsborough and Gen. Burnside, for Albemarle Sound, N. C.

13.—Steamship *Constitution* with the Maine 12th regiment, and the Bay State regiment, sailed from Boston for Ship Island, Miss., via Fort Monroe.

26.—Second " Stone Fleet " was sunk in Maffitt's Channel, Charleston Harbor, S. C.

30.—Ironclad *Monitor* was launched at Greenpoint, N. Y.

FEBRUARY, 1862.

6.—Unconditional surrender of Fort Henry to Flag-Officer Foote.

7 to 10.—Lieut. Phelps, of Foote's flotilla, commanding the gunboats *Conestoga, Tyler* and *Lexington,* captured Confed. gunboat *Eastport* and destroyed all the Confed. craft on the Tennessee River between Fort Henry and Florence, Ala.

10.—Destruction of Confed. gunboats in the Pasquotank River, N. C., also of the Confed. battery at Cobb's Point, and the occupation of Elizabeth City by Federal forces from 14 gunboats, commanded by Commander Rowan.

14.—Foote, with 6 gunboats, attacked Fort Donelson, but was repulsed, the flag-officer being severely wounded. Federal loss 60 in killed and wounded.

28.—Confed. steamer *Nashville* ran the blockade of Beaufort, N. C., and reached the town.

MARCH, 1862.

1.—U. S. gunboats *Tyler,* Lieut. Gwin, commanding, and *Lexington,* Lieut. Shirk, on an expedition up the Tennessee River, engaged and silenced a Confed. battery at Pittsburg Landing, Tenn.

6.—U. S. ironclad *Monitor,* Lieut. Worden, sailed from New York for Fort Monroe.

8.—Destruction of the U. S. sloop-of-war *Cumberland* and the frigate *Congress,* in action with the Confed. ironclad *Merrimac,* in Hampton Roads, Va. 120 men were lost on the *Cumberland,* and 121 on the *Congress.*

9.—Combat of the U. S. ironclad *Monitor* and the Confed. ironclad *Merrimac,* in Hampton Roads, Va.

11.—Occupation of St. Augustine, Fla., by Federal naval forces.

12.—Occupation of Jacksonville, Fla., by Federal forces from the U. S. gunboats *Ottawa, Seneca,* and *Pembina,* under command of Lieut. T. H. Stevens.

17.—Federal gunboats and mortars, under Foote, began the investment of and attack on Island No. 10, on the Mississippi.

APRIL, 1862.

1.—During a storm at night, Col. Roberts with 50 picked men of the 42d Illinois, and as many seamen under First Master Johnston, of the gunboat *St. Louis,* surprised the Confederates at the upper battery of Island No. 10, and spiked 6 large guns.

4.—Federal gunboat *Carondelet* ran past the Confed. batteries at Island No. 10, at night, without damage, and arrived at New Madrid.

COPYRIGHT, 1911, REVIEW OF REVIEWS CO.

HEADQUARTERS OF GENERAL Q. A. GILLMORE AT HILTON HEAD

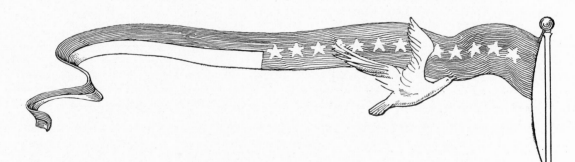

General Gillmore is not out of place in a volume that deals with the naval side of the Civil War, for almost continually he was directing movements in which the Federal navy was operating or was supposed to lend assistance. Had many of this splendid officer's suggestions been adopted, and had he received better military support from Washington, Savannah and Charleston could not by any possibility have held out, with all the bravery in the world, as long as they did. Had he been given supreme command at the time that he was ranked by General Thomas W. Sherman and had he commanded 50,000 men instead of a small army, the Federal naval victories might have been followed up by army successes. General Gillmore conceived and superintended the construction of the fortifications at Hilton Head, and also planned the operations that resulted in the capture of Fort Pulaski. Transferred to western Virginia and Kentucky, and brevetted for gallantry, he once more returned to the coast as commander of the Department of South Carolina, where he succeeded General Hunter. It was greatly through his efforts that Forts Wagner and Gregg, near Charleston Harbor, were finally silenced. During the latter part of the war he was successively in command of the Tenth and Nineteenth Army Corps.

Important Naval Engagements of the Civil War

11.—Confed. steamers *Merrimac, Jamestown,* and *Yorktown,* came down between Newport News and Sewell's Point, on the Chesapeake, and captured 3 vessels.

14.—Potomac flotilla ascended the Rappahannock River, destroying several batteries. Three vessels were captured.

—Foote's mortar-boats opened fire on Fort Pillow, on the Mississippi.

18 to 24.—Bombardment of Forts Jackson and St. Philip, on the Mississippi.

24.—Federal fleet passed Forts Jackson and St. Philip, destroying 13 Confed. gunboats, the ram *Manassas,* and 3 transports.

25.—New Orleans captured. Confed. batteries on both sides of the river destroyed.

28.—Forts St. Philip and Jackson, La., surrendered; Forts Livingston and Pike abandoned, and the Confed. ironclad *Louisiana* blown up.

MAY, 1862.

2.—U. S. S. *Brooklyn* and several gunboats left New Orleans, ascending the Mississippi, to open the river and connect with the Western Flotilla.

8.—Ironclad steamer *Galena,* assisted by the gunboats *Aroostook* and *Port Royal,* attacked and silenced two Confed. batteries a short distance from the mouth of the James River, Va.

9.—Pensacola, Fla., evacuated by the Confederates after setting fire to forts, navy-yard, barracks, and marine hospital.

10.—Federal gunboats in the Mississippi, under the command of Acting Flag-Officer Davis, were attacked above Fort Pillow by the Confed. River Defense fleet, which after a half-hour's contest, was forced to retire. The Federal gunboats *Cincinnati* and *Mound City* were badly injured, and the Confed. vessels also were considerably cut up.

11.—Confed. ironclad *Merrimac* was abandoned by her crew and blown up off Craney Island, Va.

13.—Confed. armed steamer *Planter* run out of Charleston, S. C., by a negro crew, and surrendered to Comdr. Parrott, of the U. S. S. *Augusta.*

—Natchez, Miss., surrendered to *Iroquois,* Comdr. J. S. Palmer.

15.—Federal ironclad *Monitor,* together with the *Port Royal, Aroostook,* and the mailed gunboats *Galena* and *E. A. Stevens,* attacked Fort Darling, on Drewry's Bluff, 6 miles below Richmond, on the James River. The *Galena* was badly damaged, and lost 17 men killed and about 20 wounded. The large rifled gun of the *E. A. Stevens* burst.

JUNE, 1862.

6.—Engagement between the Federal gunboats and rams and the Confed. rams in front of Memphis, in which all of the latter but one were sunk or captured. 100 Confed. prisoners taken. Memphis occupied by Federals.

15.—U. S. gunboats *Tahoma* and *Somerset,* Lieuts. Howell and English, crossed the bar of St. Mark's River, Fla., and destroyed a Confed. fort and barracks.

17.—Federal expedition up the White River, when near St. Charles, was fired into from masked batteries, and the gunboat *Mound City* received a shot in her boiler which occasioned the destruction of 82 of her crew by scalding, 25 only escaping uninjured. The Confed. works were captured by the land forces under Col. Fitch, who took 30 prisoners.

26.—Three Confed. gunboats burned on the Yazoo River by their officers, to prevent their capture by the Union ram-flotilla, Lieut.-Col. A. W. Ellet, then in pursuit of them.

28.—Flag-Officer Farragut with nine vessels of his fleet ran by the Confed. batteries at Vicksburg, through a severe fire, forming a junction with Western Flotilla on July 1st.

29.—Steamship *Ann,* of London, with a valuable cargo, captured by the U. S. steamer *Kanawha,* in Mobile Bay, under the guns of Fort Morgan.

JULY, 1862.

1.—Porter's mortar flotilla engaged the Confed. batteries at Vicksburg, Miss.

2.—Commencement of bombardment of Vicksburg, Miss., by the combined mortar fleets of Davis and Porter.

4.—Confed. gunboat *Teaser* captured on James River by U. S. steamer *Maratanza.*

COPYRIGHT, 1911, REVIEW OF REVIEWS CO.

ON THE DECK OF THE "AGAWAM"

The easy attitudes of the acting ensign, to the left of the gun, and the volunteer acting-master with him, do not suggest the storm through which the ship on which they stand, the Federal gunboat "Agawam," passed in the spring of 1864. Their vessel was called upon to coöperate in Grant's great military movement that was to bring the war to a close. In February, Acting Rear-Admiral S. P. Lee, commanding the North Atlantic squadron, was ready to assist General Butler with gunboats in the James and York Rivers. The admiral himself remained with his main squadron at Fortress Monroe to convey Butler's expedition to Bermuda Hundred. After that general got himself bottled up and, despite the protests of Admiral Lee, had sunk obstructions in the James to prevent the Confederate gunboats from coming down, the "Virginia" and her consorts came down to reconnoiter the character of the obstructions. The "Agawam," under Commander A. C. Rhind, was lying below Battery Dantzler, with several monitors. They were engaged by the fortification and by the Confederate gunboats concealed behind the Point. The Federal vessels promptly returned the fire and kept up the battle for six hours, inflicting considerable damage on the fort.

15.—Confed. iron-clad ram *Arkansas* came down the Yazoo River and engaged the Federal gunboats *Carondelet* and *Tyler,* and ram *Queen of the West.* The ram succeeded in escaping to Vicksburg.

22.—Confed. steamer *Reliance* captured by U. S. steamer *Huntsville.*

—Unsuccessful attempt made to sink the Confed. ram *Arkansas,* at Vicksburg, by Lieut-Col. Ellet, with the Union ram *Queen of the West* and ironclad *Essex,* Commander W. D. Porter.

29.—Attack on Fort James, on the Ogeechee River, Ga., by Federal gunboats repulsed.

AUGUST, 1862.

6.—Destruction of Confed. ram *Arkansas* by her commander, Lieut. Stevens, at Baton Rouge, La.

16.—Lieut.-Comdr. Phelps with 3 gunboats and 4 rams, and the 58th and 76th Ohio in transports, left Helena, Ark., sailed down the Mississippi to Milliken's Bend, where they captured the steamer *Fairplay,* with arms, &c., for 6000 men. Further captures made at Haynes' Bluff and at Richmond, La., and property destroyed.

SEPTEMBER, 1862.

5.—Ship *Ocmulgee* burned at sea by Confed. cruiser *Alabama.*

17.—U. S. gunboats *Paul Jones, Cimarron,* and 3 other vessels attacked Confed. batteries on St. John's River, Florida.

25.—Sabine Pass, Texas, captured by U. S. steamer *Kensington* and schooner *Rachel Seaman.*

OCTOBER, 1862.

3.—Confed. fortifications at St. John's Bluff, on St. John's River, Fla., captured by 1500 Federals under Gen. Brannan, assisted by 7 gunboats from Hilton Head, S. C.

—Fight on the Blackwater River, near Franklin, Va., 3 Federal gunboats, *Commodore Perry, Hunchback,* and *Whitehead,* under Lieut.-Comdr. Flusser, engaged a large force of Confederates 6 hours.

4.—Capture of the defenses of Galveston, Texas, after slight resistance by Federal mortar flotilla under Comdr. W. B. Renshaw.

NOVEMBER, 1862.

4.—Bark *Sophia* captured off N. C. coast by U. S. steamers *Daylight* and *Mount Vernon.*

18.—British schooners *Ariel* and *Ann Maria* captured off Little Run, S. C., by U. S. gunboat *Monticello.*

DECEMBER, 1862.

12.—U. S. gunboat *Cairo* sunk in the Yazoo River by a torpedo. The crew saved.

27.—Engagement between the *Benton* and the Confed. battery at Drumgould's Bluff on the Yazoo. Lieut.-Comdr. Gwin mortally wounded.

31.—Ironclad *Monitor,* Commander Bankhead, foundered off Cape Hatteras, N. C.

JANUARY, 1863.

1.—Galveston, Texas, with its garrison of 300 men, recaptured by Confederates under Gen. Magruder, and 2 steamers, *Bayou City* and *Neptune.* 6 Federal gunboats were in the harbor. The *Harriet Lane* was captured after a severe fight, in which Commander Wainwright was killed, and some of his crew. Federal flagship *Westfield* was blown up by Commander Renshaw, to avoid capture, by which he lost his life, with many of the crew.

11.—U. S. S. *Hatteras,* Lieut.-Comdr. H. C. Blake, sunk off Galveston, Tex., by Confed. steamer *Alabama.* 100 of the Federal crew captured.

14.—Four Union gunboats under Lieut.-Comdr. Buchanan, assisted by Gen. Weitzel's troops, engaged the Confed. iron-clad gunboat *J. A. Cotton,* which was aided by Confed. artillery, on the Bayou Teche, La. The *Cotton* was destroyed after several hours' combat. Lieut.-Comdr. Buchanan was killed.

16.—Confed. cruiser *Florida* escaped from Mobile.

27.—First attack on Fort McAllister, Ga.

30.—U. S. gunboat *Isaac Smith* captured in Stono River, S. C.

COPYRIGHT, 1911, REVIEW OF REVIEWS CO.

DISCUSSING THE PLANS—PORTER AND MEADE

On the left sits Rear-Admiral David Dixon Porter, in conference with Major-General George Gordon Meade. There were many such interviews both on shore and aboard the "Malvern" before the details of the expedition against Fort Fisher were finally settled. Porter had been promised the necessary troops to coöperate in an attack on the fort, but it was months before they were finally detached and actually embarked. Grant and Meade had their hands full in the military operations around Petersburg and Richmond and could not give much attention to the expedition. General Butler had more time at his disposal and proposed a plan for exploding close to Fort Fisher a vessel loaded with powder. This was bravely carried out by the navy but proved entirely futile.

31.—Confed. armed iron-clad rams, *Palmetto State* and *Chicora,* and 3 steamers, under Flag-Officer Ingraham, came down Charleston, S. C., Harbor, and attacked 3 vessels of the blockading squadron, the *Mercedita, Keystone State,* and *Quaker City,* damaging them severely, and capturing and paroling the crew of the *Mercedita.* 30 Federals killed and 50 wounded.

FEBRUARY, 1863.

1.—Second attack on Fort McAllister, Ga. Confed. commander, Maj. Gallie, killed. Federal vessels retire without loss.

2.—Union ram *Queen of the West* ran by the Confed. batteries at Vicksburg, Miss.

14.—Transport *Era No. 5* captured by Federal ram *Queen of the West,* Col. Charles R. Ellet, near Fort Taylor, Red River. The *Queen of the West,* running aground near Gordon's Landing, Red River, fell a prize to the Confederates.

18.—Mortar-boats opened fire on Vicksburg.

21.—Union gunboats *Freeborn* and *Dragon* engaged a Confed. battery on the Rappahannock River, Va. Three Federals wounded.

24.—Gunboat *Indianola* captured near Grand Gulf, Miss., by 4 Confed. steamers.

28.—Destruction of Confed. steamer *Nashville* in Ogeechee River, near Fort McAllister, Ga., by monitor *Montauk,* Commander Worden.

MARCH, 1863.

14.—Adml. Farragut, with 7 of his fleet, attacked the Confed. batteries at Port Hudson. The *Hartford* (flagship) and the *Albatross* passed the batteries and went up the river. The *Mississippi* was destroyed and part of her crew captured.

31.—Adml. Farragut, with the Federal vessels *Hartford, Switzerland,* and *Albatross,* engaged the Confed. batteries at Grand Gulf, Miss., and passed them without serious loss.

APRIL, 1863.

1.—Adml. Farragut's vessels proceeded to the mouth of the Red River.

2.—U. S. gunboat *St. Clair* disabled by Confederates above Fort Donelson on the Cumberland River. She was rescued by the steamer *Luminary.*

7.—Attack on Fort Sumter, Charleston, S. C., by 9 Federal ironclads under Rear-Adml. Du Pont.

14.—Destruction of Confed. ram *Queen of the West,* in Berwick Bay, La., by U. S. gunboat *Estrella* and others. 90 Confederates captured, and 30 lost.

16.—Adml. Porter's fleet of 8 gunboats and several transports ran past the Vicksburg batteries, losing only 1 transport and no men.

22.—Six transports and 12 barges passed the Confed. batteries at Vicksburg.

26.—Confed. shore batteries at Duck River shoals, Tennessee River, silenced by gunboats. 25 Confederates killed and wounded.

29.—Bombardment of Grand Gulf, Miss., by Porter's fleet. Confed. works greatly damaged. Fleet considerably injured.

MAY, 1863.

3.—Confed. batteries at Grand Gulf, Miss., evacuated by the Confederates, and taken possession of by Adml. Porter.

27.—Sinking of the U. S. gunboat *Cincinnati* by Confed. batteries at Vicksburg. 35 of her crew killed and wounded.

JUNE, 1863.

3.—Simsport, La., attacked by Federal gunboats.

10 and 11.—Attack on Morris Island, Charleston Harbor, by Federal gunboats and troops.

17.—Capture of Confed. iron-clad ram *Atlanta,* by monitor *Weehawken,* in Wassaw Sound, Ga. 180 prisoners taken.

22 and 23.—Seven fishing vessels captured off Martha's Vineyard, Mass., by Confed. captured bark *Tacony,* Lieut. C. W. Read.

JULY, 1863.

13.—U. S. gunboat *Baron DeKalb* sunk by Confed. torpedo in Yazoo River, Miss.

THE "KICKAPOO"
WITH TORPEDO–RAKE READY AT THE BOW

THIS NEW WEAPON OF DEFENSE WAS USED EFFECT-
IVELY DURING THE ATTACK ON MOBILE, ON MARCH 28,
1865. THE "KICKAPOO" CAME OUT SAFELY, ALTHOUGH
THE "MILWAUKEE" NEAR-BY FAILED TO DISCOVER
A CONFEDERATE TORPEDO IN TIME AND WAS SUNK

Important Naval Engagements of the Civil War

AUGUST, 1863.

21.—U. S. brig. *Bainbridge* foundered. Only 1 man saved.

23.—U. S. gunboats *Satellite* and *Reliance* captured by Confederates at the mouth of the Rappahannock, Va.

SEPTEMBER, 1863.

2.—Unsuccessful attempt to destroy by Union force, gunboats *Satellite* and *Reliance,* captured by the Confederates.

8 and 9.—An assault made on Fort Sumter by 400 men in 20 boats from the Federal fleet, under Commander T. H. Stevens. The sailors were defeated with the loss of 124.

8.—U. S. gunboats *Clifton* and *Sachem,* attached to an expedition under Gen. Franklin, grounded on the bar at Sabine Pass, Texas, and were captured by the Confederates.

OCTOBER, 1863.

5.—Confederates attempt to destroy the *New Ironsides* with the torpedo-boat *David.*

26 to Nov. 10.—Bombardment of Fort Sumter.

30.—Heavy bombardment of Charleston, S. C.

NOVEMBER, 1863.

2.—Unsuccessful attempt upon Sumter by a boat expedition.

DECEMBER, 1863.

6.—Monitor *Weehawken* founders in Charleston Harbor. Over 30 lives lost.

5.—Fight between the U. S. gunboat *Marblehead* and Confed. batteries on Stono River, S. C. Confederates defeated.

FEBRUARY, 1864.

2.—Capture and destruction of U. S. S. *Underwriter,* Actg. Master Westervelt, by Confed. attack under Comdr. J. T. Wood, in Neuse River, N. C.

18.—Federal sloop-of-war *Housatonic* sunk off Charleston, S. C., by Confed. submarine torpedo-boat *H. L. Hunley.*

16 to 29.—Bombardment of Fort Powell, Ala., by Adml. Farragut.

MARCH, 1864.

6.—U. S. gunboat *Peterhoff* sunk by collision off Wilmington, N. C.

11 to 15.—A naval expedition from Brashear City captures camp, arms, and flag on Atchafalaya River, La.

APRIL, 1864.

1.—U. S. Army stmr. *Maple Leaf* blown up by torpedo in St. John's River, Fla.

5.—Fight betweeen gunboats and guerrillas at Hickman, Ky.

12.—Adml. Porter's Red River fleet attacked at Blair's Plantation by 2000 Confed. infantry on shore, who are beaten off.

14.—Gunboat expedition from Butler's army captures prisoners and stores at Smithfield, Va.

19.—Attack on Federal vessels under Lieut.-Comdr. C. W. Flusser by Confed. ram *Albemarle,* Comdr. J. W. Cooke, at Plymouth, N. C.; sinking of U. S. S. *Southfield* and death of Flusser.

23.—U. S. gunboat *Petrel* captured by Confederates on the Yazoo River.

25.—Confederates in strong force attacked 3 of Adml. Porter's gunboats on the Red River.

MAY, 1864.

6.—U. S. gunboat *Commodore Jones* blown up by Confed. torpedo in James River.

13.—Adml. Porter's fleet above Alexandria Falls released by Col. Bailey's dam.

JUNE, 1864.

3.—Capture of U. S. S. *Water Witch,* Lieut.-Comdr. Austin Pendergrast by boat expedition under Lieut. J. P. Pelot, C. S. N., in Ossabaw Sound, Ga., Lieut. Pelot killed.

19.—The Confed. cruiser *Alabama,* Capt. Semmes, was sunk off the harbor of Cherbourg, France, by U. S. sloop-of-war *Kearsarge,* Capt. Winslow. 70 of the Confed. crew were taken on board the *Kearsarge,* and 115 reached England and France. 3 persons only were wounded on the *Kearsarge.*

A FORERUNNER OF THE NEW NAVY
THE "KICKAPOO" ON THE MISSISSIPPI

ONE OF THE FIVE RIVER MONITORS BUILT ON
ADMIRAL PORTER'S ENTHUSIASTIC RECOMMENDA-
TION, AFTER HE HAD OFFICIALLY EXAMINED
THE ORIGINAL ERICSSON "MONITOR" IN 1861

511068

Important Naval Engagements of the Civil War

AUGUST, 1864.

5.—Great battle at the entrance of Mobile Bay. The Confed. ram *Tennessee* captured after one of the fiercest naval battles on record. In the night, the Confederates evacuated and blew up Fort Powell. The monitor *Tecumseh* was blown up by a Confed. torpedo.

6.—Adml. Farragut shelled Fort Gaines, Mobile Bay.

8.—Surrender of Fort Gaines, Mobile Bay, to Adml. Farragut and Gen. Granger.

23.—Fort Morgan, Mobile Bay, surrendered unconditionally. By its surrender, Federals captured 200 prisoners and 60 pieces of artillery.

OCTOBER, 1864.

7.—Confed. cruiser *Florida* captured at Bahia, Bay of San Salvador, Brazil, by U. S. S. *Wachusett,* Commander Collins.

27.—The Confed. ram *Albemarle* sunk by Lieut. Cushing, in the Roanoke River.

31.—Capture of Confed. batteries and their ordnance and ordnance stores, at Plymouth, N. C.

NOVEMBER, 1864.

11.—U. S. S. *Tulip* destroyed by boiler explosion off Ragged Point, Va. 49 officers and men killed (all of crew but 10).

DECEMBER, 1864.

9.—The gunboat *Otsego* sunk by a Confed. torpedo in the Roanoke River.

22.—Loss of the U. S. transport *North American* by foundering at sea. 194 lives lost.

24.—Furious attack on Fort Fisher, N. C., by the fleet of Adml. Porter.

25.—Attack on Fort Fisher renewed. Three brigades of Union infantry landed two and a half miles above the fort. They were repulsed, and reembarked.

27.—Ensign Blume cuts out and takes from Galveston Harbor the blockade-running schooner *Belle.*

JANUARY, 1865.

15.—Grand assault on Fort Fisher, which was captured with entire garrison. Union loss 110 killed, 536 wounded. Confed. loss 2500 prisoners, 72 guns.

15.—U. S. monitor *Patapsco* sunk by a Confed. torpedo in Charleston Harbor. 60 of the officers and crew were lost.

23 and 24.—Confed. ironclads attempt descent of the James, and are driven back.

26.—Steamer *Eclipse* explodes on the Tennessee River, killing 140 persons.

FEBRUARY, 1865.

4.—Lieut. Cushing with 4 boats and 50 men takes possession of All Saints Parish, on Little River, S. C., capturing a large amount of cotton.

18.—Charleston occupied by Union forces.

MARCH, 1865.

4.—U. S. transport steamer *Thorne* blown up by a torpedo in Cape Fear River.

28 and 29.—U. S. monitors *Milwaukee* and *Osage* sunk by torpedoes in Mobile Bay.

APRIL, 1865.

8.—Spanish Fort, Mobile, bombarded. The Confederates evacuate at night.

12.—Mobile occupied by Union forces.

14.—Anniversary of the capture of Fort Sumter celebrated, by imposing ceremonies at the fort, and replacing the flag by Gen. Anderson.

22.—Mississippi Squadron flagship *Black Hawk* burnt at Mound City.

24.—Confed. ram *Webb* escapes past the Union fleet on the Red River; is run ashore below New Orleans, deserted, and blown up.

MAY, 1865.

4.—Surrender by Com. E. Farrand, C. S. N., of vessels under his command to Acting Rear-Adml. Thatcher, commanding West Gulf Squadron, agreed upon.

19.—Surrender of the Confed. ram *Stonewall* to Spanish authorities in Cuba.

25.—Forts Mannahasset and Griffin, and the defenses of Sabine Pass, occupied by Acting Rear-Adml. Thatcher.

JUNE, 1865.

3.—The Confed. ironclad *Missouri,* in Red River, surrenders to Lieut.-Comdr. W. E. Fitzhugh.